Praise for
THIS ENDURING GIFT

"*This Enduring Gift* is a wonderful compilation of the many rich voices and gifted poets who live in Fairfield, IA—a unique spot on the map. This anthology should not only endure, but inspire, enlighten and entertain all who touch its pages."
— MARY SWANDER, Poet Laureate of Iowa, Author of *The Girls on the Roof*

"*This Enduring Gift* is a testament to the abiding power of poetry within a particularly unique community and, by extension, speaks to poetry's universal relevance. Here, a convergence of voices from places near and far, gathered in a small Midwestern town, observe, reflect, meditate, and wonder. From evocative lyrics to compelling narratives, from precise moments of deeply felt experience to inquiries of mystical complexities, these poems resonate with individual authenticity and true collective spirit."
— WALTER E. BUTTS, 2009-2014 Poet Laureate of New Hampshire

"*This Enduring Gift* reads like a collection of polished mirrors reflecting the valor of Fairfield poets — valor born of candor and insight that takes center stage and performs a love affair with language."
— KIRA ROSNER, Author of *When Souls Take Flight*

"The poems of *This Enduring Gift*...indicate an original awareness, a sensibility, a clarity of image, rhythm, and color from a group of individuals who have lived in Fairfield, Iowa — far more than a geographical location, but more a state of mind, or consciousness, seemingly, as there is a remarkable texture-ness to them all, each one unique in its shine and feel. I am startled at the creative light found in this wonderful collection so well arranged, edited and created by Freddy Niagara Fonseca."
— RUDY WILSON, NEA Recipient & Author of *The Red Truck*, and other novels.

THIS ENDURING GIFT

© Freddy Niagara Fonseca 2010

Published by 1stWorld Publishing
P.O. Box 2211, Fairfield, Iowa 52556
tel: 641-209-5000 • fax: 866-440-5234
web: www.1stworldpublishing.com

First Edition

LCCN:2010932090
SoftCover ISBN:978-1-4218-9159-0
HardCover ISBN:978-1-4218-9160-6
eBook ISBN:978-1-4218-9161-3

All rights reserved.
No part of this book may be reproduced or utilized in any
form or by any means, electronic or mechanical,
including photocopying or recording, or by any information storage and
retrieval system, without permission in writing from the author.

This material has been written and published solely for
educational purposes. The author and the publisher shall have neither
liability or responsibility to any person or entity with respect to any
loss, damage or injury caused or alleged to be caused directly
or indirectly by the information contained in this
book.

The characters and events described in this text are intended
to entertain and teach rather than present an exact
factual history of real people or events.

THIS ENDURING GIFT

A FLOWERING OF FAIRFIELD POETRY

76 POETS WHO FOUND COMMON GROUND IN ONE SMALL PRAIRIE TOWN

SELECTED WITH INTRODUCTIONS BY
FREDDY NIAGARA FONSECA

1ST WORLD PUBLISHING

Someone, I tell you, will remember us

— Sappho 600 BC

A FLOWERING OF FAIRFIELD POETRY

SELECTED WITH INTRODUCTIONS BY
FREDDY NIAGARA FONSECA

When I peruse this glorious manuscript

Our *Master Poet* placed before our eyes,

And study how sublime the penmanship

On Earth's each flower, and night's bejeweled skies;

When I most marvel at miracles of the seasons,

At blizzards melting to a robin's song,

Then most praise I, *Him*, who with divinely rhyming *Reason*,

Authored thy temple, making *His Angels* throng.

Thou art, in sooth, a purest *Thought of God*,

Composed on the holy tablet of *His Soul*,

A violet, crowning *His Masterpiece of Love*,

Love's metaphor that fuses all *Life's* phrases *Whole*:

The glory of the Angels, translated to the eyes of Men:

'Perfection reigns, when Earth and Heaven simply, humbly, blend.'

© Brother Ludovico

Foreword by Donovan

A poem is...it cannot be otherwise...seldom explained... it spreads its words...on a page...hovering in a white sky...we give our attention to its images...or metaphors...moving in the time it takes to read...the poet's measure...Sappho's dance...upon the soft bloom of the grasses...on the prairie...this book of poets from the Fair Fields of Iowa...these sheaves of poems... just as one poet here, Steven P. Schneider says in his poem 'Prairie Air Show'...this book is indeed...

'readying itself
    for flight'

A fine accomplished set of poems, I am enthralled.

Donovan Leitch
Ireland, Spring 2010
www.donovan.ie

Introduction

A Poet is a nightingale who sits in darkness, and sings to cheer its own solitude with sweet sounds; his auditors are as men entranced by the melody of an unseen musician, who feel that they are moved and softened, yet know not whence or why.

— *A Defence of Poetry,* Percy Bysshe Shelley (1792-1822)

In *This Enduring Gift,* 76 nightingales open their hearts to emit sounds, words, and meaning to brighten these pages.

Having lived in Fairfield, Iowa for more than 20 years, I've seen this small, remarkable city transform itself from a little-known Midwest town into a buzzing and multi-faceted community. It teems with entrepreneurs, small businesses, restaurants, art galleries, artists, artisans, dancers, musicians, actors, writers, and an abundance of poets.

For many years I've wondered what makes poets happy? What effect, if any, do their poems have? Do poets write for fame, pleasure, simple recognition, or out of some deep discontent with the world around us? Millions of poems have been written over the centuries. What makes some of them more memorable than others? Is it their topic, their style, their message to the rest of us, or something more mysterious? Where do poets — and their poetry — come from?

It's likely that when speech was still in its infancy, any meaningful human utterances were little more than raw grunts, coos, and wails. Such early means of communication would form at charged occasions like hunts, births, wars, and burials. As tribal communities differentiated, language emerged. Each culture's speech eventually would shape societies, evolving to greater sophistication and complexity.

Early on, poets became prominent personae, initially as narrators and guardians of people's stories. Tribal histories and genealogies would be recounted at all-important celebrations and could last an entire day. Memorization took place through hearing and repetition.

When writing was invented and people began carving their narratives in clay, stone, or bark, poetry saw a gradual shift from auditory recollections toward absorption through the eye and the intellect. The first tendencies to record our historical and mythical past gave way to focusing more on our internal universe, individually and collectively.

Increasingly, the written word has become a powerful beacon connecting cultures throughout time. Pondering on how even a short letter, rather than speech, could form a lasting link to the future, Byron (1788-1824) wrote in his *Don Juan:*

> *But words are things, and a small drop of ink,*
> *Falling like dew, upon a thought, produces*
> *That which makes thousands, perhaps millions, think.*

Several poems passed down from ancient cultures are still enjoyed today. Think of the *Epic of Gilgamesh* from the Bronze Age (4th millennium BC), preserved in cuneiform script on clay tablets and later on papyrus, as well as the Vedas, orally preserved prior to 1700 BC when they were finally written down. There's Homer's *Iliad* written around 800 BC, Valmiki's *Ramayana* (400 BC), and many other lyrical dramatic texts by named and unknown poets.

But of all known poets, Sappho (600 BC), more than any other, embodies the mystique of antiquity's 'immortal poet,' even though most of her poetry has been lost. She might have had a foresight of that when she wrote:

> *Someone, I tell you,*
> *will remember us.*
>
> *We are oppressed by*
> *fears of oblivion*
>
> *yet are always saved*
> *by judgment of good men.*

All poets and readers can relate to Sappho's universal experience of elevation in the face of adversity. Great poems live on generation after generation because they instill a degree of timelessness. Their enduring appeal may reside in a couple of moving phrases, a few stanzas, a sentence, or even a single line. Shakespeare's sonnet, *"Shall I compare thee to a summer's day?"* and Emily Dickinson's, *"Because I could not stop for Death"* are prime illustrations. We return to poems such as these again and again as they unify diverse aspects of our common humanity.

As much as we are our own memories, we are the seeds of our future. If there is one fundamental constituent that unifies what is eternal, it is eternity itself. In his continual search of himself, man looks to find ways to reconnect with his origins. He lives to discover and embody them in his interactions with people, life, and the arts, including poetry.

Some poetry then, like Sappho's, aspires to become eternal. When presenting ideas in poetry, poets share what they find worthwhile to write down, and they are grateful when they are appreciated. They are remembered and live on in the hearts and minds of men.

Poets have a penchant for language. It's a love affair. They recognize the origins of sound and rhythm better than others. They are always alert to archetype and metaphor, and have a developed feel for how sound emerges from the transcendent to form words, language, song, poetry, structure, and meaning. The more their poetics are free of agendas, the more universal their poetry. Any agenda, however lofty, is by definition restrictive to some extent, hence not universal in scope.

In the infancy of society every author is necessarily a poet, because language itself is poetry; and to be a poet is to apprehend the true and the beautiful, in a word, the good which exists in the relation, subsisting, first between existence and perception, and secondly between perception and expression.

— *A Defence of Poetry*, Percy Bysshe Shelley (1792-1822)

Anyone, regardless of background or education, can exercise his inborn talents to create a work of art. When one writes poems, one is using his personal key to unlock doors to his potential. No matter what style in which he likes to write — contemporary, traditional, experimental, or archaic — when armed with a genuine feel for harmony, proportion, and a good ear for language, he can write attractive poetry. When gifted with a measure of genius, originality, discernment and self-criticism, he may achieve a work to be remembered indefinitely.

When I created this book of Fairfield poets, I asked the Fairfield writing community at large to submit poems based on three simple questions:

1. Which of my poems would I like to be remembered by?
2. Which poems would I *likely* be remembered by?
3. Which of these poems is really "me?"

I was merely wondering what such a selection would look like. I had no idea I would find so many poets! But what are their stories? Who are they, and what would they like us to remember?

To understand the answers to these questions, one must first look at the extraordinary cultural and spiritual community nurturing Fairfield poets. This vibrant Midwest town boasts many diverse restaurants (more per capita than San Francisco). Theatrical, musical, and dance performances — and poetry readings — abound throughout the year. A pre-eminently health-oriented community, Fairfield houses the world's premier Ayurveda health spa.

Every first Friday of the month, the arts are spotlighted during the 1st Fridays Art Walk, an Iowa Tourism Event of the Year that showcases 40 art galleries and venues in the downtown area. Hundreds, and sometimes thousands, of people come out to appreciate art and make new friends.

Culture blossoms year round. This much cultural activity is quite astounding for a town just shy of 10,000 people.

Over the past 35 years, thousands of international and US students, teachers, scientists, business people, artists, poets, and other colorful souls were drawn to Fairfield mainly because of the inspiring presence of Maharishi University of Management (formerly Maharishi International University). Since 1974, the university has offered educational programs that develop consciousness and integrate the transcendental with daily life. More than a few poets have expanded their poetic gifts while in Fairfield. This could account for why such a small town could spawn so many prolific and published poets.

This book is divided into 16 chapters, each on a different universal theme, ranging from the lyrical and spiritual to the wildly absurd. There's a brief introduction and index at the beginning of each section and an alphabetical poet's index with biographies and photos at the end.

From poem selection to design and layout, putting together this compilation of around 300 poems has been an immense joy that I will never forget. I thank all who submitted their poems, as well as those who, in many ways, have guided me in this journey. My purpose was to simply unite, within myself, the poets I've come to know here, and celebrate a flowering of Fairfield poetry that hopefully will echo in many hearts with the songs of these nightingales. Enjoy!

Freddy Niagara Fonseca, February 2010.

The Language of the Future

If ever I adopt an agenda poetica,
it will be of ever more conscious language —
that intangible, human phenomenon that has
carved out history, rivers, poems, God;
and points with you and me
. . . to the future.

Such an agenda will simply reunite
the builders and inhabitants of
all language past and present. One language,
more fluent than rivers we know, will
manifest, maturing in time
. . . in Man's future.

The language of the future will flow
with newfound ideas all our own, and
thus will we speak and sing as one. I'll
keep my wit vibrant, making sure my
every word rises to touch
. . . that great future.

© 2004 Freddy Niagara Fonseca

THESE WORDS ARE HIEROGLYPHICS

These words are hieroglyphics etched upon
    The walls and ceilings of these pages' tombs;
      Symbols, scrawled, for those candles that shall come
        Seeking to see this age's dreams exhumed.

      Here the hunt, the orgy, the rite, the ritual
        Are painted in lurid, primitive graffiti;
    Mere flights of fancy, preserved, like Pharaohs' jewels,
      A child's playthings, forfeit to death's treaty.

Thy candle, closer: these tombs are not tombs;
    Their mummies, freshly wrapped in swaddling bands;
  These, no sarcophagi, but silk cocoons,

    In which was fashioned, a new chrysalis of Man.
The cosmos spangles on these walls; laughter, on these scrolls;
  No ancient, perished age these words,
        but a new age of Man's Soul.

© Brother Ludovico

TABLE OF CONTENTS

I	*When I Peruse This Glorious Manuscript*
III	*Foreword by Donovan*
V	*Introduction*
IX	*The Language of the Future*
X	*These Words Are Hieroglyphics*

3   CHAPTER 1: The Poetry of Remembrance and Renewal

4	Chrysalis	*Donna Davison*
6	I Keep a Flowering Bough	*Brother Ludovico*
8	Fall of an Angel	*Viktor Tichy*
10	Grandma's Pancakes	*Bill Graeser*
12	Awestruck at Niagara Falls	*Freddy Niagara Fonseca*
16	Waltz	*Diane Frank*
20	New Ache	*Paul Johan Stokstad*
24	Restoring the Meadow	*Carole Lee Connet*
26	Swing Low, Sweet Pontiac	*Nancy Berg*
30	Meditation	*Karen Karns*
32	A Word for My Mother	*Leah Marie Waller*
34	Rendezvous	*Steven Druker*
36	November Repast	*Susie Niedermeyer*
38	View #45	*Thomas Centolella*
40	A White Veil	*Libbett Rich*
42	Four Memories of North West Arkansas	*Charlie Hopkins*
46	A Still Point of the Turning World	*Henry Robert Hau*

49   CHAPTER 2: The Poetry of Nature, the Cosmos, and the Soul

50	This Whisper	*Michael Hock*
52	Iowa Meditation	*Viktor Tichy*
54	Mirror Lake	*Rolf Erickson*
56	The Language of the Trees	*Freddy Niagara Fonseca*

60	Prairie Air Show	Steven P. Schneider
62	Spring Leaves	Susan Klauber
64	Forest Road at Night	William Clair Godfrey
66	Dolphin Report	Nancy Berg
70	Into the Woods	Rolf Erickson
72	Jesus in Iowa	James Moore
74	Troubles	Glenn Watt
76	The Stage	Janet Thomas
78	In the Wind River Mountains	Karla Christensen
82	On Hope	Glenn Watt
84	Walking the Loop	Steven P. Schneider
90	Shepherd on Snowdon	James Tipton

93 CHAPTER 3: The Poetry of Mysteries and Imagination

94	A Vague Feeling	Phoebe Carter
96	Imagine You're a River	Jason Walls
98	There Is a Secret	Rolf Erickson
100	Love Poem to a Chinese Tallow Tree	Charlie Hopkins
102	Where I Walk	Bill Graeser
104	The Rain Is Sun When It Falls in Ireland	Leah Marie Waller
106	The Doe	Freddy Niagara Fonseca
108	Lullaby for the Universe	Nynke Passi
110	Tumbling Planets	Janet Thomas
112	The River Stone	Henry Robert Hau
114	Caught	Karen Karns
116	The Other Side	James Tipton
118	Something to Know	Bill Graeser
120	Like the Robin's Egg	Paul Johan Stokstad

123 CHAPTER 4: The Poetry of Whimsicality and Simple Things

124	While You Were Gone	Tom Le May
126	Zinnia	Elizabeth McIsaac
128	The Moor Park	George K. Attwood
130	The Puzzle Tale	Viktor Tichy
132	Sneaking Free	Tony Ellis
134	Fairy Trifle	William Clair Godfrey

136	Water Wings	*River Dog*
138	Five Haiku	*Ken Chawkin*
140	Toilet Poetry	*Jordy Yager*
142	Lullaby Baby Frog	*Karla Christensen*
144	When I Die	*Viktor Tichy*
146	Trying on Your New Hat	*Tom Le May*

149 CHAPTER 5: The Poetry of Darkness and the Eerie Nocturnal

150	Riding with Ludwig	*James Tipton*
152	El Dia de los Muertos	*Karla Christensen*
154	Under Orion	*Brother Ludovico*
160	Cold Wet Night	*Ken Chawkin*
162	Ode to Dry Starlight	*Robin Lim*
164	Night Sketches	*Para Steinmann*
166	The Coyotes	*Susie Niedermeyer*
168	Feeding Cats	*Leah Marie Waller*
170	Rite of Passage	*Patricia Regan Argiro*
172	Swimming through Brooklyn	*Jordy Yager*
176	Night Vision	*Susie Niedermeyer*
178	Marbles at a San Francisco Sunrise	*Barry Rosen*
182	Stricken	*Michael Hock*
184	The Beginning of Real Time	*Roger Pelizzari*

187 CHAPTER 6: The Poetry of Angels, You, and GOD

188	Spirals	*Patricia Regan Argiro*
190	Lalla	*Carole Lee Connet*
192	The Orders	*Thomas Centolella*
196	The Master	*Susie Niedermeyer*
198	When Will I Awaken	*Sharalyn Pliler*
202	Communion	*Viktor Tichy*
204	I Need to Feel You Every Moment…	*Charlie Hopkins*
208	Shopping	*Einar Olsen*
210	Atman's Jesus' Buddha's Krishna's…	*Matthew A. Bovard*
212	Like a Seed	*Glenn Watt*
214	In Defense of Angels	*Brother Ludovico*
220	I Once Met a God	*Tony Ellis*

22	He	*Diana Quinlan*
24	God Bless the Universe	*William Clair Godfrey*
26	The Picture of You	*Paul Johan Stokstad*
28	Gaea's Wedding Kiss	*Viktor Tichy*
32	On a Medieval Painting of the Fall...	*Freddy Niagara Fonseca*
34	In the Evening We Shall Be Examined...	*Thomas Centolella*
36	Good Night	*Patricia Regan Argiro*

39   CHAPTER 7: The Poetry of the Anecdotal and Domestic

40	Melons	*Rustin Larson*
42	Waving Man #1	*Allen Cobb*
44	Cereal Cold Wars	*Phoebe Carter*
46	Magic Carpets	*Carole Lee Connet*
50	Bug in My Pants	*Viktor Tichy*
52	Protection	*Tracy Chipman*
54	Wild Rabbit in the Woods	*James Moore*
58	Hero	*Leah Marie Waller*
60	Red Paste and Rice	*Carole Lee Connet*
62	The Bottom of Glass	*Judy Liese*
64	To the Clown Who Had His Eye...	*Anne Hildenbrand*
66	New Delhi Street	*Linda Egenes*
68	Chanukah Lights Tonight	*Steven P. Schneider*
70	Blue Heron	*Henry Robert Hau*
72	My Cambodian God	*Tony Ellis*
74	This Is How You Hang up Clothes	*Judy Liese*
76	House Painter Sitting on the Roof of...	*Charlie Hopkins*

81   CHAPTER 8: The Poetry of Animals, Pets, and All of Us

82	Simon	*Jeffrey Hedquist*
86	Ant Warrior	*Phoebe Carter*
88	An Animal of Ancient Ancestry	*Anne Hildenbrand*
90	Smallest Dog in the World	*Nancy Berg*
94	When Ninja Sits	*Carol Olicker*
96	Cleo	*Rustin Larson*
98	Night Heat	*Ann Du Bois*
100	The Whale's Song	*Andrea Dana Stevens*

302	The Love of Horses	*Megge Hill Fitz-Randolph*
304	Squirrel Brain	*Jeffrey Hedquist*
306	The New York City Zoo	*Freddy Niagara Fonseca*
312	The Gerbils	*Rustin Larson*
314	Mushikarati: The Mouse's Poem	*Angela Mailander*
316	So Say the Wise	*William Clair Godfrey*
318	On the Angels among Us	*Brother Ludovico*
326	Doin' What Comes Naturally	*Richard K. Wallarab*
328	The House Sparrow	*Henry Robert Hau*
330	How They Sometimes Show up	*Glenn Watt*

333 CHAPTER 9: The Poetry of Strife, Grief, and Conflict

334	Caught Looking at the Moon	*Rolf Erickson*
338	The Black Hearse	*Bill Graeser*
340	The Terminal Temple	*Carole Lee Connet*
342	Statue of an Enraged Lion	*Freddy Niagara Fonseca*
344	One Moment	*Tony Ellis*
346	Mumbling	*Bill Graeser*
348	Dying	*Karen Karns*
350	What Will Never Dry	*Robin Lim*
352	Ice	*Glenn Watt*
354	How Many?	*Michael Hock*
356	Tornado	*Judy Liese*
358	After the End After the Beginning	*Margo Berdeshevsky*
360	My Hands	*Tom Le May*
362	Sole of the Shoe	*Matthew A. Bovard*

365 CHAPTER 10: The Poetry of Erotica, the Body, and True Love

366	I Lie Down	*Libbett Rich*
368	My Body	*Leah Marie Waller*
370	Photograph from Okinawa	*Diane Frank*
374	Carnival in Rio!	*Freddy Niagara Fonseca*
376	Advent of Autumn	*Susie Niedermeyer*
378	The Feminine Mystique, and the...	*Brother Ludovico*
388	Song	*Megan Robinson*
390	Chinese Ghost Wedding	*Nancy Berg*

94	In the Herb Garden	*Rustin Larson*
96	Sparks Flying	*Patricia Wood*
98	Wild Woman	*Barry Rosen*
100	The Sixth Day of Creation	*Viktor Tichy*
102	We Are Drunk	*Nynke Passi*
104	The Raptors	*Thomas Centolella*
108	You're the Most	*Paul Johan Stokstad*
110	Seed Time in Fairfield, Iowa	*Charlie Hopkins*
112	To a Young Waiter	*Sharalyn Pliler*
114	Tenth Anniversary Prayer	*Charlie Hopkins*
116	The Master's Gift	*Michael Hock*

119	**CHAPTER 11: The Poetry of Abundance and Times Well Spent**

120	Samoset	*Meredith Briggs Skeath*
122	Maine Song #4	*Allen Cobb*
124	Platte River Liftoff	*Steven P. Schneider*
126	The Fool	*Glenn Watt*
128	Sometimes	*Tony Ellis*
130	Middle-Aged Man	*Charlie Hopkins*
134	Father in His Coffin	*Bill Graeser*
136	To a Cumulus Cloud	*Brother Ludovico*
142	Lines of Force	*Thomas Centolella*
144	Michelle Kwan	*Jason Walls*
146	One Hundred Years	*Elizabeth McIsaac*
150	Drug Books	*Matthew A. Bovard*
152	Hammock	*Linda Egenes*
154	Teacher	*Rustin Larson*
156	Someday I Will Have a Mountain Cabin	*Christopher Seid*
158	Three Non-Haiku	*Brian Stains*
160	"A Fossil, Dad!"	*Viktor Tichy*
162	Morning	*Allen Cobb*
164	Always a Good Time to Grow up	*Meredith Briggs Skeath*

167	**CHAPTER 12: The Poetry of the Mildly Nutty (Humor Included)**

168	The Gray Dress	*Raven Garland*
172	The Trees Striptease	*William Clair Godfrey*

474	I Could Have Danced All Night if I...	Nancy Berg
480	Junk Pile	Bill Graeser
482	Buildings	Allen Cobb
484	Some Really Nonsense Poems	Elizabeth McIsaac
486	Fishy Doggerel	Angela Mailander
488	Louie the 14th	Tom Le May
490	High Coos and Buddhist Leanings	Ann Du Bois
492	Toad to My Gray Hairs	Ruthie Hutchings
496	Beauty Hard to Believe	Henry Robert Hau
498	Bareback English	Viktor Tichy
500	If You Want to Drop Your Body	William Clair Godfrey
502	My Elephant	Gale Park
504	The Love Song of J. Alfred Frog Prince	Angela Mailander
508	Laughing Leaves Retreat	Barry Rosen

513 CHAPTER 13: The Poetry of the Arts, Poems, and Books

514	Birth of a Poem	Leah Marie Waller
518	Tag Sale	Bill Graeser
520	Poetry Dances, Olé!	Freddy Niagara Fonseca
524	Iowa Omen	Diane Frank
526	These Words Are Wounds	Brother Ludovico
528	Lady with an Ermine	James Tipton
530	Poetry: The Art of the Voice	Ken Chawkin
532	Somebody Has to Play Mozart	Silvine Farnell
534	Paper Music	Elizabeth McIsaac
536	If I Could Write	Jasmine Bartolovic
538	Elvin Ray	James Moore
540	Open Readings on Other Planets	Bill Graeser
542	Advisement	Patricia Regan Argiro
544	Poet as Art	Matthew A. Bovard
546	Books	Freddy Niagara Fonseca

551 CHAPTER 14: The Poetry of the Wilderness We Harbor

552	Radio City Hall	Laurie Sewall
554	I Turn My Back	Paul Johan Stokstad
556	The Deer	Susie Niedermeyer

558	Night Birds	*Andrea Dana Stevens*
560	You Left Me	*Sharalyn Pliler*
562	Untitled	*Tom Le May*
564	Blackberries All Dried up Now	*Carole Lee Connet*
566	Territorial Waters	*Viktor Tichy*
568	Creatures Nobody Recognizes	*Rustin Larson*
570	And if It Happens	*Susie Niedermeyer*
572	Retreat from Kandahar	*Carole Lee Connet*
574	Where They Hung a Crucifix	*Robin Lim*
576	We Seep into This World	*Brother Ludovico*
578	The Sandbox	*Richard K. Wallarab*
580	Window Decoration	*Susan Klauber*
582	Three Poems out of Southeast Iowa	*Charlie Hopkins*
584	The Forgiven	*Glenn Watt*

587 CHAPTER 15: The Poetry of the Exalted and Transcendent

588	This Lamplight Falling on My Child's...	*Brother Ludovico*
590	These Highest Dreams	*Allen Cobb*
592	The Divine Abode of My Own Buddha-...	*Leslie Gentry*
594	This Balloon of Joy	*Graham de Freitas*
596	Hymn of Praise to the Divine Mother...	*Charlie Hopkins*
600	Metamorphosis	*Megan Robinson*
602	To the River Is a Place I Go	*Henry Robert Hau*
604	A Vision	*Gale Park*
606	Giant Sequoia - A Hymn	*Freddy Niagara Fonseca*
610	Delphi	*Allen Cobb*
612	The Temple	*Catherine Castle*
614	Seeking to Hide	*Angela Mailander*
616	Lament for Lost Silence	*Allen Cobb*
620	The Egrets	*Henry Robert Hau*
622	A Hymn to the Moon-Mother	*Brother Ludovico*
632	Gates of Dawn	*James Tipton*
634	Poem Written Dream-Side (Qin Guan)	*tr. Angela Mailander*
636	Unexpected Call	*Meredith Briggs Skeath*
638	Brother Sun Sister Moon	*Matthew A. Bovard*
640	At the Speed of God	*Michael Hock*

643 CHAPTER 16: The Poetry of Transition, Surprise, and Ascension

644	The Citadel	*Tom Le May*
646	Death Is Coming	*Charlie Hopkins*
648	Shards of Future	*Jason Walls*
650	Lyrebird Song	*Janet Thomas*
652	The Flight	*Libbett Rich*
654	Death's Inheritance	*Brother Ludovico*
658	Days Are Short	*Gale Park*
660	A Man Will Abandon His Face	*Charlie Hopkins*
664	Salaat	*Elizabeth McIsaac*
666	Columbia	*Nancy Berg*
670	Icarus' Lover's Dream	*Andrew Josephs*
672	Consider the Tracks	*Tom Le May*
674	For the Life of Me	*Tom Kepler*
676	View #2	*Thomas Centolella*
678	When a Vessel Breaks	*Patricia Regan Argiro*
680	Near Lindos, Rhodes	*Allen Cobb*
682	Sat Guru	*Michael Hock*
684	When My Body Dies	*Sharalyn Pliler*
686	Falling	*Gale Park*
688	When I Lay Down My Treasures at...	*William Clair Godfrey*
690	Fire Dance - An Invocation of the Light	*Freddy Niagara Fonseca*

- 697 **EPILOGUE Who We Are**
- 699 **Poets' Index and Biographies**
- 731 **Acknowledgements**
- 732 **About Freddy Niagara Fonseca**

The Poetry of Remembrance and Renewal

THE POEMS

CHAPTER

I

*Any healthy man can go without food for two days
— but not without poetry.*

— Charles Baudelaire, French poet (1821-1867)

THIS ENDURING GIFT

CONTENTS

4	Chrysalis	*Donna Davison*
6	I Keep a Flowering Bough	*Brother Ludovico*
8	Fall of an Angel	*Viktor Tichy*
10	Grandma's Pancakes	*Bill Graeser*
12	Awestruck at Niagara Falls	*Freddy Niagara Fonseca*
16	Waltz	*Diane Frank*
20	New Ache	*Paul Johan Stokstad*
24	Restoring the Meadow	*Carole Lee Connet*
26	Swing Low, Sweet Pontiac	*Nancy Berg*
30	Meditation	*Karen Karns*
32	A Word for My Mother	*Leah Marie Waller*
34	Rendezvous	*Steven Druker*
36	November Repast	*Susie Niedermeyer*
38	View #45	*Thomas Centolella*
40	A White Veil	*Libbett Rich*
42	Four Memories of North West Arkansas	*Charlie Hopkins*
46	A Still Point of the Turning World	*Henry Robert Hau*

*Life is not measured by the number of
breaths we take, but by the number of moments
that take our breath away.*

— Anonymous

Chapter I
The Poetry of Remembrance and Renewal

Minerva, a fictional poet in Edgar Lee Masters' (1868-1950) *Spoon River Anthology*, has these lines on her tombstone:

Will some one go to the village newspaper,
And gather into a book the verses I wrote?—
I thirsted so for love
I hungered so for life!

Like Minerva, who doesn't cherish a fond desire to be remembered forever? An engineer likes to be honored for the bridges he built. Doesn't every mother want to live forever in the hearts of her children? Chefs enjoy hearing praises about their culinary efforts.

And poets? Tell a poet how much you enjoyed his books or ask about his next one, and you'll see gratitude beam in his eyes.

One poet's quiet words can make an enduring impact on many peoples' lives, even if for a duration as brief as the reading of a poem....

Chrysalis

Donna Davison

Chapter 1: The Poetry of Remembrance and Renewal

Who knew I was in pupae stage?
I thought I was in life...

As I spread my still damp wings
The smallness of the chrysalis is revealed.

Where once my home, my walls of protection,
It now lies in pieces at my feet.

Longingly, I look upon those broken limbs of life.
I had no idea they would one day be gone.

They look so small, so lifeless now,
No longer imbued with the juice of doubt and confusion.

So suddenly emerged into the light,
I feel vulnerable, naked, unsure yet curious.

I know not if the chrysalis will suddenly reform about me...
Yet it looks so still, so dead as it lies broken at my feet.

Quite hesitant I am to move from this spot of security
Amongst the shards of my former home.

I feel different, formless,
Unsure of who I am.

I sense something breathing within me...
I feel the desire to explore.

I attempt to move with my caterpillar body.
It no longer responds.

My eye beholds a butterfly gently hovering over me.
How exquisite it looks!

It seems to smile upon me
As if we are sisters.

Another has landed next to me.
It seems to be speaking my language.

Suddenly, I notice my wings, wet with newness—
They work!

I Keep a Flowering Bough

Brother Ludovico

CHAPTER 1: THE POETRY OF REMEMBRANCE AND RENEWAL

I KEEP
    a flowering bough within my *Heart*,
  Branched over the calm wide ocean of *Time*,
So that a *singing bird* will come at dark,
  And pour sweet notes to the moon's slow soft climb.
There no ache, no desire, no breath stirs the calm,
  No rude breeze rustles the moon-dappled leaves,
Though far below men's kingdoms rise and fall,
  This *Bird* still warbles with sweet-throated ease.
When first the silver moon sailed over Earth,
  And stirred the country-side with *Love* sublime,
When first lips prayed, and *Man* praised *God* for *Birth*,
  These clear notes pierced the night with a *Joy Divine*.
Ah, sweet and low, this endless melody,
Our Soul's the nightingale of Eternity.

Fall of an Angel

Viktor Tichy

A Sculpture by Auguste Rodin

Chapter 1: The Poetry of Remembrance and Renewal

Sudden as a Cairo sunrise,
the arch of her spine
airbrushes an undulating shadow
on the ledge beneath her marble skin.
Wings washed from the star dust
by a cascade of Carrara white hair,
the woman without a face
is being devoured in a kiss.

In twilight that belongs to lovers and predators,
her captor's hand warm with full memory of breasts
clutches her armpit like a deprived talon.
How many times did the earth shake
under the fall of an angel?
We all came from such a grasp.

What is the action that pervades the cosmos?
To a small child, everything is growing.
To you, my son,
the universe is never ending motion,
but if you ask your father
who can't save one star from collapsing,
everything in Creation is growing older.

He will not abandon you. His job is finished
when gradual as a Copenhagen sunset,
you abandon him.
You too one morning will look in the mirror
and see your own image
turn and fade away.

Grandma's Pancakes

Bill Graeser

Chapter 1: The Poetry of Remembrance and Renewal

Even in old age when Death comes to the door who would let him in?
Inundated as we are with living we think there's still laundry to do,
a book to finish, a video to return. So it was with grandma withering
on the bed, and why not—she still with the strength to sit up.

Then, tired of ringing the doorbell Death raised his fist to the door
and grandma spoke of the funeral parlor she remembered from streets
she roller-skated as a child, a place that unless the son and grandson
of the undertaker took up the business was long gone.

"Yes, grandma, yes," I said, then seeking her smile I spoke of her
pancakes, how her trick was to prepare the batter the night before,
mixing the white of the egg with the flour first, then the yolk,
and placing it overnight in the fridge.

As I spoke the ninety-three birthday candles of her life glowed
in her eyes and happily she said—"When I get to heaven the first
thing I'll do is make everybody pancakes!"

So it was one perfect morning that my grandmother having prepared
the batter the night before made all the free and joyous souls pancakes,
a heavenly feast that I already have been so privileged as to enjoy.

Awestruck at Niagara Falls

Freddy Niagara Fonseca

Chapter 1: The Poetry of Remembrance and Renewal

The shattering din and ever-louder roar
on approaching the waterfall,
ear-splitting almost to the max;
the steep drop of megazillions of gallons of growling, crashing water;
and the sheer, awe-inspiring wonder
the first time I saw
the turbulent magnitude
of Niagara Falls

had my little boy asking me that day, "Daddy,
what's a waterfall?"
As I was thinking hard what to
tell him of my mounting impressions of that massive outpouring of water
and the deafening, hypnotic power
of it all, almost pulling you clear over the edge,
he showed me in his own simple way, as we were getting closer,
what Niagara Falls

meant to him in his wide-eyed face at seeing
how much water was falling;
and how he covered his ears—his tiny
silhouette etched against that huge backdrop of roaring water,
aghast at the sly and enticing allure
of the beckoning abyss;
and how he flung himself into daddy's big arms to safely
watch Niagara Falls!

Awestruck and thunderstruck, but fiercely together—
my son holding on to me for dear life, and I to him—
we watched the overwhelming, shatter-splattering,
water-whelming walls upon walls upon walls
of clattering, clash-blasting, raging tons and tons
of water never-ending,
bowling us over, almost hurling us downward into
the Savage, Merciless, Rock-
Splitting,
ROARING, DRONING,
WRECKING, THUNDERING,
ROAR - RUMBLING,
M A E L S T R O M
of

T-O-T-A-L P-A-N-D-E-M-O-N-I-U-M—
mounting to huge, primordial, clang-towering soundscapes
of blangering, rattling, thundering bragh and droning brang;
obliterating every sense of self I've ever known
with the most cataclysmic, heart stopping vistas of clashing clangor—
ever-louder—
loud beyond comparison or conception even;
rending any lurking memory of quietude to bits and pieces, and
any reasonable thought to a jumble of noiseless nothings—
impossible to describe in words,
as words get completely ripped apart, chopped off, bent out of shape
to become unrecognizable,
lose their meaning,
thunderously disappearing, reappearing,
but differently, and
resembling nothing, not even sound,
roaring away again without trace—
back into the crashing, crazy chaos of noise
blasting downward at Niagara Falls!

How could I ever tell my son what a real waterfall is,
as everything I ever thought it was, was being made ridiculous
by this untamable power
bursting wide open with just all-out sound, sound, ongoing sound,
undifferentiated, primal, tribal, and intense;
bordering almost on madness;
simultaneously incomprehensible and making some sort of sense,
yet totally unfathomably so;
washing over everything,
drowning out and eroding everything in its path,
and shatter-shaking the very earth under Niagara Falls.

In the midst of all that infernal cacophony
where you cannot hear your own voice,
even if you screamed your lungs out for help,
my son pointed on high to the
many, many rainbows arching over clouds of spray bubbling up and away
to where the old Niagara River once must have decided
to go over the edge, and start falling down,
down, down, down, forevermore down,
to fall, fall, and fall,

Chapter 1: The Poetry of Remembrance and Renewal

and then indeed fell, fell, fell;
kept falling, tumbling, rumbling, thundering;
is still falling, crashing, and droning;
falls, falls, and
falls;
recklessly
falling
crash-shattering into
the seething, thundering, awesome cauldron
of Niagara Falls;

and then to proceed,
gradually becalming,
becoming a river all over again,
beyond the clamor,
beyond the thunder
where once it fell,
flowing toward a quieter distance to
where we all are headed,
far beyond anything
like Niagara Falls
faintly echoing,
still echoing
inside our ears,
and in
the back of our
minds
as I was safely driving
my son back
home . . . .

Waltz

Diane Frank

Published in *The Winter Life of Shooting Stars*, by Diane Frank.
© 1999 by Diane Frank.

Chapter 1: The Poetry of Remembrance and Renewal

The comet discovers a blue path
over your shoulder,
spinning through outer space
above the wood porch railing.

We are whirling to the harmonies of
"Star of County Down,"
your arm in the midheaven
of my back, holding
burgundy velvet.
A violin is weaving through
the flute,
but your eyes hold me to
a deeper melody.

Around the borders of
my seeing, your hair
curls into a halo of memory.
Maybe it is the full moon
or the thunder clouds gathering
out of season
over the rolling Wisconsin
cow pastures
predicting tomorrow's snow.

As we circle around each other,
the wind swirls over
the red barn
next to the 18th century
school house,
a terrifying beauty
that will blow the walls apart.

If I invite you into my house,
I know you would take the time
to find the trilobites
and the seashell fossils,
to see how the curve of the cello
fits my leg.
I'd watch you fold the prayers

This Enduring Gift

you have almost forgotten
into the saffron wrapped around
the bare feet of the Buddha.

And in your eyes
I might find the blue imprint
of a comet,
a message from a planet
near the Pleiades
etched by a ten-year-old
with a switchblade
into your largest finger,
an almost forgotten memory
of the way back home.

CHAPTER 1: THE POETRY OF REMEMBRANCE AND RENEWAL

New Ache

Paul Johan Stokstad

Chapter 1: The Poetry of Remembrance and Renewal

There's a new
ache in my heart
like a balloon,
growing, pushing
trying to get out
and float free

and it's just because
of your baby hand
resting in mine,

your climb,
still a bit awkward
up onto the couch
only to sit on my lap
and have me read you
the book you brought

your head, finally
giving up to rest
on my shoulder
as I bounce you
hoping for sleep
to the Norah
Jones album
again

it's your tiny bite
from my sandwich

your shriek of delight
while galloping around
the living room

your every tear
for hitting your head
for mommy leaving
for being up too late
(I dream of saving
every one)

This Enduring Gift

There is no gold
to outweigh or value
this feeling

as you lean over
in your high chair
to give me a little
broken piece
of your
avocado

Chapter 1: The Poetry of Remembrance and Renewal

Restoring the Meadow

Carole Lee Connet

For Carolyn Sims

Published in *The Iowa Source* 2001.
NFSPS Martin J. Prouty Award 2nd prize, 2004, *NFSPS Review*.

CHAPTER 1: THE POETRY OF REMEMBRANCE AND RENEWAL

Sowing tallgrass seed in the sunrise meadow—
big bluestem, Indian grass, switchgrass,
laced with purple coneflower,
evening primrose, prairie sage.

Tramping the abandoned pasture
in my straw hat and green Wellies,
chased by blue belly clouds,
broadcasting seeds by the handful.

Rampant with thistle, poison ivy, multiflora rose,
the gypsy meadow where the deer sleep
has been mowed, the wild thorns chopped,
though the insidious roots live on.

Today I am thinking about yesterday,
the hospital wedding I arranged in one day
for my friend with the half-shaved head,
her last unfulfilled wish.

A year ago the surgeon extracted a tumor
the size of a twelve-week fetus from her brain.
Now new growth is strangling her spine,
poison ivy in a run-down pasture.

The room is crammed with angels.
We are standing at the foot of her bed,
playing the part of her mother and father.
I speak for the mute bride, you give her away.

Today I am writing a poem for my friend,
wandering the worn out pasture,
sowing red clover, angelica,
blazing star.

Swing Low, Sweet Pontiac

Nancy Berg

for the late, great Roger Kaputnik

Published in *Oracles for Night-Blooming Eccentrics,* by Nancy Berg.

Chapter 1: The Poetry of Remembrance and Renewal

My father said there's a tollbooth
on the way to the Sweet Hereafter
and I have to say I'm strangely honored
that in at least one Vicodin vision
he chose to be carried to infinity
in my red 17-year-old Pontiac Sunbird
with its dirty white *schmata*-top
three hubcaps
and the continual high-pitched squeal
of a drill at a discount dentist.
This is one sunbird that never learned to fly,
I want to tell him;
it crawls from zero to 25
in a little more than an hour and a half.
But my father's in no rush, I guess,
and I'm thinking if good intentions
can be converted to currency *anywhere*,
it surely must be there,
at that dazzling tollbooth.
In this case the currency's all in the bumper stickers:
"Practice Random Kindness and Senseless Acts of Beauty"
on its field of purple
directly above the license plate;
"Wage Peace" scrawled in white letters on aquamarine;
"Save Tibet" on that flag of twin snow lions
and fierce geometry of light;
and over to the left, the tender, if prosaic,
"A Home for Every Animal Begins with a Place in the Heart."
I'm glad I never found the anti-nuclear classic
that said *"The Meek Don't Want It"*
beside a drawing of the earth,
since this might have offended the character in the tollbooth.
While it's true that here, in this temporal realm,
my earnest bumper stickers
at best provide reading material
for the rare bored driver not texting or applying mascara,
I think my father tried to see them
as proof that his sad-eyed daughter
turned out to be a relatively magnanimous person after all.
Mistaking my mother for me,

he asks if we will be taking the top down for this journey,
and I'm thinking,
if not now, when?
The heavenly cartoonist and I
can inch our way to timelessness
with the wind in whatever hair we have left,
singing "Beauty is Truth; Truth, Beauty,"
preparing to trade all we needed to know on earth
for all we need to know hereafter.

Chapter 1: The Poetry of Remembrance and Renewal

Meditation

Karen Karns

June 2009

I'm older now, and in harsh light
my crusty edges are dull, twig grey.
So, like a miner, I lower the light
into my cave, slide down, rock by
slippery rock, into a succulent
pool of sap, and bathe for hours.

Exploring, I lift the lantern
to the cave wall and Ah,
Inside, I'm a perfect rose petal pink.

A Word for My Mother

Leah Marie Waller

Published in *Under the Cedar Tree*, by Leah Marie Waller.

Chapter 1: The Poetry of Remembrance and Renewal

You were the hug when everyone was crying.
You called when the boys didn't.
You paid for all the things
I never told you
I always wanted.
You pulled my shoulders back
and my spirit up
when I didn't believe in myself.
You taught me how to bake cookies
and how to make a family.
You nourished me
so I could nourish him.
You will be the most beautiful woman
in the world.
Since the beginning
the mountains of your heart
echoed down
an unwavering note.
So I just have one thing to say:
I love you mom,
you gave me life.

Rendezvous

Steven Druker

"Rendezvous" was written in 1984

Chapter 1: The Poetry of Remembrance and Renewal

I stand in a languid place,

    My soul billowed by your remembered breath.

I stand in an arid place,

    My nostrils bedewed by the soft bouquet of your skin and hair.

I stand in a barren place,

My heart ripened with the essence of yours;
the tender feelings which so sweetly swarmed from yours to mine
now nested there, swelling the inner chambers with honeyed nectar.

I stand in a distant place,

    So close to you, so filled with you,

        And missing you so.

November Repast

Susie Niedermeyer

Published in *Under a Prairie Moon,* by Susie Niedermeyer.

I hate the cold gravel roads
that crisscross the quadrants of my day.
As I drive I shriek at the cows
clumped like raisins in lumpy oatmeal fields,
the green scraped off the landscape
like uneaten spinach off a plate.

How angry I've been at the predator wind
that yanks at my scarf
and the leaves that levitate in doorways
and ghost across the highway.
I'm collecting Japanese beetles in jars,
the ones that bite my neck
and fall from the ceiling into my tea.

Inside the weather's just as bad-futile acts
of contrition, guilt thick as grits.
You hole up like a drowsy snake
in front of your computer, and we send emails
through a 1910 plaster wall, reconfiguring
the parameters of a marriage.

I feel heavy as a rotting persimmon,
bleeding vital juices onto a plate.
I don't know how to live any life
other than this, here in frigid Iowa.
The chill clings to me like shrink wrap
and my limbs are stiff as celery.
Can't we just go home?

View #45

Thomas Centolella

After Hokusai and Hiroshige

Published in *Views from Along the Middle Way,* by Thomas Centolella. This poem was read at the United Nations as a part of Poets Against the War.

I dreamt half my life was spent
In wonder, and never suspected.

So immersed in the moment
I forgot I was ever there.

Red-tailed hawk turning
resistance into ecstasy.

The patrolmen joking with the drunk
Whose butt seemed glued to the sidewalk.

A coral quince blossom in winter,
Pink as a lover's present.

And tilting my bamboo umbrella
Against the warm slant

Of rain, was I not a happy peasant
Crossing the great bay on a bridge that began

Who knows when, and will end
Who knows when?

A White Veil

Libbett Rich

Chapter 1: The Poetry of Remembrance and Renewal

A white veil whirling
round my body
I am carried
to an altar
for a sacrifice

My body is charred
and yet a new one rises
and I remain alive outside
my burned body

Myself splits into two slices
and a lotus springs up in the middle of me
It is handed to me
and I am open wide

Four Memories of North West Arkansas

Charlie Hopkins

for Ananda Lorca Hopkins

Chapter 1: The Poetry of Remembrance and Renewal

one

I am 24 years old again.
Ananda in the moonlight room
spring wind blowing through her from an open window.
She is wearing a little gown the color of the moon
pulling herself up by the bars of her crib
using the power of the moon.

She is crying she is crying!

People have told us let her so she can learn to be
alone.

We are crying.

two

I walk in wet fields toward end of day
sun setting fire to water in the ruts.
Follow hoof prints of a white calf through oak trees
into the pasture higher up where long grass whispers

"Jesus saves... Jesus saves..."

To the south black crows caw from the hollow
where the spring creek empties into corn.
I hear them beating something on a rock and later find
the skull of a squirrel broken open with the marrow eaten out.

In the quiet after a crow caw there is a hollow in my chest
the size of an open hand.

Below me now red furrows in the dusk.
The field a barren woman with streams of menstrual blood.
I kneel to drink water the color of fire and blood from the hoof print
of the white calf.

This Enduring Gift

Turning home my first wife is kneading dough again.
I look down at our rent house built of creek rock with flag stone porch
where copper heads like to sun themselves.
Suddenly my hands are beside my mouth
my lungs letting out bursts of air from the hollow in my chest
imitating a crow!

Dogs in all directions lift their heads and look into trees!

three

Something is wrong with the pregnant cow!
She walks in circles bellowing!
From a distance it looks like a tree limb sticking out behind her.
She lies down gets up.
I run over see the hoof of her calf coming out.
She lies down in pain again.

Run to the road yell at an old farmer driving his tractor to town
a man whose teeth are like children dead to him now.
Shows me how to put both hands inside the cow
take hold of the calf's head and pull it into place.

Then we all pull together!
Shelley runs from the house and we all pull on the calf's legs
our hands cut by razors of wind!

The farmer says sometimes he hooks them to his tractor and pulls.
But the calf shoots out like my daughter did
steaming blue and white membrane and blood!
The cow gets up licks the eyes of her calf
licks out the nose and mouth.

Everybody is happy!

four

Then come long horns of evening
crow caws flattened over pond water and carried deep in earth.
I get up in the dark stars falling like figs from the Bible.

Walk around the rent house knowing ten years before
that I will loose everything
be picked up by county cops walking towards Texas
shirtless with an oak bow strung across my chest
and a quiver full of hand whittled arrows
shouting

"I am the white calf! I am the Mother of the calf!
I am crow caw!"

Everybody laughing!

A Still Point of the Turning World

Henry Robert Hau

Published in *For the Bird Sings,* by Henry Robert Hau.

Chapter 1: The Poetry of Remembrance and Renewal

Jogging up a hill in High Park
one morning late March
I saw four scarlet tanagers
riding shoots of black oak
like musical notes in the wind

The world crashed in silence
I entered the tableau
fell into the Chinese painting
at one with eternal artifice
and nature

O Beauty, time stopped
I was born and died

Imagine,
I ran up that hill to meet them
in that moment, transcendence

... and the birds just flew away

The Poetry of Nature, the Cosmos, and the Soul

Chapter 2

If the universal is the essential, then it is the basis of all life and art. Recognizing and uniting with the universal therefore gives us the greatest satisfaction, the greatest emotion of beauty. The more this union with the universe is felt, the more individual subjectivity declines.

— Piet Mondriaan, Dutch painter (1872-1944)

Contents

50	This Whisper	*Michael Hock*
52	Iowa Meditation	*Viktor Tichy*
54	Mirror Lake	*Rolf Erickson*
56	The Language of the Trees	*Freddy Niagara Fonseca*
60	Prairie Air Show	*Steven P. Schneider*
62	Spring Leaves	*Susan Klauber*
64	Forest Road at Night	*William Clair Godfrey*
66	Dolphin Report	*Nancy Berg*
70	Into the Woods	*Rolf Erickson*
72	Jesus in Iowa	*James Moore*
74	Troubles	*Glenn Watt*
76	The Stage	*Janet Thomas*
78	In the Wind River Mountains	*Karla Christensen*
82	On Hope	*Glenn Watt*
84	Walking the Loop	*Steven P. Schneider*
90	Shepherd on Snowdon	*James Tipton*

A work of art has an author and yet, when it is perfect, it has something which is essentially anonymous about it.

— Simone Weil, French philosopher, mystic, and social activist (1909-1943)

We are all in the gutter, but some of us are looking at stars.
— Oscar Wilde (1854-1900)

Chapter 2

The Poetry of Nature, the Cosmos, and the Soul

Nature, or the natural world, is a favorite subject of most poets, along with such alluring topics as Love and Night. It is primarily regarded as the outdoors — grass, trees, hills, rocks, animals — things we can touch in our physical world.

But aren't all these closely related to what's inside us? Feelings, the psyche, the Soul, Self? Isn't everything we define as 'outdoors' just that because we build walls in order to create a dwelling around *our inside world?*

Whether living in rural or urban surroundings, poets become inspired to write after looking through a window at the sky or hearing a bird warbling a song.

In little more than an instant, some fine aspect of Nature, the Cosmos, or the Soul may show up scribbled on a piece of paper and turn into an ode, a stanza, a haiku, or maybe just one thrilling line of wonder.

this whisper

Michael Hock

Dedicated to Sri Gary Olsen, current Living Master, and founder of the MasterPath.

© 2009 Michael Hock.

Chapter 2: The Poetry of Nature, the Cosmos, and the Soul

the song of the morning star
or the nectar of sage smelled
shook loose by rain like the finest comb
this turning one thing to another
day to night, summer to winter
such indelible sweetness, joyous greeting
the you of god always there, joining
joining all, connecting, transcribing
the one upon the other, endless
no stop, no gap, no matter what holds back
holds on, struggles and anguish aside
change and transcendence your magic sword
your constant blessing of there and not there
all this serving, this constancy of
the magnificent you in all, the sound
at the base of every concept
yes! this you come to meet, give back
that holy moment transfixed upon another
give back even self transcended, the holy
you becoming this one being also
the world singing its joy no concern
no focus, but there upon the simplest stillness
time's crinkling and quaking cast loose
like the doppler fade of a long past truck
the whine almost gone into forever gone
while here You are, bright with greeting
this secret whisper, finally, after so long
resounding like a whole universe speaking

Iowa Meditation

Viktor Tichy

When the tune is so pure, the hearing dies
beyond the silken thread of frozen sound,
when winter oaks shed their silver garb
and a starling tweets the countdown,

when licorice eyes bathe and shine
in the quarry pools of mine,
and your lips tame my flooded gaze,
then gasp into a smile,

when the void in the navel
explodes into a shower of poppies,
too unbearably red
not to shutter the mask with their softness,

it's time to root the fingers into meadows
and listen for the birth of fireflies.

Mirror Lake

Rolf Erickson

Chapter 2: The Poetry of Nature, the Cosmos, and the Soul

One
trout
rises

to nibble
a
reflected star

sending ripples through the universe

The Language of the Trees

Freddy Niagara Fonseca

I never saw a discontented tree.
— John Muir

I

I asked the trees one summer
What they had been thinking of all year.
They wouldn't say,
But then I heard them wave
And whisper of the ages—
Seasons—
Years, and months, and days—
And countless hours
Of abundant happiness!

II

I like the tales they tell me.
Autumn makes them talk of leaving all,
And yet they stay,
And as they drop their leaves,
They muse for weeks on April—
Thrushes—
Stars and lingering Indian summers—
Rain—
And latent loneliness . . .

III

Their voice is low in winter.
Snow and icy winds are on their minds,
And they withdraw;
But in their winter dreams
You hear how branches sing,
And think of dawn—
The sun in distant countries—
Warmth—
And summer peacefulness.

IV

How grand they are each season—
Often have I seen them stand like kings!
A certain awe
Surrounds their splendid forms,
And so they wait for spring—
For flowers—
Verdant prairies—
Butterflies in May—
And simple loveliness.

V

And then they speak of lovers!
Sudden colors spread their message fast,
And every year
Their many stories bloom,
And nourish noble pages—
Poems—
Gorgeous music—
Heart and mind
With endless youthfulness.

VI

And so we welcome summer . . .
All day long they stand and think and dream,
And all we hear
Is how they wave again
And whisper of the ages—
Seasons—
Years, and months, and days—
And countless hours
Of unending happiness . . .

Prairie Air Show

Steven P. Schneider

First appeared in *A Prairie Mosaic: An Atlas of Central Nebraska's Land, Culture and Nature.*
Published in *Unexpected Guests*, by Steven P. Schneider.

Just because
   no one sees

the pods
   of the milkweed

slowly open
     on the prairie

on a cold October night
   doesn't mean

we should ignore
   their white silken treasure

readying itself
   for flight

on a sunny afternoon
   when the cottonwoods

are turning gold.
   Who can say

if the prairie dogs
   sun-bathing

on the hillside
     have come to see

the air show,
   but when a trio

of pods burst open
and the white silk parachutes

float over the prairie
   meadow

even the sharp green tips
   of the yucca

crane in anticipation.

Spring Leaves

Susan Klauber

I shed my winter boots,
and perch on the gray rocks,
listening to the lake
laying her offerings at my stocking feet.

Leaves I wouldn't let go last fall,
hung onto all winter
like the last mole of my identity,
slip into the wind unnoticed.
I spot the first one float over the lake,
nestle down close to the water,
within breathing distance
of the gentle lapping of its skin.
Then they kiss,
a soft and instant marriage,
drifting off together,
the leaf carried on the tender canopy of water.

Then two, three, four leaves follow,
rippling brown tiaras in the monastic air,
curling into the plush seats
of the moving carriage.

The silent return of comets continues,
interludes of invisible wands
releasing a diary of used stars
to the care of the wind and the water.

It is so simple.
When it is time, we notice.
We don't know what, or why,
but we notice,
the background of our fussing.

Forest Road at Night

William Clair Godfrey

Chapter 2: The Poetry of Nature, the Cosmos, and the Soul

I have walked the forest road at night,
Alone, without a light.

Dolphin Report

Nancy Berg

Published in *Oracles for Night-Blooming Eccentrics*, by Nancy Berg.

Look inside the center of my heart.
You'll find a newspaper clipping of yourself
in your white First Communion veil
or a snapshot of your grandson at his Bar Mitzvah,
smiling in front of the chopped liver swan.
I am in love from the moment I am born
until the moment I die.
Why else would I leap thirty feet in the air,
whistling and clicking,
spinning seven times
before I touch down in the dark sea
where I am born, tail-first
and nudged to the surface to breathe;
before I even taste the rich milk of my mother
I fall in love with everything above and below sea level.
With the currents pressing fast on my soft, new skin,
with the sun sending shafts through the top of the ocean,
with the woman on the boat in the yellow scarf
shouting, pointing,
holding a drink and a camera in one hand.
When I am in love I swim like a fish,
fly like a bird,
and breathe like a man.

Listen to the center of my heart.
You'll hear that quiet song you used to sing over and over
in a thin, high voice
when your mother thought you were asleep.
The awkward, tinny piano of your first recital.
You'll hear the joke about the sailor
that will still make you laugh
five minutes before
you close your eyes for the last time in this body.

It patterns my face in a fixed grin
and lets me glide and play on the waves from your ships,
falling backward
into joy crackling like early electricity.
But that same love

makes me need to guide those ships
every night for twenty years
through the sharp coral reefs of Australia.
The same love that lets me hold you to the surface
when you're drowning
makes me cling to an abandoned dinghy
like a giant rag doll.
It makes me haunt one beach for ten years
waiting for a dead boy to ride on my back.
That which lifts me up also weighs me down,
but you already understand this.
I live only to breathe in unison.

So I learn to speak without vocal chords
and recognize geometric shapes in waterproof books.
Small things like this make you so happy.
But look inside the center of my heart.
You'll find a hologram
of the part of you you've been wanting to worship
for a long, long time.

Chapter 2: The Poetry of Nature, the Cosmos, and the Soul

Into the Woods

Rolf Erickson

Published in *Leaves By Night, Flowers By Day.*

Heading north
just over
the ridge

you'll
find
the lake

wide as a world

deeper
than
mind
can
be

patiently
waiting
for

you alone

it's
your
home

it's where
your dreams go
to come true

it's the reason sometimes
not knowing why
you stop and listen

the trail
heads
north

into
the
woods

day
and
night
it calls you

Jesus in Iowa

James Moore

Published in *Lyrical Iowa*.

Iowa is rusty brown, windy and clear
   this St. Patrick's Day.
Mustaches of dimpled snow, still white,
   die alongside the highway.
Unseasonable warmth, sixty-eight degrees
   till midday, low of twenty-five tonight.
The pools of water in the flat, muddy farm fields
   look hopeful if a bit naïve.
There's no green save for the road signs,
   perhaps a hint beneath the dead grass.

Nature appears reluctant, hesitant,
   like a first-time expectant mother,
   a nervous kind of eager.
It's a sunny day but even the sky seems pale.
Hwy 1 lays disinterested, listless,
   a bleak grey flattop river mindlessly winding.
If Jesus were to suddenly reappear,
   it wouldn't be here,
at least not today.

Troubles

Glenn Watt

Published in *The Contemporary Review*.

Chapter 2: The Poetry of Nature, the Cosmos, and the Soul

I take mine back to the garden
where I can sit among these things that grow –

the purple sputterings of the iris
as they flare up against an orange wash
of poppies woven
into a latticework of weathered cedar,

thin drifts of columbine
hovering like lavender clouds
above white clumps like snow,

pale blue saucers spinning
on their tall poles –

until my preoccupations with the world quietly lift
like a second lid,

until they stand, rusting, like this scrap iron Kokopelli
on its solitary stalk
among the withering stubs and the late-blooming fringe
of the festive tulips,

until all I want
is to be here, in the garden, in the moment,
where my soul

is a thick succulent quilted tuber unraveling
its violet tresses downward

into my upstretched many-fingered palms.

The Stage

Janet Thomas

Five deer dance on snow,
a blue rhythm commanding
the moon to follow.

In the Wind River Mountains

Karla Christensen

I go swimming because the water holds me up
because the water touches me all over.
It is a lovemaking,
the way it slides past my sides, calves, knees
cools the top of my head,
Jellos thick around me until
I am fruit encased in cold green translucency.

Give me a wind, a river, a mountain a lake,
covered with granite rocks,
all the trees dead, burned
and the lake cold,
so cold it takes me four days to get in,
becoming a prayer, a revolution, a ritual cleansing.

Why does the lake still exist
in air so dry it could suck the lake into it
and contain it all without rain
as the wind contains without a shimmer
the unwilling offering of the edge of my lips
and the plump of the skin on my hands?

My body is an uncomfortable thing
to take on a long hike, still, I like
to watch the scenery change:
poised on the edge of a limestone cliff
I wonder whether to cry or to trust the trajectory
of my body through air and trust the willingness
of my feet to find one balance point at a time.
I prefer always to be close to the ground
choosing to scratch through wild berries and
crush the wild mint under muddy legs

or to climb tiredly stomach over a log, swing one leg,
watch the broken-off knife of branch as the last
thigh goes by. I could be hopping lightfoot
log to log as the others have, to leave me a quarter
mile behind, panting in a field of blue lupine
that merges into dusty sky made of my breath.

I like to sweat. Pores open, evaporation is its own revolution
a happy event, not like struggling with breath. Climbing
the boulder strewn drop next to the rapids I know
that when I catch up the others will leave before I rest.
Here, God has made a flagged stone walkway
into the river where a bear could easily
crawl out and drink from the river without wetting his feet—
though I suppose he doesn't care about that.

The kids go on, promising to return in three hours.
I think of grizzly bears while I pant and sweat.
I wet my hat, bathe my face, head spinning, look for shade,
fall onto the underlip of a boulder
in the stars of heat prostration. If a bear comes,
the burnt tree trunks will not offer refuge
not that I could climb a tree anyway
and I sure as hell can't run: I'd be staggering
on the edge of the mountain. If a bear comes—
if the kids don't come back, or don't stop for me—

Inert under stone shade, flesh on granite,
my mind becomes element-air miles across—
If a bear comes, if the kids don't return—
I am willing, flesh like fruit, so different from stone,
cells with nerves to sense themselves,
cells into the Wind River Mountains
can melt and evaporate
until no messages start or end.

I dream of an undersea life,
of a boat in a harbor
or rock pilings under a pier,
of the ebb & flow of shadowy green waters
and the ectoplasmic sensing of sea food on a rock.

I like to swim because water surrounds me,
holds me up while I struggle with breath,
I like to be submerged in the water under thoughts.
It's a kind of lovemaking, flesh in the water,
flesh walking through air, flesh lying on a rock.

On Hope

Glenn Watt

Published in *The MacGuffin*.

Chapter 2: The Poetry of Nature, the Cosmos, and the Soul

One spring, I spent several evenings among the mule deer on Warm Springs mountain. They seemed so happy then, having just survived another hard death by starvation or by the bullet to wander down and graze peacefully on the tender leaves of timothy and clover that grow there along the base of the mountain. As legend has it, an Indian could at one time walk right up and touch one of these sleek brown creatures as it browsed unsuspecting in the gathering dusk before me. I tried that, working my way carefully down through the dry sage and loose rock of a hillside, stopping dead still when they looked up, sometimes caught balanced awkwardly on one leg for long moments while they leisurely tested the air. I don't think I ever really intended to touch one. I just wanted to see how close I could come. Their lives, like my hopes, were so quick and supple there, so vulnerable in that high open country in the sun.

Slow and clumsy, I came within a hundred yards before they wandered down to the river to drink.

Walking the Loop

Steven P. Schneider

First published in *Critical Quarterly*.
Published in *Unexpected Guests*, by Steven P. Schneider.

Chapter 2: The Poetry of Nature, the Cosmos, and the Soul

1.

You are out walking the loop, a 3 mile circuit
along elderberry, fir and wild blackberry—
water on all sides. Though you have walked this loop
many Sundays, nobody knows your name
or who you are.

It's a question of beginning again.
Of finding that place within
where you can give yourself to what you see,
to what you hear,
where you can say "hello"
and not mind if anyone is listening.

The Western gulls that hover near the shore
have rehearsed the geometry of flight.
They cruise above the lake, dip
when a piece of bread
is tossed into it.

Sometimes you bring your son here.

He is happy to see the boats bobbing
afloat with software engineers, investors, retired teachers—
their caps, visors, and sunglasses
shielding them from the sun
and one another.

2.

For the tightness inside of you to uncoil,
you must learn the secret of walking the loop.
Take this group of Vietnamese refugees,
smiling, talking back and forth
as if their lives depended upon it.

They are happy to be in the park today,
away from some South End side street
with its litter and mangy cats.
They are dressed as if it were a holiday,
their cotton pants ablaze with the color
of pink and orange water lilies.

One of them plans to catch a fish.
He carries his pole in one hand,
his line in the other.
He will stand by the shores of Lake Washington,
far out on one end of the loop
where he can see the city.

He will toss his line out
toward the skyscrapers, the open air markets, and dry cleaners—
out into the lake, and for a moment
forget that he must have this fish
to feed his children.
He will drink in the jagged beauty
of the snow-capped mountains in the distance
and forget
that his wife never returned
from her parents' village.

3.

It used to be every Sunday meant going on an outing together.

Often, the road led to a sandy beach,
or a path through the woods.

But now you are relearning the necessity
of finding your own way.
She spends her Sundays in the garden,
spraying the bugs off raspberries, building mounds of dirt,
pinching the flowers off strawberry plants.

In her straw hat and dungarees,
she is sounding her own depths.

A neighbor tells you he's tried to count
the different kinds of wild flowers
she's planted in the bed beside your driveway.
"More than you see up in the summer mountain meadows," he says.

This space between you now
"is a kind of answered prayer."
Not a cold and stony peace,
but warm, like the evening air in August
out on the loop.

4.

Half-way around, there's a small stone house
that sits close to the shore.
Set back on a wooded hill
is the fish hatchery.

You can hear the sounds of water
trickling over rocks down the stream bed:
a slow, steady stream today.
In cool, dark pools beneath the fir and hemlock
sleek, bright-orange salmon
dart among the shadows.
Who knows what dreams they spawn?
And when the fish hatch,
they will make their way into the stream,
down the hillside and out into the lake.

5.

The letter S makes a loop
that if you follow to a logical conclusion
will close.

The fishermen who wait
in the shadows by the shoreline
make a loop of their lines
into which a hook may be hooked.

The Blue Angels in full aerial display
dazzle the viewer with their daredevil antics,
leaving a loop of smoke in the air behind them.

A loop must return, and because it does
you can keep walking
without ever losing your way.

6.

When twilight turns the chittering of the birds to music,
and the ducks out on the lake huddle for evening prayer,
you make your way back.

Beneath a waterside weeping willow,
a group of Cambodians sit cross-legged on the grass,
eating rice and fried fish out of blue bowls.

After dinner, dessert: rhubarb
pie on paper plates.
After that they will fly a kite,
its green and black tail fluttering over the lake.

Their children will curl into their mothers' laps
and dream.
Not an unhappy dream,
but a kind of reverie,
a blending of wind socks and chimes.

One old man will sit apart from the rest,
his teeth missing, and look out onto the lake.
He will be watching for the terns.

If you listen closely,
you will hear the wind moving off shore.
In the distance, bells are sounding,
a kayak glides through the water.
You have been walking the loop,
drawing you out even as it takes you in.

Shepherd on Snowdon

James Tipton

In another life I awoke at dawn,
tended the sheep,
climbed the mountain after them
wrapped in fog, wind piercing
my cape of hide. I sang
for the pinnacles revealed
by the blowing mist.
I danced for the tunes
of bleating sheep and the bells of the lost streams.
I spoke poetry to the giant of the cliffs.
And no one heard, no one saw,
but I was happy, by myself
with all of that mountain
                      for me alone.

The Poetry of Mysteries and Imagination

Chapter 3

The most beautiful thing we can experience is the mysterious. It is the source of all true art and all science. He to whom this emotion is a stranger, who can no longer pause to wonder and stand rapt in awe, is as good as dead: his eyes are closed.

— Albert Einstein, German scientist (1879-1955)

Contents

94	A Vague Feeling	*Phoebe Carter*
96	Imagine You're a River	*Jason Walls*
98	There Is a Secret	*Rolf Erickson*
100	Love Poem to a Chinese Tallow Tree	*Charlie Hopkins*
102	Where I Walk	*Bill Graeser*
104	The Rain Is Sun When It Falls in Ireland	*Leah Marie Waller*
106	The Doe	*Freddy Niagara Fonseca*
108	Lullaby for the Universe	*Nynke Passi*
110	Tumbling Planets	*Janet Thomas*
112	The River Stone	*Henry Robert Hau*
114	Caught	*Karen Karns*
116	The Other Side	*James Tipton*
118	Something to Know	*Bill Graeser*
120	Like the Robin's Egg	*Paul Johan Stokstad*

Do something that nobody else has done, something that will dazzle the world!

— Paramahansa Yogananda,
Indian yogi and guru (1893-1952)

Chapter 3

The Poetry Of Mysteries And Imagination

Francisco Goya (1746-1828), the famous Spanish painter, wrote a caption for one of his etchings, *"Fantasy, abandoned by reason, produces impossible monsters; united with it, she is the mother of the arts and the origin of marvels."*

Poets love the impossible. Don't talk to us about logic. We demand freedom to imagine, find, reject, explore, choose, and make the impossible possible.

We want mists, veils, mystery, secrets, and ambiguity in a language that's precise and unambiguous. We create an imagery of words impossible to define.

Imagination! Who can sing thy force? Or who describe the swiftness of thy course?
– Phillis Wheatley, American poet (ca. 1753-1784)

And if we create a monster and not a marvel? So what? We'll beget a wonder the next time. Leave fantasy and imagination to us, and we'll etch a parade of marvels in the tablet of your soul.

A Vague Feeling

Phoebe Carter

Chapter 3: The Poetry of Mysteries and Imagination

A vague feeling
More foreign than India.
The spectral sound of the tambourine
The beautiful laugh,
The butterflies —
They intertwine anonymously.
Trying to remember to breathe
With a serenade of dangerous emotions.
Trying to maintain the order
And yet...continue to imagine.

Imagine You're a River

Jason Walls

Chapter 3: The Poetry of Mysteries and Imagination

Imagine you're a river... you fight through life wriggling your way through sharp bends, but this is okay for you, until you catch a glimpse of the upcoming ocean. It's so vast and beautiful. You're excited, you're afraid. Which is right? Both. Imagine that rapids represent your heart, and the river's flow represents your mind. You begin to descend down a steep slope toward the vastness of the ocean. Your mind is excited about the possibility of becoming something immeasurably great, but your heart is afraid because this isn't an ordinary bend. Your heart clings to familiarity and beats faster, and more rapids form. Concurrently, your mind picks up speed and the flow becomes immeasurably faster. When your heart and mind finally agree, and the tumult of the descent finally finds peace, you understand yourself in a new way. You're still a river, but now you're connected with all other rivers, and you're all flowing together in one ocean. Your heart becomes content as it accepts the change, and the rapids disappear. Then your mind, sensing that the heart has let go, begins to spread out into a new, more profound flow. And you come to realize that other hearts and other minds are just like yourself. They went through different yet similar paths to reach this boundless state. You understand this, your different parts agree, and you reach out to agree with other parts of other rivers. And you clasp together... and find bottomless peace... and you no longer have to imagine you're a river.

There Is a Secret

Rolf Erickson

Chapter 3: The Poetry of Mysteries and Imagination

There is a
secret
in this poem

where

one line ends
and
the next begins

where

nothing is
and
everything is possible

don't
be
misled

by mere words

Love Poem to a Chinese Tallow Tree

Charlie Hopkins

Chapter 3: The Poetry of Mysteries and Imagination

Tonight the moon is rising up the back of my spine.

I go without a shirt on to the Chinese tallow tree

in the yard.

I want to bend her down in my arms and ride her

like I did when I was a boy.

But she is above me now

her branches full of yellow pollen.

Where I Walk

Bill Graeser

I walk where the rusted car
sits at the edge of the field—
grass as high as the fenders.

The shout of the engine
and rumble of the road
have gone

that now the grass is heard—
chaff bells chiming
in the wind

and birdsong—bugles
of a feathered cavalry.

Beyond the field are trees,
the earth sloping down
to a stream

with water enough
to hear what water says.

This is as far as I've come.
No further have I been.
As many have not

but a field mouse,
a hawk,
an oak holding

the sun in its arms
and a poem,
though not this poem,

but one you write
in a field
not far away.

The Rain Is Sun When It Falls in Ireland

Leah Marie Waller

From *Poem A Day For A Year Journal*

Chapter 3: The Poetry of Mysteries and Imagination

Heavy and sudden
on the grey street without apology.
How can I hold an umbrella to this majesty?
This is a country where the ugly sister is beautiful
and her puddles are bowls of silver wine.
Here the clouds are evening gowns
resting on the shoulders of the cities
and the view looks barren without them.
Here the sun doesn't rise or set down to the fields;
she falls proud and soaking
from the smiling Irish sky.

The Doe

Freddy Niagara Fonseca

For my Daughter, for a Doe

The thirst of the soul is sweeter than the wine of material things, and the fear of the spirit is dearer than the security of the body.
— Kahlil Gibran

Chapter 3: The Poetry of Mysteries and Imagination

Why so afraid to bow down,
My dear, dear daughter?
Does not the doe daily go down to her spring?
Doesn't the spring, brimming with water,
Flow like a river down to the sea?

Why so afraid to look up,
My dear, dear daughter?
Does not the sea always look up at the sky?
Doesn't the cloud, heavy with water,
Rain in cycles back to the sea?

You are thirsty—I know it,
My dear little doe.
You're thirsty and lonely, and yet you resemble a
Cool oasis brimming with water
Where birds gather and sing.

I am trustful—you know it,
My dear little doe.
Be your journey as trustful, for I'll be going,
Like a river receding, like water
Flowing back to its spring.

Don't be afraid to look up,
My daughter, my dear one.
Have my hands not always dried all your tears?
Be on your own now, dear daughter.
It's time for me to go.

Don't be afraid to bow down,
My daughter, my dear one.
One heaven spans all over your tears, you know.
Won't you come down to the water
Now and drink, dear little doe?

Lullaby for the Universe

Nynke Passi

Chapter 3: The Poetry of Mysteries and Imagination

If my eye were placed high as God's eye—
sky with its pupil of light—
I would know the stories of this world
and translate them to poems

My eye would see the night sky,
a meadow of soft, black grass,
and the frozen stars exploding from it,
white puffs of dandelion

My eye would see planets, helical shells
slow as slugs in pace,
crawling no faster than inch by inch
up the wall of space

My eye would see the orbiting moon,
a glass bubble blown
from the perfectly round mouth of Earth,
floating and glowing till dawn

My eye would see the sun, a bride
trailing her veil of rays,
waiting at the altar—no groom in sight—
waiting like that all her days

If my hand were as large as the hand of God
I'd part the curtained blue sky
Then shifty clouds could enjoy the show
and trees might take a bow

If my hand were as large as the hand of God
I'd cup the lonely moon's face
I'd hide with the moon in the universe
behind nothing, in no place

Tumbling Planets

Janet Thomas

Chapter 3: The Poetry of Mysteries and Imagination

I am the Pear Princess
I climb the purple tower,
I see the Mother's wheel
shatter the knife-edged skies of men.

I stand toe-deep in wet sand,
silver air seeps
through my outstretched fingers.

I inhale the white smiles of squirrels,
the eyes of bees,
and the swirling tails of sea-stars.

My words soar with swallow-tailed certainty,
tilting the tumbling plumage of the planets.

The River Stone

Henry Robert Hau

Published in *For the Bird Sings,* by Henry Robert Hau.

Chapter 3: The Poetry of Mysteries and Imagination

I gave you a blue river stone
cut to hold your rings
and the Dalai Lama's petals

It is a tomb now
for the ashes of our Karma

----

  far away
I will become now snow

  to dissolve
on the white leopard's paw

Caught

Karen Karns

Caught in a fine silken netting of bliss, I struggle
no more. Body and mind float downward beneath
the swift current and sink deep into the downy
membrane of ocean floor, like lost buried treasure.

Held by neither land nor sky, the sea envies me.
It can not follow into that primordial stir, that first
whirling of darkness into light, or play midwife as
bubbling births dance their way into figure and form.

The Other Side

James Tipton

Chapter 3: The Poetry of Mysteries and Imagination

The other side of the galaxy —
Over its wall a stream runs
Where I hear dancing —
Jingle of anklets
Flute sounds
Tiny cymbals
And from there
Indescribably far
It comes to my ears
And I know the feet dancing
Bare in the new green grass
I know the smile, the blue eyes,
The wave of dark hair
And the dancer departs
On a ripple passing
Downstream

Something to Know

Bill Graeser

Published in *Lyrical Iowa* 2006.

Chapter 3: The Poetry of Mysteries and Imagination

The old tree by the old school
knows something—look at it
and you'll see.

A city of leaves built high
above a single trunk, and the way
the sun comes to it, and the rain,

and roots—a cellar full
of monks making wine, while
in any weather wearing but

a simple bark-robe. But more
than this is the stillness, the poised
Grace, as if the best place

it could be is right where it is
and if ever it needs move...
a breeze comes.

Like the Robin's Egg

Paul Johan Stokstad

Chapter 3: The Poetry of Mysteries and Imagination

Like the robin's egg
Waiting at the edge
Of being blue
And not being

Your skin approaches
The junction point
Of Being
And becoming

Like candy for the fingers

Touching you
I can never be sure
Whether I've touched
The truly real

Or it's just
That my fingertips
Are dreaming

The Poetry of Whimsicality and Simple Things

Chapter

4

*A first-rate soup is more creative
than a second-rate painting.*

— Abraham Maslow, American psychologist (1908-1970)

Contents

124	While You Were Gone	*Tom Le May*
126	Zinnia	*Elizabeth McIsaac*
128	The Moor Park	*George K. Attwood*
130	The Puzzle Tale	*Viktor Tichy*
132	Sneaking Free	*Tony Ellis*
134	Fairy Trifle	*William Clair Godfrey*
136	Water Wings	*River Dog*
138	Five Haiku	*Ken Chawkin*
140	Toilet Poetry	*Jordy Yager*
142	Lullaby Baby Frog	*Karla Christensen*
144	When I Die	*Viktor Tichy*
146	Trying on Your New Hat	*Tom Le May*

I don't like to commit myself about heaven and hell — you see, I have friends in both places.

— Mark Twain, American author and humorist (1835-1910)

Chapter 4
The Poetry of Whimsicality and Simple Things

Now for something different. Here's what Chinese Zen master Yunmen (ca. 864-949) advised mankind long ago, *"In walking, just walk. In sitting, just sit. Above all, don't wobble."*

But seriously, it's sometimes argued that only the serious deserves to carry the label of 'High Art.' But *that* kind of art looks high only because some influential critics placed it upon a pedestal, and you believed them.

Whimsicality has its own platform, and 'it ain't' high at all. It revels in making fun of the austere, academic, and pedantic.

If it is true that Art imitates Life, there must be room for simple things as well.

Now if High Art tries to tell you what's best for you, don't believe a word of it. We can be down-to-earth and have a ball with Low Art anytime!

Just make sure you don't wobble.

While You Were Gone

Tom Le May

While you were gone
The roosters didn't crow.
We got up late and were grumpy all day,
                              every day.
The corn refused to grow even one inch!
Heroes wouldn't rise to the occasion and
there were no silver linings in any of the many clouds.

While you were away joy evaporated
like rain in the desert
                leaving reservoirs at dangerously low levels.
Responsible public officials are alarmed; alarming!

Thank God, you've returned.

Zinnia

Elizabeth McIsaac

Published in *A Sun Palette of Song'ans, Book I*, by Elizabeth McIsaac.

Chapter 4: The Poetry of Whimsicality and Simple Things

You don't go out for perms,
never hassle combs,
your glory shapes in layers
coifed and pulled back tight,
fresh and crisp this morning,
lustrous silky mauve
around your sunny eyes.

You toss your ribboned head
        to beats of horsey hoof
        and kiddee jumper rope,
        the breeze, the bee,
        my passing by —
so by the end of day
you've tousled with delight
your ruffled flutter strips.

Too soon
your starch will slacken,
less formal,
head inclined,
your bob a little frowzy,
their tips a smidgen furled
poofed and rolled awry,
and color toned to mute
with moon and starry light.

My buxom daytime Zinnie,

Good night.

The Moor Park

George K. Attwood

Published in *Into The Pulse of the Golden Turtle*, The Live Poet's Society, 1989.

Chapter 4: The Poetry of Whimsicality and Simple Things

My mind reels with thoughts of
The luscious fragrance
Of ripe, golden apricots.

And not just any apricots will do,
But most especially those named Moor Park.
Large, golden orbs of apricot juices.

Swarming through my mind —
The fruit's ambrosial nectar,
Redolent of some hypnotic perfume,

As the juices of the Moor Park,
Are again flooding down
My lips, and chin, and chest.

The Puzzle Tale

Viktor Tichy

Tribute to the Lowe Family

First Prize in *Ohio Poetry Day*.

Chapter 4: The Poetry of Whimsicality and Simple Things

A girl who lived in our land
received for her fifth birthday
a jig-saw puzzle of the world.
She wanted to put it together right away,
but her father said:
"Darling, this is way too complicated.
It can take the rest of our lives.
I will go to the store for a today's paper
while mom is cooking spaghetti.
After supper we can start".

He returned half an hour later,
but his daughter completed the puzzle by herself.
"How on Earth did you do it?"
The grown man asked, amazed.
"It was easy, dad, look!
On this side of the world is our little house.
Once I put the home together,
the rest of the world fell in place in minutes."

sneaking free

Tony Ellis

Published in *There is Wisdom in Walnuts,* by Tony Ellis.

Chapter 4: The Poetry of Whimsicality and Simple Things

perhaps I can sneak
unobserved
into the light
and become accidentally aware
slip around a thought
and become somehow undefined
lie flat and undiscovered
while a cloud of recognition rolls over me
trip and fall into space
like a leaf
hovering from a tree—
free

Fairy Trifle

William Clair Godfrey

> A poem of the Nabishswam
>
> *The "Nabishswam" is that time, about four in the morning, when the stars begin to fade. It is the best time to meditate as the events of the day are beginning to take form.*
> — Maharishi

Published in *Lyrical Iowa*.

Chapter 4: The Poetry of Whimsicality and Simple Things

In a large yellow tulip:
    mix up a batter of little girl giggles
    2 hp tsp full: puppy tail wiggles
    2/3 cup grandmother's double chin jiggles
    stir by the light of the moon
    set mixture aside

In a Pink Lady's Slipper: combine equal parts of
    bunny nose twitches
    cartwheels and skipping
    whirling and twirling and sliding and slipping
    tickling and teasing and squealing with glee
    tea parties pouring invisible tea
    leap frog and somersaults
    goldfish and snails
    inch worms and ladybugs
    pollywog tails
    toes through the clover
    and leaf jumping piles
    mud pies and butterflies
    dimples and smiles

    sift through a fuzzy cocoon

    fold into tulip mixture

    bake at dawn –– IN THE LIGHT OF JESUS ––

    serve at sunrise

Water Wings

River Dog

from Grandma with Love

Chapter 4: The Poetry of Whimsicality and Simple Things

Barely five and worldly wise, flipping hair in beaded braids:
Jamaican beach surprise!

Coppertone cold upon her back
awakens chilly goose bump tickles.
Laughing, she giggles and skips away
flotations squeezed 'round her tiny arms.
Swimsuit lines on skin so fair crisscross her golden tan,
the sweetest hue I've seen: smooth as see-through vellum.

Risky, her voyage, she trades her inner tube
for plastic water wings, puffed by Grandma-Wind-Bag:
"Trust your buoyant plastic bubbles, navigate the
waves of stormy days, bobble bravely on a sea of hope.
Dare enormous oceans, invite the taste of brackish breeze,
sink or swim ablaze for courage. Forget the bellybutton rule!
Confront caution boldly, face the random splashes,
sail to new horizons, follow stars to victory!"

Crazy-blue Jamaican bay, Reggae swaying purple Rumba:
Rhythms ebb the tides of moon, rolling beaches silver tumble,
broken shells on twinkle toes dance in time to sandy letters written,
washed to sea, yet burning still in memory.

Crimsoned coral fast asleep, cracked from ruddy beds,
lazy, rolling over, turns a beaded prize:
Strings of tuneful treasures, fingers counting mala ties,
spinning sacred chants 'round faithful rosary,
invoking blessings for my love, blessing from the sea.

Maritime surprise! A finny dolphin fine salute!
Intoning benediction, he hails the joyous child and lifts her on his back.
High in garland circles splashing laurels in the air,
waving fare-thee-well to water wings, she calls,
"Look! Grandma, I'm swimming!"

Five Haiku

Ken Chawkin

From *13 Ways to Write Haiku: A Poet's Dozen*

Previously published as part of a group in The Dryland Fish, An Anthology of Iowa Poets.

Chapter 4: The Poetry of Whimsicality and Simple Things

Defined

3 lines, 2 spaces,
17 feet to walk thru;
then,   the *un*ending

Translated

(Inspired by Australian artist Gareth Jones-Roberts's painting
Egrets in Morning Light)

on the edge of space
two egrets in morning light
woken from a dream

The Fall

sudden drop of leaves
a negligée to the floor
trees stand stark naked

Winter Memo

On seeing snowflakes
written on a piece of bark
I copied this down

Forest Flowers

tiny white flowers
a constellation of stars
so low yet so high

Toilet Poetry

Jordy Yager

Chapter 4: The Poetry of Whimsicality and Simple Things

When I say, "toilet poetry"
I don't mean a "potty mouth,"
Nor do I mean
Daily verbal movements
That range from
Sputtering constipation
Of gaseous entanglements,
To the oil-slicked
Espresso shots of diarrhea,
Nor do I mean
The type of poetry
That reeks of a three-day old
Vomit-stained porcelain god,
Nor do I mean the type
Of toilet experience that feels
So damn good
That it should be poetry,
No.
Quite to the contrary,
When I say, "toilet poetry,"
I mean very literally
Poetry written into fruition
While on the toilet,
It is in these moments
Of pristine deliverance
When the distractions of the hour
Take their respective order,
Lining themselves outside
The door,
While the words
That jigsaw their puzzle
Throughout your soul
Are granted the necessary
Time-space ratio
Needed for me to actually
Begin to think of myself as a poet,
Albeit a toilet poet,
And the assurance arises
That if all else fails
I at least know that I have
Extra toilet paper
(from the almighty poet-tree).

Lullaby Baby Frog

Karla Christensen

Chapter 4: The Poetry of Whimsicality and Simple Things

In the green-faced mountains,
the mountains near the moon,
where the bony Brahman cows
nurse their hundred calves,
and the boys in white shorts are walking
boys and dads together walking
that's where I would plant you,
my pollywog,
in your own private pool;
the soft pink cup
of an orchid
hanging high in the moss-
covered gavolon tree.

In the milk green breasted mountains,
in the curve of the scythe like the moon,
that's where I would raise you,
my love,
where the fence posts grow arms
into branches, lashed together
through tropical storms,
leafy arms reaching
through your empty spaces.
In the spring green mountains
I would plant you near the moon.

When I Die

Viktor Tichy

Published in *100 WORDS*.

Chapter 4: The Poetry of Whimsicality and Simple Things

I wake up in a city without strangers,
where streetcars ride topless
and girls wear Sweet William,
Wild Rose, and Black-Eyed Susan,
the names of their children
braided in their hair.

No soldiers live there, no policemen,
only grandfathers, lovers, and boys.
In that city you know me.
We drink milk from street fountains,
wear clothes to ski slopes,
and love in rooms without walls.

Trying on Your New Hat

Tom Le May

Chapter 4: The Poetry of Whimsicality and Simple Things

Your hat, although new, already smells like you,
  subtly floral, clean and warm.
Feeling a bit silly and a bit guilty,
  I put it on my big and round head
  which sits on the buttress of my shoulders.
I worry that I might stretch the knit of the hat but
  I find I like having something of yours gently clasping my skull.

Maybe I should worry that this is some kind of weirdness on my part,
  an area of my brain that has a street sign that says "Forty Second Street"
  and I am a hick in the big city, exploring the seedy and vaguely shameful
  venues.
But this gentle thrill is tinged with delicate hues of
  embarrassment,
          hints of unmanliness.

I like the way the new chapeau matches your scarf, a deeper, more potent
  periwinkle (a color, a word I will forever associate with you)
  and your freshly painted fingernails.
I like your feminine wiliness.

How do you keep your mysteries coexisting all together, that's what I want to know.
I disperse mine — I shoo them away
  like geese or puppies.
I am a comic gargoyle, all bluster and rout
  in the intermingling of faith and fear.

But you seem to bind your mysteries to you:
  Sometimes with colors,
  Sometimes with graceful dance or exotic ragas from far away,
  Sometimes with a voice as soft as the careless slap of harbor chop
  against the hull of a boat tied snug to it's mooring
  rocking gently
        under hoary
               Constellations.

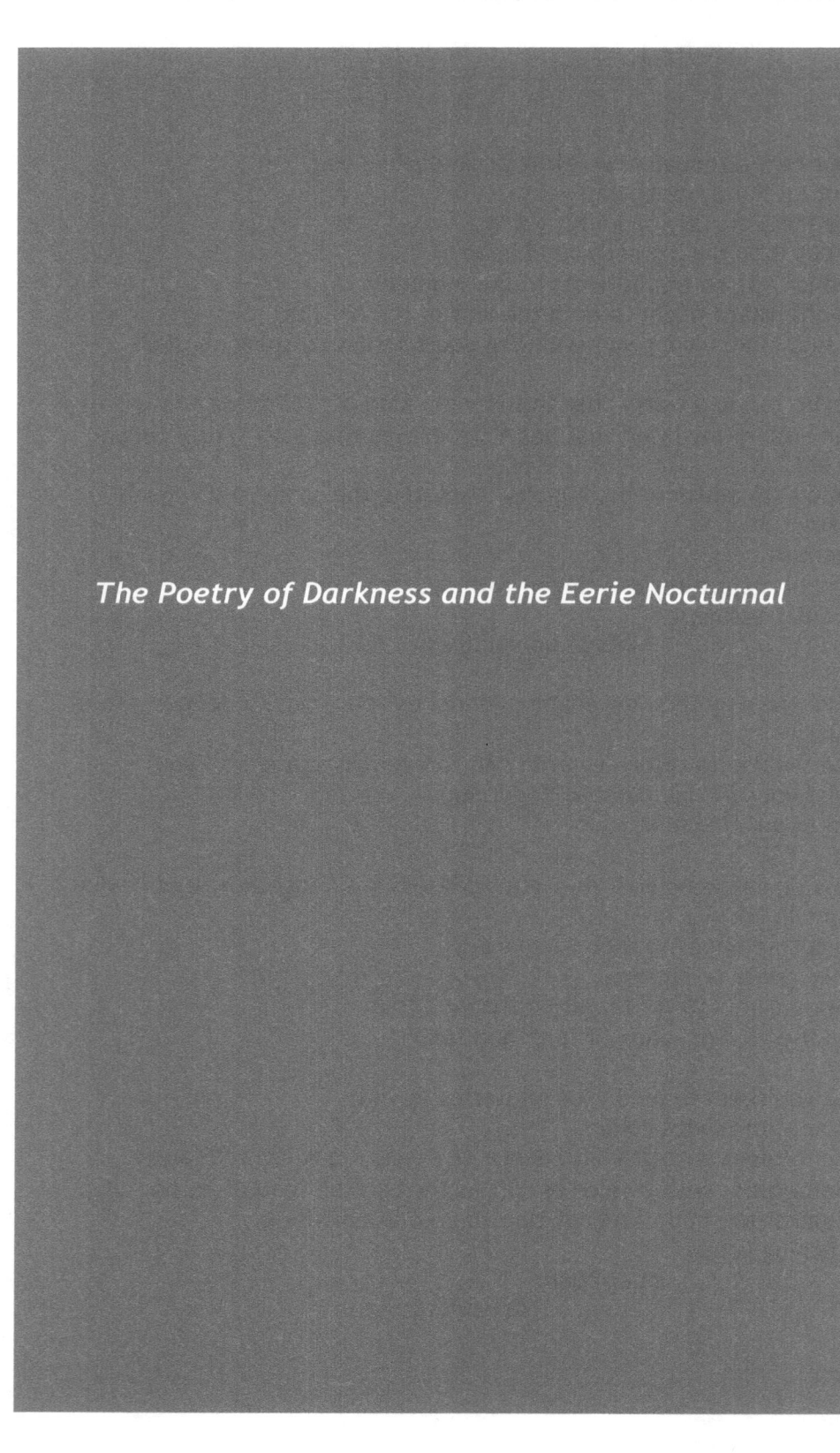
The Poetry of Darkness and the Eerie Nocturnal

Chapter

5

We have all nursed illusions: give us the right ones!
And all of us dream Dreams: let us dream bright ones!

— Joe M. Ruggier, Maltese poet (born 1956)

CONTENTS

150	Riding With Ludwig	*James Tipton*
152	El Dia de los Muertos	*Karla Christensen*
154	Under Orion	*Brother Ludovico*
160	Cold Wet Night	*Ken Chawkin*
162	Ode to Dry Starlight	*Robin Lim*
164	Night Sketches	*Para Steinmann*
166	The Coyotes	*Susie Niedermeyer*
168	Feeding Cats	*Leah Marie Waller*
170	Rite of Passage	*Patricia Regan Argiro*
172	Swimming through Brooklyn	*Jordy Yager*
176	Night Vision	*Susie Niedermeyer*
178	Marbles at a San Francisco Sunrise	*Barry Rosen*
182	Stricken	*Michael Hock*
184	The Beginning of Real Time	*Roger Pelizzari*

You are made of stars!

— Serbian Proverb

Chapter 5: The Poetry of Darkness and the Eerie Nocturnal

Darkness, represented by Night, Death, and the Nocturnal, has been a recurring poetic theme throughout all ages and cultures.

'Night' poems may be about simple nocturnal elements, or they may subtly draw us towards dawn and the advent of Light. Other poems begin with Light only to gradually fade metaphorically into the Unconscious or Death.

Typically, we expect a poem to end with a strong final statement. But Night poems are often about indecision, posing unanswered questions as their sub-themes. The main subject always is the eternal struggle between Light and Dark. To deny this struggle means a protracted descent into deeper darkness.

Yet, the Dark remains an awesome motivator, and a good Night poem has the power to stir forces needed to face our spiritual dilemmas.

Our greatest glory is not in never falling, but in rising every time we fall.
– Confucius, Chinese thinker (551-479 BC)

Riding with Ludwig

James Tipton

Chapter 5: The Poetry of Darkness and the Eerie Nocturnal

The darkness is made of mist
and rain and I drive relentlessly
deeper and deeper into it.
I have stopped behind taillights
reflected in the asphalt, with green
and yellow shining crisscross
on the black road. Now only
far red blurs of other cars;
pale headlights: fish eyes, luminous
underwater, coming from the other direction.
The world has receded and only
this night and I, alone in my car
going north, going north, exist.
Memory is a phantom that crosses
through my brain and is gone.
One whom I love and who has died
visits my thoughts and is gone.
There is a mystery I love
as the night deepens. How is it
that this moment, propped on all
the others, has its sway, then too,
vanishes in the mist
that settles all else down
to the bare essentials of moment
and moment passing and ancient days
stacked on one another,
yet knowing no chronology:
the comfort of all times as one
flooding in with the unceasing
rain on the windshield.
Then Beethoven comes on the radio—
strident, confident movements
that accompany the downpour,
throbbing bass notes of the past,
the steady stream of the present,
and I'm riding with Ludwig
on and on into the night.

El Dia de los Muertos

Karla Christensen

Published in *The Source* and the author's chapbook *Mazatlan*.

Chapter 5: The Poetry of Darkness and the Eerie Nocturnal

I want to go home
to that mysterious part
of the dark earth
where witches watched
with burning eyes,
canoes turned to stone
and rode the tides

and we danced our communion
in the silver arms of the dead
eating sugar skeletons
on the moonlit graves of our friends.

Dirt was not
a synonym for sin.
Dirt was what rose
from under our feet
like a holy mother
touching our clothes,
our hands,
our faces
reaching out her arms
to fold us in the night-
moist,
fecund,
deep.

Under Orion

Brother Ludovico

Under Orion was composed in the small town where the poet lives. Arguably the most spectacular of all constellations, Orion is especially dazzling when seen hung in the southern heavens, in the cold, clear, late January airs. It is a special celestial vision to see it sparkle, as it were a living god, over the frozen lake that this poem describes, even as it were returning from a triumphal hunt at the world's beginning.

THE poetry of motion is a phrase much in use, and to enjoy the epic form of that gratification it is necessary to stand on a hill at a small hour of the night, and having first expanded with a sense of difference from the mass of civilized mankind, who are dream-wrapped in a disregard for all such proceedings, quietly watch your stately progress through the stars. After such a nocturnal vision, it is hard to get back to Earth, and to believe the consciousness of such majestic speeding is derived from a tiny human frame.
From *"Far From The Madding Crowd"*
— Thomas Hardy

Chapter 5: The Poetry of Darkness and the Eerie Nocturnal

I

THE
    January night is still, clear, and cold;
    The deep snow, sparkling like an immaculate ash
Belched from a celestial volcano,
    Has made a moonscape of these streets I pass;
This frozen lake, a glacial blanket of ice,
    Mantling leviathans in its dark belly;
This small, one horse town, monumentalized,
    A *Pompeii* buried in Eternity,
In the alabaster lava of this white night.
    I lift my eyes unto the firmament,
Unto the stars, that, like crickets chirruping light,
    Sing of some absolute reign of Innocence.
No hunter, but a *Daniel*, in a den of angelic lions,
Before me wakes, rises, smiles, the majesty of *Orion*.

II

THE
    water tower, band shell, ice fishers' shacks,
    The weather-beaten cottages on the shore,
Seem like toys tumbled from a playroom's sack,
    Scattered upon a kindergarten's floor
Beneath the colossus of his magnificence;
    A child's things: wind turbines, satellite dishes, barns,
Mere tiddlywinks erected in adolescence,
    A toddler's first steps to his mother's arms.
And what am I, here, bundled in coat and boots,
    A straw wind-swept across these frozen steppes
Of an unfathomable infinitude?
    A thing to wake, love, know, only to forget?
Is Truth a hocus pocus of astrologers' amulets?
Mere legends? Doodles on a chalkboard called the zodiac?

III

I LIFT
>   my sail beneath *Orion*, a fairy
>   With broken wings, bound to a sinewy mast,
> A bone-built schooner, loosed on a limitless prairie,
>   Uncharted, kingdom-less, *Oceanus* vast;
> A gypsum-white desert of dimensionless sand
>   No sextant, compass, or *Pharaoh's* host may measure,
> Free-sifting through the nomadic soul of Man
>   A bounty, whose each grain's a boundless treasure.
> Sunrises, moonrises, seedtimes, harvest-tides,
>   *Andromeda, Hercules, Cassiopeia;*
> Green Summers, gold Autumns; wails, smiles, curses, sighs,
>   The cavalcade of Life's cornucopia;
> A mariner most foundered, tangled in riggings and rusted irons,
> Most found when most Stilled, anchored here, at the feet of *Orion*.

IV

HE
>   arches high on yon proscenium,
>   Frozen mid-stride, in a hinterland of stars,
> A hunter garbed in a hunter's regalia
>   Of girdle, lion's skin, club, and scimitar,
> The dog-star, *Sirius*, panting at his heel;
>   A longing fixed *Forever* in his eyes,
> Aimed at no bear or eagle, but with appeal
>   At *Atlas's* virgin daughters, the *Pleiades*,
> That *Zeus* enchanted to a flock of doves:
>   This *Beowulf*, or *Goliath* of the spheres,
> Knocked cuckoo for eternity with Love,
>   A puppet, with comets whizzing through his beard.
> Not nebulae, not asterisms, but a Man through and through,
> From *Betelgeuse* on his club, to *Rigel* buckled on his shoe.

Chapter 5: The Poetry of Darkness and the Eerie Nocturnal

V

I DREAM
    of small Italian train stations,
  In southern *Puglia* and *Calabria,*
The roses and finches, the goldfishes in the fountains,
  Old men, vending *gelati,* and singing *tarantellas;*
The brown-eyed children, olive-skinned maidens,
  The marble, genuflecting *Madonnas;*
My closed eyes, dry wells drinking tears of Heaven,
  Hearing in laurel hedges Earth's hosannas.
I dream of kissing you in the warm rain,
  Holding the fruits of your wet breasts the while,
My heart, breaking, at the jolt of that train,
  Losing forever your Audrey Hepburn smile.
Men squander pearls, scrounging like swineherds for their *Zion,*
Brought to their knees, like boys, beneath the loving Eye of *Orion.*

VI

I PRAY
    beneath *Orion.* At his feet
  I lay my brow upon a cloud of white,
Upon a snowdrift of Divinity
  That drowns each dark fear with Transcendent Light.
Slowly the turnstile of the cosmic stage
  Lifts its celestial circus of constellations,
Parading heaven with hero, god, beast, and sage,
  Awing Earth's children, with the dazzling procession
Of a bestiary of dreams: snake-handlers, dragons,
  Centaurs, hydras, pegasi and unicorns,
Bears, bulls, lions, serpents and scorpions,
  Andromeda, Hercules, Cassiopeia, all born
To wheel their legends 'round Truth's indivisible Pole,
Stars, swirling like snowflakes, through the cosmos of Man's Soul.

VII

TONIGHT
    the Earth a perfect jewel gleams,
  An island, in an infinite archipelago,
Heaven's ceiling, frescoed with bright myths and schemes,
  By an archangelic *Michelangelo*
Recumbent on scaffolds of mountain-crests,
  Adorning the dome of this divine *Sistine;*
Inhaling opium of cosmic consciousness,
  While spangling night with hieroglyphic dreams.
A spinner of myths, unwinding mummy Reason,
  Sowing the fallow night, from seed-sacks of dreams;
His thoughts, first shepherds of the Signs and Seasons,
  His dust, combusting fires of quenchless Being.
Man is a nightingale, who sings the hearts of lions,
Flesh, fledging to an Angel, for those Eyes beaming through *Orion*.

VIII

THE
    pizzeria, drug store, cinema,
  This main street derelict with *Zhivago* snows,
Greed's beast, swearing its bloody tracks, stigmata,
  Only to lead down alleys to hookers' ghosts.
The seedy corner tap, at closing time;
  The jukebox, the beer signs' neon penumbras,
The dizzied drunks, stumbling out dumb, deaf, blind,
  Into a universe of virgin tundras.
Cliff dwellers, high on some Himalayan peak,
  Their altars, sacrificing Santas and cheap Angels,
These lovers, babblers, brawlers, Earth's first priests,
  Their curses and kisses, holiest rituals.
War's kite-picked bones, guillotines, genocides, pestilence;
Ages and kingdoms forgiven, by a confetti of pure Innocence.

IX

I LAY
    upon my bed, my arms spread wide,
      Staring at the candelabrum of night,
My body, nailed with stars, here crucified,
      My wicked thorns, bleeding forth roses of light.
Slowly the myths of what I have believed
      Propel their zodiac through my mind's eye:
First sins, first labors, cradles, altars, graves,
      Your nightgown, first unveiling your *Venus* thighs.
Sunrises, moonrises, seedtimes, harvest-tides,
      Andromeda, Hercules, Cassiopeia,
Snow softly sifting clean as veils of brides
      Through an hourglass vaster than *Siberia.*
Pouches of berries, grails, thrones, and posies of dandelions;
Hunters come from the hunt, at the last, sparkling like *Orion.*

Cold Wet Night

Ken Chawkin

A Tanka

Chapter 5: The Poetry of Darkness and the Eerie Nocturnal

Rain on the trailer
Beating down its dismal song
Drop, by cold, wet, drop

A monotonous rhythm
Driving home ... the loneliness

Ode to Dry Starlight

Robin Lim

Chapter 5: The Poetry of Darkness and the Eerie Nocturnal

Today I saw a galaxy behind my dream.
Many million pinpoints of light
bled through my eyelids, in the newborn day.

I can't be sure if this beauty
was due to my over fifty years of seeing,
or perhaps all the stardust from the babies
I have received, has been rubbed roughly
by my hands into my eyes.
Eyes so tired and scratched.
Eyes open to see a fifteen-year-old girl
push an unwanted boy into our world of noise
and light.

When I was twenty-seven, invincible
still insulated by health and energy,
A dying father said to me, "Enlightenment is nothing
more than accepting the unacceptable."

I did not cry for the girl or her baby.
Enlightenment is a drying up and hardening
of the eyes.

June 2009

Night Sketches

Para Steinmann

Chapter 5: The Poetry of Darkness and the Eerie Nocturnal

1.

Leaves
silhouetted on my windows
by a crescent moon

2.

A single birdcall
in the forest
like a flute in the silent air

3.

Rain
striking the pebbles
in a waterfall of song

4.

A breath of wind
in the tulip poplar
rippling through my dreams

The Coyotes

Susie Niedermeyer

Published in *Under a Prairie Moon*, by Susie Niedermeyer.

Chapter 5: The Poetry of Darkness and the Eerie Nocturnal

It was birthing time and the barn rose
luminous under an eggshell moon.
In the half light I could see them
streaming by and hear the laughing
yip and howl of them.

Then silence, but for the skitter
of a rat in the manger
and the heavy night sighs
of the does.

I told myself the fence is sound,
mice and fawns are plenty,
but my fear that night
was not of flesh and blood,
but the oldest fear...

the myriad forms
of shadowed
darkness.

Feeding Cats

Leah Marie Waller

Published in *Under the Cedar Tree*, by Leah Marie Waller.

Chapter 5: The Poetry of Darkness and the Eerie Nocturnal

I pull into the drive way
listening tentatively for soft paws
on the dew covered grass.
I call their names,
they do not answer.
The movement sensor light
comes on
and I gasp
slightly.
I slide my copy of the key
into the fake gold knob
and twist.

I grab a can of Newman's Own cat food
and a feeding plate.

Soon I can just make out
the first pair of yellow eyes
ascending on the horizon.

They plant themselves around the small green dish
poking their bumpy toughs
at the wet lump
and it slowly vanishes.
They press their bellies
into my knees
and press their faces
on my hands.

I look towards the dark woods
and the hush of some ancient tong
whisper to me.
Suddenly I just want to run
through those black thickets all night,
to catch the small animals there
in my mouth,
and be part of the mystery
that goes on while I am usually
sleeping.

Rite of Passage

Patricia Regan Argiro

Published in *Toward Sunset*, by Patricia Regan Argiro.

Chapter 5: The Poetry of Darkness and the Eerie Nocturnal

At night a child finds red
ribbons on her bed, feels
clutches in her belly, and
stands to welcome
streamers down her wet,
awakened thighs.

She hears no drums. No
chanting sister-mothers come
through fullest darkness to
braid pearls in her
long, long hair.

Only the moon, the pearly moon,
appears from covering cloud to
watch as one more woman
takes her rightful place in
time's long, long turning.

Alone, the young one
makes her ritual. Drawing
out her treasured pen, her
sacred diary, she writes
her strong new secret
into song.

Swimming through Brooklyn

Jordy Yager

Chapter 5: The Poetry of Darkness and the Eerie Nocturnal

As I swim
Through the streets of downtown Brooklyn
I'm surrounded by
Spiritual gypsy cabs
Who operate and capture
The light of the night,
They stop and question
The intention of my direction,
With eyes flickering
Like Argentine candles
Made from the wax of the drooling moon
Who looks on with envy
At the planetary willingness of us all
To shout out
Our block,
Our haven,
Our celebrated tendencies
Of identifying places with meaning,
And where before stood
Towering tenements in my heart
Now stand flagrant fragrances
That speak of nudist birthday parties
Celebrate at dawn
Within the confines of our fortified city streets,
The same streets that testify
To the universal structure
Of my post mortem beliefs,
The same streets
That pronounce the friction
Produced between our androgynous thighs
Every time we take a step
And circumnavigate this global wonder of a mother,
It forces me to prostrate forth
With my head bowed beneath
The intersection of my evolutionary streetlights,
And praise myself
For all the times
That I chose to doubt an idea
Just to unveil the subtleties
Of its delicacies

This Enduring Gift

Within the frontier of my own beliefs,
Cuz I never thought that I could ever know
What Borges meant when he said
That philosophy isn't
"clear and precise understanding"
but rather it's the
"organization of the essential perplexities of man"
and I never thought that I could
ever understand Talib when he said
"I'm not a human being in some old spiritual shit
I'm a spiritual being manifested as a human, that's it"
And so swim we must
Amongst our streets
Swim with the swirling words
Of our comrades in arms,
Words that speak of a stronger tomorrow
And arms that harness the ability to make it so,
And I promise you
That these streets,
Whether Nostrand Avenue
Or Highway 34,
Will bounce back
And televise the revolution
Of these spiritually filled human pinata's,
That's why we keep each other
At arms length,
To make room for the swinging sticks
Of our own consciousness,
And so swim we must
And "when all art is signed anonymous"
Mr. Sage will get his chance to
"turn that Big Bang theory
into a small pop hypothesis"
But until then I stand corner-stricken
With my back to the wind chimes of human expression,
And my genitals facing East
Accepting the heat of Ra's chariot
With the knowledge that we must all
Let go eventually
And make do with our journey,

Regardless of our final resting ground,
You see,
I keep my life in the cargo pockets of my intellect,
Who counterbalances the winged messengers
Upon my feet,
That carry messages back and forth,
Until the goal becomes the course,
And so allow poetry
The opportunity to dance we must
But words are actions
And actions are poetry in motion
And thus any worker that chooses
To enter the confines of the Dexter factory
Deserves the acknowledgement of speaking the truth
With regards to these aquatic tendencies
Of ours
And so I come here to you tonight
To humbly apologize for any wrong doing
That I have committed upon you and your stars,
And I come here to you tonight
To sincerely ask for your forgiveness
For all the times that I was unwilling
To mount up the will power
To change those things that I could have but didn't
And I come here to you tonight
To thank you for not murdering my dreams in their sleep.

Night Vision

Susie Niedermeyer

Published in *Under a Prairie Moon,* by Susie Niedermeyer.

Chapter 5: The Poetry of Darkness and the Eerie Nocturnal

Snow falls softly
and the last rosy cloud greys,
abandoning the mind's horizon.
The shoulders of hills
hunch against the cold, the field
a flat belly, punctuated by the navel
of a frozen pond. Skirting dark
clumps left by a plow,
two dogs trot a hedgerow
as the veil of night pours
over eyes that turn within.
Remembering the fire
of the invisible
I feel the body of the earth
becoming my body, my body filled
with quiet stars and snow.

Marbles at a San Francisco Sunrise

Barry Rosen

Chapter 5: The Poetry of Darkness and the Eerie Nocturnal

In the quantum mechanical world,
the neon cosmos flashes fluorescent
hues of greens and blues.
Sometimes on.
Sometimes off.
Always blinking into the cool summer mists
of a sleepy city.

In smoky jazz clubs
drunken crowds
dissolve in rhythmic blues
of flying feet
while clarinets caress
boisterous bingers.
At sunrise,
they crash onto cream down pillows
shouting sleepy sonnets
to the rising sun.

At the zoo a crazed housefly
clings to an elephant's leg
feeling like the most
important fly in town.
Oblivious,
the pachyderm,
as kingly as Brahman,
stomps solidly
through the green ferns.

A few exhibits away,
a baby fawn
hungover from a
long night's nap
rises from her mother's lick.
A frog croaks and rolls
over in the mud
while church bells ring
and a city awakens.
On the 12th floor the worried maid
dusts old glass shelves.

Her cluttered mind whirls
like the endless trash
blown by bay winds bellows
"How will I pay the rent?"
Her rebellious niños ask mama
if she will wash the dirty sun.

In the Palisades
a zaftig housewife
clings to her Laura Ashley sofa
gobbling Hershey kisses and wiping tears
as the world turns.
At Palisades Park, a 4-year-old
dribbles his lime Popsicle juice
onto mounds of hardworking ants.
His blue and green marbles
bounce off of concrete curbs and
sandy mounds.
He ponders:
"What city is down there?"

Thick fog and ocean waves
pound the shores at the Zen monastery.
The Master strikes contemplative monks
stuck in the sound of
one-hand clapping.
"Wake-up."
"Dissolve."
Tilt your eyes and see.

To God,
Jupiter must be a giant marble,
rolling in the dunes
bouncing off of a sandy foot,
that has caressed a
mossy rock
drenched by misty fog
rolling over an awakened metropolis.

4-29-06

Chapter 5: The Poetry of Darkness and the Eerie Nocturnal

stricken

Michael Hock

> Dedicated to Sri Gary Olsen, current Living Master, and founder of the MasterPath.

© 2008 Michael Hock.

Chapter 5: The Poetry of Darkness and the Eerie Nocturnal

moon slips away
pouring into the cleft
between the white hills west
while moonbeams ricochet
into my kitchen

night is cloven;
Sol gathers his might
beneath the white hills east
and betwixt these two.....
the giving and the adoring.....
we have the moment's freedom to trek the circuit
That pale pale azure radiance
infuses my snowy world-
2 hour delay pauses industry
kids snoozing oblivious
plows doing their labor-
while I climb into the electric blue
the day not yet come

I am stricken by your beauty
Thursday's moon rising
sunset's fading glow
clouds caressing the luminous hills
the earth bathed; effulgent
world halts, but does not stop
the moment of immaculate conception is now
too pure for praise
or to hold to memory
thus I wax silent
and behold the enduring
resplendent within
shimmering through you
like starlight upon a thousand distant peaks

The Beginning of Real Time

Roger Pelizzari

© 2007 Roger W. Pelizzari.

Chapter 5: The Poetry of Darkness and the Eerie Nocturnal

Almost morning,
somewhere along the edge of March,
I woke to a moment so still,
I heard the ice cracking
on the frozen waters of the world.
Rising from the valley
between night and day,
I opened my eyes and saw my watch
sleeping on the table,
stopped at midnight.
It was a signal for the beginning
of real time.

Here and now the world is new.
We see by the light of the sun
that shines in the middle of the head,
while invisible winds
blow everything false away.
Who will miss the shadows of our old lives?
This is how we enter the future,
through the door of the present.
This is where we find the place
we have longed for,
where no one needs to ask,
"Where am I? Which way should I go?"
We are made of green earth and gold fire.
The blue sea flows through us,
and the sweet, silver air.
The stars flash from the mind
to the sky,
growing brighter as we look.
Soon, we will not even remember
the time when we were asleep,
dreaming that this would happen.

The Poetry of Angels, You, and GOD

CHAPTER 6

Thou glorious mirror, where the Almighty's form glasses itself in tempests...The image of eternity, the throne of the Invisible...

— From *Childe Harold's Pilgrimage*
Byron, British poet (1788-1824)

Contents

188	Spirals	*Patricia Regan Argiro*
190	Lalla	*Carole Lee Connet*
192	The Orders	*Thomas Centolella*
196	The Master	*Susie Niedermeyer*
198	When Will I Awaken	*Sharalyn Pliler*
202	Communion	*Viktor Tichy*
204	I Need to Feel You Every Moment in My Heart	*Charlie Hopkins*
208	Shopping	*Einar Olsen*
210	Atman's Jesus' Buddha's Krishna's God's...	*Matthew A. Bovard*
212	Like a Seed	*Glenn Watt*
214	In Defense of Angels	*Brother Ludovico*
222	I Once Met a God	*Tony Ellis*
224	He	*Diana Quinlan*
226	God Bless the Universe	*William Clair Godfrey*
228	The Picture of You	*Paul Johan Stokstad*
230	Gaea's Wedding Kiss	*Viktor Tichy*
234	On a Medieval Painting of the Fall of Man	*Freddy Niagara Fonseca*
236	In the Evening We Shall Be Examined on Love	*Thomas Centolella*
238	Good Night	*Patricia Regan Argiro*

All the fish needs is to get lost in the water.
All man needs is to get lost in Tao.

— Chuang Tzu (4th Century BC)

Chapter 6

The Poetry of Angels, You, and God

Dante, Milton, and other spiritually-oriented poets wrote from elevated planes from which each word seems to vibrate a classical harmony. They gave us works of rare beauty and genius, structured and proportioned with accomplished meter, rhythm, and tone. The ornate structures used in such poetry tend to charm and sedate the reader, making his mind receptive to the poems' intended profundity.

As the medieval mystic Saint Catherine of Siena (1347-1380) wrote, *"There the soul dwells — like the fish in the sea and the sea in the fish."*

In today's hectic age we have little time for the greater attention needed to absorb classical poetry. Modern poets like to experiment with different phrasings that suit a poem's particular subject matter, or they borrow methods and themes from older schools to create unexpected hybrids.

Whether using traditional or modern styles and language, some inspired poets invoke the divine regardless of idiom, transcending poetics' many challenges to reveal an inherent symmetry and order pervading all life.

Spirals

Patricia Regan Argiro

Published in *Lyrical Iowa* 2001.

Chapter 6: The Poetry of Angels, You, and God

A small child, given a marking instrument
(crayon, pencil, pen) for the very first time
will frequently make a spiral to occupy the
large white space they face. They'll do it
hurriedly, starting near dead center and
skirling outward, to use up, boldly,
all the empty space. Is this because inside
they know that galaxies are fashioned in this form,
that doubling and rising vertically, this form
allows for all the samenesses and differences,
the individuality that we call life?

Is this form God to them, or is it the knowledge
spilling forth that God, too, faced with the
nothingness before creation, put a finger
at the center and, laughing, let it whirl
outward in just-off concentric circlings to
form the Universe?

Lalla

Carole Lee Connet

14th c. Kashmir mystic poet

Ohio Poetry Day Society Ontology Award 3rd prize 1999, published in *OPDA Review*.

Wrapped her bones in skin,
went about naked,
dancing and singing
in silence.

What she heard
she gave to the infants
of sleep.
What she touched
she released from under
the mask.
What she saw
she laid at the gate
of emptiness.
What she tasted
she left
for the ants.
What she smelled
she engaged
with her breath.

One morning she slung a strip of cloth
on each shoulder,
tying knots on one
for ridicule,
on the other,
for respect.

In the evening
the cloth merchant's scales hung
balanced.
Neither scorn nor praise carried
weight.
She wrapped them around
nothing.

The Orders

Thomas Centolella

Published in *Lights & Mysteries,* by Thomas Centolella.

Chapter 6: The Poetry of Angels, You, and God

One spring night, at the end of my street
God was lying in wait.

A friend and I were sitting in his new sedan
like a couple of cops on surveillance,
shooting the breeze to pass the time,
chatting up the daydreams, the raw deals,
all the woulda-coulda-shoulda's,
the latest "Can you believe that?"
As well as the little strokes of luck,
the so-called triumphs, small and unforeseen,
that kept us from cashing it all in.

And God, who's famous for working
in mysterious ways and capable of anything,
took the form of a woman and a man,
each dressed in dark clothes and desperate enough
to walk up to the car and open the doors.

And God put a gun to the head of my friend—
right against the brain stem, where the orders go out
not only to the heart and the lungs
but to consciousness itself—a cold muzzle aimed
at where the oldest urges still have their day:
the one that says eat whatever's at hand,
the one that wants only to fuck,
the one that will kill if it has to . . .

And God said not to look at him
or he'd blow us straight to kingdom come,
and God told us to keep our hands
to ourselves, as if she weren't that kind of girl.

Suddenly time was nothing,
our lives were cheap, the light in the car
cold, light from a hospital,
light from a morgue. And the moments
that followed—if that's what they were—

arrived with a nearly unbearable weight,
until we had acquired
a center of gravity
as great as the planet itself.

My friend could hardly speak—
he was too busy trying not to die—
which made me chatter all the more,
as if words, even the most ordinary ones,
had the power to return us to our lives.

And behind my ad-libbed incantation,
my counterspell to fear, the orders
still went out: keep beating, keep breathing,
you are not permitted to disappear,

even as one half of God kept bitching
to the other half that we didn't have
hardly no money at all, and the other half barked,
"I'm telling you to shut your mouth!"
and went on rummaging through the back seat.
And no one at all looking out their window,
no one coming home or going out . . .

Until two tall neighbors came walking toward us
like unsuspecting saviors . . . And God grabbed
the little we'd been given, the little we still had,
and hustled on to the next dark street.

Chapter 6: The Poetry of Angels, You, and God

The Master

Susie Niedermeyer

Published in *Under a Prairie Moon*, by Susie Niedermeyer.

Chapter 6: The Poetry of Angels, You, and God

A galactic silence
drifts over the world
during these, the Master's last days.
Each moment a button coming undone,
the jewels of the mind
exposed to float endless in time.

So many decades, obedient, we reached
for the satin muscle of truth
stretched long by invisible hands.
How we wanted to be changed,
to be absorbed. Eyes closed,
we opened the door
to silent chasms of ice,
the mists of the moon.
Everything we touched
dissolved.

Today and forever his light burns in us,
soft as a fontanel, the place
where light collects under the skin.

When Will I Awaken

Sharalyn Pliler

Chapter 6: The Poetry of Angels, You, and God

I have slept in Tennessee
On a mountainside
Alone,
Swallowed in a sea of grass,
A small speck shivering in an ocean
Of undiluted stars.
Lord, lord, when will I awaken.

I have lain on beds of pine needles
At the furthermost Key
Delirious beyond sleep
In exaltation
With the sounds of wind song and tree whispers
And the immortal rhythms of sea water.
I thought it surely was
Divinity,
To feel so high
But just like yesterday
The sun came up
And it was just plain life again,
Only now,
More tired.
Lord, lord, when will I awaken

I have slept, fitfully,
My head buzzing from time zones
On an airplane
Seven seats wide,
Facing,
Like a church congregation,
That silver alter
Playing Tarzan of the Apes,
With no one thinking about miracles,
About this magic bullet,
This sliver of metal between the full moon
And a black ocean, this oldest of oceans,
Too ancient to comprehend,
Too far below to even see.
Lord, lord, when will I awaken.

I have slept in Canada
On my honeymoon
On a waterbed in a third rate motel,
The night of the day we saw the moose,
The night of the day I realized
That I didn't love my husband.
The moose was ugly but real.
The fantasy was beautiful but not.
Lord, lord, when will I awaken.

I have slept
Sometimes surreptitiously
Sometimes with slacked-jawed verve,
In lecture halls and churches,
In traffic and out,
More than once while making love,
More than once while making promises,
More than once without closing my eyes,
(Most of my life, without closing my eyes).
What is dream and what is Truth?
Lord, Lord. When will I awaken.

Chapter 6: The Poetry of Angels, You, and God

Communion

Viktor Tichy

1st prize in *Ohio Poetry Day*.

Chapter 6: The Poetry of Angels, You, and God

I want a God
to sink my teeth into.

A sacrament that tumbles
out of a psalm

in lose hungry shorts
without panty lines

and a T-shirt too tight
to tolerate any mysticism.

When you touch me,
my crown of thorns is lifted.

When I drink you,
the priest can keep the wine.

I Need to Feel You Every Moment in My Heart

Charlie Hopkins

For Carol

Published at http://www.realization.org/page/doc0/doc0092.htm

Chapter 6: The Poetry of Angels, You, and God

Forgive me if I tell you I am lost.

Even though you hollowed out the rock
and made a temple in my chest
my heart is still sometimes a slaughter barn
where dogs fight over ribbons of blood.

Though I have heard angels singing clear syllables
that can change a stone into a man
and bring him crying to his knees
I am lost.

So many times I have been saved by Grace
heard the ringing of invisible bells
that covered the laughter of demons and drove them away.
I have killed demons by the thousands with a sword
and baptized this world in their blood
but I don't know for sure what my own name is.

Mother Mary smiles at me using the faces of grocery clerks.
The Mother and Father of the Universe tell me
I am their child.
But I am lost because I can't remember every moment
in whose arms I am held.

Two times I felt a presence behind me
and turned to see a god seven feet tall
whose open face was a shotgun blast to the heart.
But twenty-three years later I come to your door
like a boy crying with a fish hook caught in his hand.
I need your help to go deeper.

I have seen Jesus Christ laughing inside an oval of light
the color of lavender.
I have seen Lord Krishna dancing inside a conch shell clear as ice
saw him float over the Gulf of Mexico
while seagulls mimicked his name
and mullet leapt out of waves to reach him
but I could not reach him.

This Enduring Gift

Shree Maa told me, "I am you. I am nothing."
Shivabalayogi said to me, "I am who you are.
You can never forget your own Self."

But every moment I don't remember I am in love with you
is like living in a bombed city.
There is an emptiness in rooms where you have lived and danced
then left them behind
that hurts like a pulled tooth.
I need your help to go deeper.

For a long time I was afraid to give myself to you
knowing I would be eaten alive.
Now the sound of my bones snapping between your teeth
is salvation.

I want to walk in the perennial garden
and gather into my wide face the light of the sky
coming down at sunset to kiss me on the mouth
and leave my lips red as a girl's.
I want to give back light to you like the moon.

My beard is white.
My belly like a woman's three months pregnant.
But in my heart I am a lover.
I am a bridegroom with a handful of flowers.
If the one I love is Shiva
then he can be the groom and I will be three months pregnant
with his child.

Take these flowers from my hand and put them in my hair.
I am talking to the God who lives in the body of Carol.
I am singing these words to my wife.

Chapter 6: The Poetry of Angels, You, and God

Shopping

Einar Olsen

dedicated to Maharishi

Even in Brooks Brothers I can
think of God
and be with You in
my heart in
the thick cologne and sales prices
creating that cloud of subtle excitement,
swirled in the wine of 1940's muzak—
You must be Being
throughout thoroughly,
untied in the glossy ties
free in the separates,
filling up the shorts,
long in the elegant aisles
of the stores of significance;
the colored cloth of Purchase floats in
the sea of omnipresent consciousness,
while I
buy
and save myself
money and more than money
by memory
and more than memory
by the good Grace
of my Master
who has never worn a tie,
a belt,
a pair of pants.

Atman's Jesus' Buddha's Krishna's God's Flying Spaghetti Monster's Jahweh's Great Spirit's Love

Matthew A. Bovard

Chapter 6: The Poetry of Angels, You, and God

Lost myself finding myself.
Here in the now.
Slight smile. Happy fulfilled.
Truly fulfilled feeling
a little more day by day.
Happiness in doing.
Doing what?
Doing it.
What ever happens upon my journey
to beyond beyond.
Gotta a lot of love to spread.
Now all I can do is go spread
a smile and a hug.
Get to know all the family.
Just groove through time and space
till you can't groove any more.
Then you will be ready to
submit to the self. Find the self.
The real self, the self you see inside
the love you feel.
Your truth, Your justice, Your love
   The one the only
      Yours
        Which we all have
       and is the same
         Love
Jesus' Buddha's Krishna's
Flying Spaghetti Monter's God's
Jahweh's Great Spirit's Love

Like a Seed

Glenn Watt

Like a seed planted in the dark

> a seed not unlike a desire
> in a dark not unlike our own

Planted as if in the void

> between thoughts
> between words

Which is a kind of ground beneath them

> a fuel in which they burn

Placed there with tenderness and care

> for what calls up more tenderness
> than to give one's self over
> into another's keeping

And placed there with utter abandon

> for what requires more abandon
> than to give one's self over
> so completely

As if our lives themselves could be planted

> folded like all things are folded finally
> back in upon themselves

This of course where all our stories end

> giving up their host like a husk
> into grief and glory

And where all begin

> kneeling here before the altar
> of what was, is, and always will be.

In Defense of Angels

Brother Ludovico

> Written As A Confession, Testimony, And Argument,
> For Those Who Have Repeatedly Attempted
> To Have This Poet Incarcerated,
> Disinherited, And, Or, Confined In An Insane
> Asylum: And For Those In His Former
> Brotherhood Who Have So Endeavored
> To Vilify His Person, And Deride His Art,
> Maintaining, In The Mazes Of Their Reasons,
> That Simplicity And Stillness,
> Are Tantamount To Lunacy.

"If the end brings me out all right, what is said against me will not amount to anything. If the end brings me out all wrong, then a legion of angels swearing I was right will make no difference."
— Abraham Lincoln

Chapter 6: The Poetry of Angels, You, and God

I

NOT
    merely as my midnight guardians,
   That stir the ethers with such dulcet thunders,
  Winged shepherds of this flesh, that wake me from,
   To take me to, the pastures of fresh slumbers;
 Not as Love's troubadours in smitten airs,
   Who serenade my dreams with arias sweet
     And soft, so soft more soft than dulcimers,
   With lutes, and flutes, and harps so rarely rare,
'Twould make a *Judas* fall to his knees and weep;
    Neither those posted at sainted sepulchers,
   Nor those whose hosts *Iniquity* rend asunder,
     Nor those who over the dying gently hover;
 Not as the darling muses of my verses,
   Mixing ink, blood, gall, to rapture on these pages,
   Warbling hosannas midst Earth's aches and curses,
   Holding Heaven's candle as Hell rages;
More, far more, signify thy bosoms' flood of such sweet singing:
Thy minstrelsies are tidings, promising Man new Meaning.

II

IF
    I be mad, my madness then shall scream:
   "Madness is the sweetest-most beatitude!"
 If I be touched, and scourged with base esteem,
   I say *"touch, nudged me to exalted moods!"*
 If poisoned by a cockatrice's venom,
   My blood fomenting till my mind's deranged,
     Then, frothing with rabid might,
 I say *"cherubim are the idiots of Heaven,*
And by gorging manna, I have gone insane!"
    'Tis no tarantula's toxic bite,
   Nor some peyote crazing wild the blood
     That frenzies souls to fevers full of Light!
Madness is a word; *Truth*, a deathless kingdom;
   One seals a tomb, the other, all Heaven discloses!
 If madness courses through my father's son,
   It sings like nightingales and blooms like roses!
If it be mad for ear, to hear, the echoes of Eternity,
I pray each mother's womb, be a cradle of Insanity!

III

I SHALL
    not solitary be confined,
      For these are those that step through stone and steel;
No reason shall brainwash them from my mind,
      For midst Man's myths and mirrors, they are most Real.
They can not from my soul be exorcised,
      For devils, not Angels, buckle to twisting screws!
        Not starved till the tent of this flesh faints,
      Not blasted from these ears, burned from these eyes!
What I behold is deafening, blinding, True!
      I fear no posse knocking with complaint,
    No jury snickering with mock appeal,
        No sheriff issuing orders of restraint!
For asylums may not bar the wings of Grace,
      Straitjackets may not shield Love from Man's Heart,
    Like a harlot, stone me in the marketplace!
      Bound to two horses, tear my flesh apart!
My Father's Mansions teem with playgrounds full of children,
Who shimmy down sunbeams, bearing balm for Earth's blind Pilgrim.

IV

THEN
    I renounce all hating brotherhoods,
      All *Pharisaic* cynics and vilifiers,
Those whose wrists trickle avaricious bloods,
      All who scoff, and denounce Truth's Child a liar!
And in their stead, I beckon my winged brothers,
      Knitted not by flesh, but steeliest threads of Spirit
        That bind with One Law and Dominion,
      Not biters of shekels, but Light's singing lovers,
Who stroll the gardens Earth's steward shall inherit!
      Come, Heaven's royal sons!
Thy harps thy swords! Moonbeams thy chariots!
        Come, singing army of sweetest Angel-dom!
Send arrows of music deep into Man's Heart,
      That wounded, it may Awake Man's Mind!
Announce unto Man's Flower, sprung from dust and dark,
    "The dews ye sip, weep from Wellsprings Divine!"
No! No! Not shamed! But proud to uttermost humility!
To blast the ram's horn that shall bring *Jerichos* to their knees!

CHAPTER 6: THE POETRY OF ANGELS, YOU, AND GOD

V

COME!
    Angels! To thy earthly brethren's need!
    We, who so deeply dungeoned in dull flesh,
  Are shackled in slavery of posh gross greed,
    By bloating *Mammon* starved to ghostly death!
Forsake us not! Unbind our blithe wings bound
  By links of trinkets and the knots of Reason,
    We, Light's lost child and forlorn lover,
  Who mining for ingots, snakes and skeletons found,
Whose blindness, was our race's mindless treason!
    Our spirits, bound like twin-birthed brothers,
  To share one lineage of *Blessedness*,
      Divinely suckled by one Life-Mother,
Come! Mounted on stallions of the breeze and thunder,
    Quaking the valleys, cymbaling through flowers,
  Spill from cloud parapets to earthily plunder
    With Immortality Man's dust-chained hour!
Legion upon legion, wing from celestial battlements,
Conquer Earth's Kingdom, with *Alleluias* of thy Innocence!

VI

WITH
    balm and harp-song, come to our babes' cradles,
  In midnight vigils, kneel on stones of air,
  Feed their first slumbers, hungers for parables,
    Smother their brows and buttocks with kisses rare.
Their hearts unto thy bosoms fold with wings,
  With milks of Heaven, our earthly foundlings nurse,
    With lullabies lilted soft as psalms,
    Thunder through rafters of their temples' dreams
The *Silence* pillaring the Universe!
    Teach them Earth's riches are Heaven's alms,
  That each possession that this world deems fair,
    Is a sparrow fallen broken to their palms:
That whether they wield sword, or pen, or plough,
  Each bears the mighty mission pulsed through flowers,
To blossom Light's kingdom from dark seeds endowed,
  To smile Eternity through their fleeting hours.
Whisper the *Wisdom* that must dawn deep in our kinde:
"That to be truly Human, is to truly Be Divine."

VII

COME
>to our wounded! Heal our temples whole!
>>Weep in our dust, the miracle of Love's leaven!
>
>Broken in body, blinded in soul,
>>Unguent each anguish with the Grace of Heaven!
>
>Kneel to kiss clean the soldier's gaping gashes,
>>Victor with vanquished, together dress, and bind,
>>>And soundly binding, brotherly seal!
>
>>With thy tongues lick stripes left by wicked lashes,
>
>Tell all who bleed, they bleed a nectar Divine,
>>That Spirit, each bodily lesion may congeal!
>>Tell each who feels Fate pierce flesh with nails driven,
>>>"The Hand that crucifies, Eternally heals."
>
>Come to our lonely, crippled, fearful, and poor,
>>Dwellers of hovels, brothels, sewers and trestles,
>
>The sickly, addicted, beggared, starved, and whored,
>>Fill to the full with Love, their exhausted vessels.
>
>Come, Nurses of Light, to the litters and gutters of our dying,
>Tell them God hears, like pealing bells, last whispers and last sighings.

VIII

COME,
>>Angels, to thy Brothers bent in the Sun,
>>To those whose bones and dreams sow the dark soil,
>
>Whose spirits stoop to thistle, stone, and dung,
>>Anointed in the sweats of brutish toils.
>
>Come to our fields and forges, benches and folds,
>>Unto the anvil, oven, and olive-press,
>>>Roll up thy radiant sleeves,
>>And in the blizzards of Earth's heats and colds,
>
>Pick the ruddy apple, milk the udder's tenderness,
>>Bind fruited grasses unto sheaves!
>>With he who weathers storms, and droughts, and broils,
>>>Stomp the purple grape until it holy bleeds!
>
>In tandem with Earth's Tiller tell Man's dreams:
>>"Man groans behind the ox for higher Reason!
>
>*Through Man Earth culminates its intricate Scheme!*
>>*Man's Soul, Waked, Is the harvest of the seasons!*
>
>*Tell Man his dull dead dust may fledge the miracle of wings!*
>*Through Man, the tongues of stones break their hard hearts to sing!"*

IX

THEN
    curse, revile, spit, jail, anathematize!
  Burn Love's scriptorium in your trash barrels!
What you so drearily drone and sermonize
    These ears hear like virgins' midnight madrigals!
Such bile the honeycombs of their hearts translate
  To kisses rained like petals on your face!
    They steal to us in our dark night,
      Children, soft-parting *Misery's* wretched drape,
To choir pure *Jubilance* to our sad race!
    Your curses can not stanch the dike
Of Heaven's rising, smiling, all-embracing Tide,
      That seeps in darkest slumbers dreams of Light!
Not tucked beneath pillows, buried in vaults,
  But showered like *confetti* on all heads!
Not for me, not for you, but to right the faults
  Dealt all flesh yoked to drudgery and dread!
More revelatory than the wheel, the plough, the wind-bellied sail:
Man is a Brother of the Angels, when his Unseen Truth's unveiled!

X

TRUTH'S
    Trumpet must sweet-whisper to each Heart!
  To the enslaved, the beaten, and the bent,
To those who gnash, moan, lust in alleys dark,
  Those wrapped in newspapers foul with excrement.
The paralytic's nerves must tingle like new wings,
  Those blinded with doom, must behold *Hope's* Smile.
    The death-bed, marriage-bed, cradle-hood,
  Must drench with dews of One Love's christening!
All races, faiths, all fear and doubt and guile,
    Must melt into one crucible of Love,
A distillation of *Original Innocence*
      That thaws its drops divinely through Man's blood!
Sing! Angels! Sing to each dust-deafened Heart,
  As Ye to these ears Heavenly rehearse!
Sing through Man's age-old temples of doom and dark,
  Love's pulse, that throbs its heartbeat through the Universe!
No! No! Not shamed! But proud to uttermost humility!
To tell my earthly brothers: *"Man Wakes to Heaven's Fraternity!"*

I once met a god

Tony Ellis

Published in *There is Wisdom in Walnuts,* by Tony Ellis.

have you ever stood naked as the dawn
but huge as cosmic space
and with all the universe within you?

have you ever looked in a mirror
and seen infinity
cloaked in a stranger's mask?

I once met a god
in the woods of Holland

he appeared before me
radiant and bejeweled
like Krishna
with a shining gold crown
and a kind smile

I thought of all the Indian paintings I had seen

he was inside and outside me
at the same time
and his form was both solid and clear
his appearance was brief
and his blessing short
but I have never forgotten him
though it was many years before
I revealed his secret

he hovers in my thoughts
as a gentle presence
inexplicable and unimaginable
but real as flesh

He

Diana Quinlan

Chapter 6: The Poetry of Angels, You, and God

    Listen...
        He sings an ancient song
        So long hidden
           In an empty room

God Bless the Universe

William Clair Godfrey

Tune: *God Bless America*

Published in *Lyrical Iowa*.

Chapter 6: The Poetry of Angels, You, and God

God bless the Whole Wide World,
All of Mankind.
Stand inside her, beside her,
Above, below, and before, and behind.
From the Yangtze, to the Ganges, the Mississippi, to the Rhine
God bless the Whole Wide World,
And all Mankind.

God bless the Universe.
All — THAT — I love.
Dwell throughout her, about her,
Be the light of the stars up above.
From the Microcosm, to the Macrocosm,
     through all the dimensions, seen and unseen
God Bless The Universe,
And all sentient Being.

God — IS — the Universe, and all

The Picture of You

Paul Johan Stokstad

Chapter 6: The Poetry of Angels, You, and God

The sun is on the screen
behind your shoulder

This pastel blouse
striped red, blue

That little arm, barely
visible

And, mouth parted slightly
there's a subtle shade of
pink on your cheek

You may not believe in god
but, you are everything divine
to me.

Gaea's Wedding Kiss

Viktor Tichy

> *The kingdom of heaven is inside you,*
> *not in the buildings of wood or stone.*
> *Split the wood, I am there.*
> *Lift the stone, you will find me.*
> — Jesus in the Gospel of Apostle Thomas

* Schuman resonance is a standing wave in ionosphere powered and in sync with every lightning discharge. The frequency of 7.83 Hz (the light speed divided by the circumference of the globe) and its harmonics (around 16 Hz) seem to trigger bursts of synchronized neural discharges on the EEG scan during the TM and flying sutra of the Sidhi Program. It can help explain the physics of Super-radiance, which could be amplified by the power of global lightning discharges.

Chapter 6: The Poetry of Angels, You, and God

I

The Earth was a part of heaven
ever since we burned Giordano Bruno,
but Heaven on Earth? A frightening metaphor.

When the heavens shrink
to light-years of darkness and fire,
and the antimatter rocket sets our fist on Mars,
the final frontier remains where we come from.
Women live to share that place,
but men must die to return there.

The only thing preferable to loving a woman
is being one. But who can compress a hurricane
into a Coke bottle –
a womb into the skull of a man?

Washington, Tel Aviv, Baghdad,
Teheran, Pyongyang, Kabul,
clash of cut godlings.
As long as we know grief or greed,
the Earth will be a ground for crusades.
That's why in the last two thousand years
we had two hundred eighty five days
without war.

II

Jacob fell off his ladder once,
but how many times the earth shook
under the fall of an angel?
We all came from such a crash.
When I wrestled with my angel, I got her pregnant.
Then I learned to find her face on my pillow
and remain breathing,
We drank milk from street fountains,
wore clothes to ski slopes,
and loved in rooms without walls.

With two sons, two daughters, and peace,
my family, the cone of a tornado,
will grow five-thousand-fold every three centuries.

Will the Milky Way contain you, my children,
by the year three thousand,
when at the cusp of the avalanche of lovers
every breathing human
will be a direct descendant of mine?

My fairy tales, the lyrics of her lullabies
plotted the charts of your universe,
the road map for our lives the continental divide.
We strayed.

III

Money blinks from monitor to monitor
with the speed of light.
Odessa goddesses, China dolls of Shanghai
are the prize. Love breaks Mach One.
The carousels of matrimony click another notch,
but a honeymoon at the airport
turns every prince into a frog.

When the gaze in the mirror tells me
how it feels to live in a well so deep,
you can see stars at noon,
I receive a jolt from the Himalayan spine –
an email offer of a meditation course.

The darkest place in a human body
is inside the skull, so I picture enlightenment
as if TM wired Christmas lights in my head.

Sun rays incarnate into maples.
Silos, hog farms, and phone pole dendrites
embroider the horizon of an Iowa town
where every affair is incest.
Skylights nipple the meditation domes,
two heroic mandalas of sunrise turned cellulose.
Two thousand close their eyes in sync,
backbones coiled like sea horses in limestone.
Matter unrolls the DNA of God.

Behind our eyelids we join the soundless choir
where every thought is a lie.

Chapter 6: The Poetry of Angels, You, and God

As the low voltage orgasms of the flying sutra
wash each brain,
Moses, Christ, Mohamed, and Buddha
toast with soy milk above the poplars.
No use for sepia on compressed tree pulp,
no fodder for crows in drying trenches,
no spores for plutonium mushrooms.

Sagittarius and Virgo cohabit a breathing void.
The planetary magnetic kitten
purrs in Schuman Resonance*
at the back of my head.
My restructured body becomes a galaxy.
Nail polish flashing at the keyboard,
an overload.

When I come out of the Dome,
the world has taken a shower
and changed into play clothes.
A turquoise hacky sack time-warp away
from the auction. We are seven billion neurons
in one galactic brain.
There are more paths from one heart to another
than atoms in the universe.

You sleep on my shoulder
with all our lovers and children.
Our hearts float naked in the stellar tide.
The whole night we look forward
to opening our eyes.

I adore all your fingers and all your eyes.
My every exhale whispers a wedding vow.
I lift the bobbin-lace veil.
Gaia is the bride.

Pianissimo, as with an apology,
a hand alights on my shoulder.
A curly white hair and beard
mask a Moses-like face behind me.
"Viktor, you are snoring."

On a Medieval Painting of the Fall of Man

Freddy Niagara Fonseca

Chapter 6: The Poetry of Angels, You, and God

The Angel turned them out of Paradise,
And God withdrew within.
A glorious Realm receded from their Eyes—
They shrank from loving Him.

The World is like a Darker Sphere until
We meet His Love within.
An Angel full of Grace is waiting still
To lead us back to Him.

"In the evening we shall be examined on love"

Thomas Centolella

— St. John of the Cross

Published in *Lights & Mysteries*, by Thomas Centolella.

Chapter 6: The Poetry of Angels, You, and God

And it won't be multiple choice,
though some of us would prefer it that way.
Neither will it be essay, which tempts us to run on
when we should be sticking to the point, if not together.
In the evening there shall be implications
our fear will change to complications. No cheating,
we'll be told, and we'll try to figure the cost of being true
to ourselves. In the evening when the sky has turned
that certain blue, blue of exam books, blue of no more
daily evasions, we shall climb the hill as the light empties
and park our tired bodies on a bench above the city
and try to fill in the blanks. And we won't be tested
like defendants on trial, cross-examined
till one of us breaks down, guilty as charged. No,
in the evening, after the day has refused to testify,
we shall be examined on love like students
who don't even recall signing up for the course
and now must take their orals, forced to speak for once
from the heart and not off the top of their heads.
And when the evening is over and it's late,
the student body asleep, even the great teachers
retired for the night, we shall stay up
and run back over the questions, each in our own way:
what's true, what's false, what unknown quantity
will balance the equation, what it would mean years from now
to look back and know
we did not fail.

Good Night

Patricia Regan Argiro

Published in *Toward Sunset,* by Patricia Regan Argiro.

Chapter 6: The Poetry of Angels, You, and God

Our breath
flowers in
moondark air,
gathering silence.

"Sleep with
the angels,"
you say
and I,
quite suddenly
near dreaming,
murmur that
I am.

The Poetry of the Anecdotal and Domestic

Chapter 7

*Don't listen to what they say.
Go see.*

— Chinese Proverb

CONTENTS

Page	Title	Author
240	Melons	*Rustin Larson*
242	Waving Man #1	*Allen Cobb*
244	Cereal Cold Wars	*Phoebe Carter*
246	Magic Carpets	*Carole Lee Connet*
250	Bug in My Pants	*Viktor Tichy*
252	Protection	*Tracy Chipman*
254	Wild Rabbit in the Woods	*James Moore*
258	Hero	*Leah Marie Waller*
260	Red Paste and Rice	*Carole Lee Connet*
262	The Bottom of Glass	*Judy Liese*
264	To the Clown Who Had His Eye Blown out...	*Anne Hildenbrand*
266	New Delhi Street	*Linda Egenes*
268	Chanukah Lights Tonight	*Steven P. Schneider*
270	Blue Heron	*Henry Robert Hau*
272	My Cambodian God	*Tony Ellis*
274	This Is How You Hang up Clothes	*Judy Liese*
276	House Painter Sitting on the Roof of a...	*Charlie Hopkins*

The bed is a bundle of paradoxes: we go to it with reluctance, yet we quit it with regret; we make up our minds every night to leave it early, but we make up our bodies every morning to keep it late.

— Ogden Nash, American poet (1902-1971)

Chapter 7

The Poetry of the Anecdotal and Domestic

Some poetry lovers pooh-pooh the anecdotal for being too insignificant to write about. They argue that such poetry resembles prose and doesn't involve very profound ideas. Ditto for domestic subjects. Some poets, however, find it suits their writing style very well.

No matter how commonplace our feelings can sometimes be, they are all composed of basic experiences that make up the daily grind.

The word 'anecdote' is derived from the Greek *anekdota* which means things unpublished.'

How many potential stories are crying out to be heard, but remain unwritten in poetry? Must that be?

We all share core narratives waiting to be retold again and again. So doesn't everything begin as a feeling looking to be shared, all in good time, expressing simple miracles of ordinary life?

If an unheroic story is told in bold terms, its value may well transcend the 'merely anecdotal' and be praised as quite poetic when published.

Melons

Rustin Larson

Published in *Cimarron Review*.

Chapter 7: The Poetry of the Anecdotal and Domestic

You bought one, perfectly ripe,
but within days
little holes appeared
and it began to shrink from inside
like a consumptive.
Time after time we'd buy the sweet smelling globes
and they'd rot.
You said we had bad luck with melons.
I said we were cursed,

and so it was we wandered the earth dreaming
of the perfect incorruptible melon.
We would walk by a woman
and think of melons. We would walk by a man
with large knees and think of melons.
Even when we were spending money on clothes
we would think we were dealing out melon leaves,
thick and prickly, always leaving
a trace on our hands. Our shoes became
melon rinds, and our fingers, slivers of ripe
yellow melon. So when was it we stopped
thinking of these things? I think it was
the day in the supermarket when
you said to me, "Rus, I can't live
like this anymore!" and walked off,
leaving me to contemplate the absence of melons
and their traces, their juices and their mold.
"Why should I live like this either?" I thought,
and sat down on a crate, and weighed
my big round head in my hands.

Waving Man #1

Allen Cobb

Published in *Cave Paintings,* by Allen Cobb.

Chapter 7: The Poetry of the Anecdotal and Domestic

In my town
at the corner
of one street and another
an old man stands and waves.
He waves at every passing car and person.
Maybe he is looking for a lost lover,
parent, son, or daughter.
Maybe he has nothing left but friendliness.

Cereal Cold Wars

Phoebe Carter

Chapter 7: The Poetry of the Anecdotal and Domestic

It is not often a question
of right or wrong
With the two of us.
We would much prefer to sip our cereal in silence
Than plug our noses and take that leap of faith
Into the baby pink swimming pool that is
Forgiveness.
You'll smile at me
and I'll pretend not to notice.
A word may slip out
here and there.
But I'll snatch it back
and swallow it whole with my cheerios and milk.
We don't share our off-white reasons for our magenta mistakes.
We've already made up our minds:
There are better ways to die
Than by our own poison.

Magic Carpets

Carole Lee Connet

Published In *Contemporary Review* 1999.

Lying in the parcel tray of a humpbacked
   whale, a lacquer-black Hudson Terraplane
      with a shelf just the right size
for my eight-year-old body covered by a bubble
   of stars. We slip past derricks dipping ponderous
      beaks along a narrow road so rutted the wheels lurch
sideways whenever slight seizures shake Dad
   off track. Chubby big sister beached
      on the back seat soft as Cocker Spaniel ears,
baby sister swimming the whole way
   in Mom's belly while we eat baby red bananas
      cruising through damp mountains to the silver
shops of Tasco and a black-eyed boy selling emeralds
   for a quarter, which Dad won't give me
      because he says they're cut from Coca Cola
butts. Circling Chapultapec Hill to Grasshopper Castle
   where Diego Rivera stops painting
      the Revolution to sign my postcard.
Landing at the Sun Pyramid, which Dad will
   not let me climb because he says Quetzalcoatl
      unfriezes in so much heat
and the plumed serpent will eat
   my heart for supper.

Riding high on the back of a red and white
   tiger, a brand new Corvette convertible,
      top down, clutching the chrome trim,
legs pressed together tight
   against the leather seats, frizz-permed hair
      tangling in the wind as Daddy roars
away from the curb at Lockwood Elementary
   after picking me and my sister up from school.
      All the kids gaping in awe, even
the rich brats, as we hit 60 in half
   a block, the shiny molded plastic body
      of the test car reflecting late afternoon
sun into shards of light,
   stabbing their jealous hearts
      while we grin and try to look cool
like we're definitely not
   wetting our pants.

This Enduring Gift

Sleeping on the rump of a chestnut
    Clydsdale, a Ford "Woody" with oak strips
        for traces, on top of flip-top Budweiser
cartons allotted us kids one each for suitcases.
    Sister brother sister squashed
        peanut butter between Blue Bunny bread
in the middle, Mom up front moaning
    her bursitis, Dad growling shut-up all the way
        from St. Louis across salt-sweating orange
sands to the sound-sucking humus of feathery
    clippings dropped by red giants
        paring their fingernails, to the wake-up
pines of Pemigewasett Lake. My oars cleave
    mats of white water lilies with yellow hearts
        around an island big enough for a willow
wigwam but too far from harbor in a sudden squall
    that panics Mom into sending a cheeky boy
        in a Coast Guard cutter to rescue a red-faced
"ninny" not old enough, he says, to be out
    so far without an adult
        and if you claim you're grown up
then you're not smart enough to be out
    of your playpen.

Learning to back up in a faded brown
    June bug, Dad's re-tired Mercury with the perpetual
        grin full of nickel-chrome fillings. Scuttling the gravel
driveway in first gear to Kirkwood, boomeranging
    backwards to Essex, over
and over, past Mom's bearded iris, past the patio laid
    with bricks named Purington Paver, Egyptian, LaClede,
        collected by Dad from all over the world.
Past the prickly holly trees guarding
    the front door where I stepped out in a strapless
        hand-me-down from cousin Kacky tulle gown
on the tuxedo arm of a red-headed
    monkey who gave me a wrist corsage
        of yellow roses in a cellophane box,
a ride in his old man's rusted out Buick and my only
    chance to go to the Senior Prom.

Body splicing in the front seat of a snub-nosed
   shark, a baby blue Studebaker
      my steady—whose class ring I wear wound with yarn
to fit—calls the Virgin Trap, holding the wheel
   while he holds me around the waist, one hand clutching
      my breast while I try to stay on my side
of the road. He says aim the fender at the yellow line,
   which I can't see in the passing headlights.
      So he says keep your eyes on the white line
on the right side of the blacktop. Now pull
   in at the overlook but don't look while I pull
      down your panties and I promise, baby, I won't go
all the way in. But he's pushing too hard
   and there's something wet and red between my legs.

Bug in My Pants

Viktor Tichy

You tickle in my groin
under the fabric of my underwear.

If I knew you were a bumblebee, a wasp,
or a Desert Storm veteran,
I would gently extend my hand,
let you crawl on my finger,
and take you out of my house.

If you were a cockroach, a cricket,
or a Catholic priest looking for God
in the shorts of school boys,
I would imprison you in my fist
and delighting in your ticklish protests
I would set you free outside the door.

If you were a run-away teen,
a wife, or a tax fraud convict,
I would vacate my office
and offer you dinner.
I would kill you
only if you were a mosquito,
my history teacher, or a fly.

But you are an unidentified stranger,
an intruder without a map, visa, or green card.
How do I know you are not ready
to bury your stinger,
into my pelvic floor,
and inject your venom or progeny
under my skin?

In a panic of ignorance
I crush your chitinous shell.
I feel your texture through the fabric,
the wetness of your exploded heart,
but when I tear off my trousers
to identify your cadaver,
like a paycheck, like childhood,
like the scent of an Indian dancer,
you're gone.

Protection

Tracy Chipman

Chapter 7: The Poetry of the Anecdotal and Domestic

Down the red granite gravel road
to a cul-de-sac of white birch,
white pine
white light
open to the Divine.
Ice cream pails tied
to our waists,
old scarves tied to our heads.

Meaty deerflies
dived and butterflies danced
as we three; Grandma, Grandpa and me
made our way into the raspberry's dense
sharp sweetness.
In silence we picked
while the air hummed
heavy with humidity.
Holding,
holding us close.
So still.
Softly we picked,
breathing in sync,
fingers stained with
berry blood.

We found a place
where the bushes sank.
Pushed low by a heavy force.
Bear, here, only heartbeats ago.
Nose and paw
fruit and tongue
stained with
berry blood.

Wild Rabbit in the Woods

James Moore

Chapter 7: The Poetry of the Anecdotal and Domestic

6:39 am Sunday morning,
moist, cloudy, 65 degrees,
seventh of may two thousand.

Into a late spring, I bolt out of sleep,
down the loft ladder,
flicking a dead roach from a chair
into an old tea cup,
out the big wooden front door,
to relieve myself in a hurry.

As I pull my pants down I spy a wild rabbit
startled into frozen-statue mode.

The sweet relief flows and completes itself,
the round black eye of the rabbit
riveted on me, not a single whisker stirring.

With one hand behind my back, teacup in tow,
the other supporting my flaccid domingo,
I play statue as well,
weight shifted slightly onto the right foot,
rabbit maybe twenty feet away.

Five minutes we both stay perfectly still,
eyeing each other like our lives depended on it.

The morning symphony is in full swing,
the woods loud, alive with sound:
mourning doves on the perimeter,
a rooster in the distance,
tweets, shrieks, toots and whistles of
cardinals, sparrows, geese, swallows,
jays, robins, blackbirds, occasional crows,
construction site hammering of woodpeckers.
I'm startled to hear an outboard motor—
no, it's a mammoth fly.

Birds crowd the hanging feeder 30 feet away.

The two frozen statues continue to stare each other down.

A whisker stirs once in ten minutes, now a second time,
me, with teacup behind back and penis in hand,
throat tickles but careful swallowing stifles desire to cough.

Finally, the rabbit resumes eating,
munching its fresh garden salad, leaf here, grass there,
even a dandelion stalk fuzzy end and all,
biting, eating, chewing, swallowing, ears hyper-alert, radar screening noises,
nervous eyes everywhere at once, head twitching incessant.

It creeps closer to me now oblivious, or accepting, non-threatened,
as close as ten feet, five feet, eating, eating.

The symphony continues in full swing
enhanced by more bird-wing flutters, tree rustles,
and cricket clatter (or am I imagining the crickets?)

I remember as a boy, at three of four years old,
waiting in a car in the Wisconsin countryside
to meet my father for lunch (he delivered dry cleaning),
my mother and I sitting with windows open off the side of the road
as redwing blackbirds led the other birds in song and swoops,
the same lovely birdsongs I'm hearing now.

As the rabbit continues breakfast, munching and looking around,
chewing cud-like, smug and floaty as a carp,
legs sometimes pawing up and down in mock getaway,
I think of Saint Francis who could understand the talk of wild animals,
communicate with them, befriend them
(they would come out of the wild into his hands),
and the saints in India who live in forests and meditate
with scorpions and cobras and lions and tigers,
and stories of holy men doing *tapas*, austerities,
like standing on one leg for hours, days, years even,
sometimes in water up to the neck, all to gain equanimity,
universality, oneness with nature and the divine.

As I remain motionless, pondering thus, eyes locked to the skittish hare,
weight still shifted onto the right foot,
insights quietly dawn under the one-cloud stone grey sky.

Chapter 7: The Poetry of the Anecdotal and Domestic

Surrounded by the new greens of foliage and fauna,
happy buds, still growing, bursting with joy,
grass not yet cut this year,
I completely lose track of time,
but the rabbit, whose back is now to me,
suddenly passes wind and lurches straight upward in a violent bound.

Having never heard a wild rabbit fart before,
my mouth contorts and eyes widen to keep from laughing out loud.
(Is it the fart itself, or the fact that a sound from one's own butt
causes such a panic, that seems so funny?)

A second small fart (all that salad I guess) causes only a head twitch,
but to my utter bemusement and delight, another loud blast
sends the rabbit skyward once again,
proving it wasn't a hallucination.

Oh, the secrets the woods can reveal!

[Of course, rabbits fart.
Why shouldn't they?
All God's creatures fart, no doubt, including the Son of God himself,
all the prophets and saints, rodents, mammals of all shapes and sizes,
even birds and snakes and insects and fish?]

Heavy with realization, or not,
by now my foot is getting heavy.

The rabbit, whether embarrassed,
or simply full, hops out of sight,
white tail bobbing up and down, just like that,
disappearing into the woods.

I collect myself, and head inside, laughing.

It's 7:10am.

Time flies when you're standing still.

Hero

Leah Marie Waller

Published in *Under the Cedar Tree*, by Leah Marie Waller.

CHAPTER 7: THE POETRY OF THE ANECDOTAL AND DOMESTIC

Little black ant from the oak tree
a suicide jump—
saved by my shoulder

Red Paste and Rice

Carole Lee Connet

NFSPS Connecticut Poetry Society Award Honorable Mention, 2002.

Chapter 7: The Poetry of the Anecdotal and Domestic

In the smog of Kathmandu,
tourists breed beggars,
skeletons with rag-wrapped babes,
wooden crutches, milky eyes.

Snot-nosed children swarming
like flies on sugar cane,
small hands stretched out,
banking on guilt.

On the steep steps to the monkey temple,
a sadhu swaddled in orange
daubs red paste and rice between my charmed eyes,
showers marigold petals on my head.

Holds out his right hand.
"Fifty rupees," he advises me, in English.
Fifty rupees, less than a dollar,
small change for a tourist.

"What happened to you?" my ex-pat friend laughs,
seeing my smeared brow.
"You gave fifty rupees!
That's half a day's wages for a man pulling a riksha."

The next sanyasi catches me on the outskirts of Thamel
just before the bridge over the Bagmati
as the sun slides into the holy river
of turds to wash away the diesel fumes of the day.

I decline to be blessed.
Instead, I drop a bread roll in his begging bowl.
"Fifty rupees," he implores, tucking away his petals.
I am incensed. "They only charge *ten* at the temple!"

My Buddhist friend laughs when I complain.
"In his sandals, wouldn't *you* ask for more?"
Then softly, "He is like that
because you are like this."

The Bottom of Glass

Judy Liese

Chapter 7: The Poetry of the Anecdotal and Domestic

She skates alone
over the thick ice of Goose Lake
under a full Alaska moon.

Her skates glide silently
across a clear virgin surface
beyond the boundaries
of the ice rink.

The toothy toe of her ice skate
catches on an icy protrusion.
tossing her face down on glass.

Blinking, dazed, she lifts her head,
looks through impossibly clear ice
at etchings of ferns and stars,
feathers and galaxies,
illuminated by moonlight
all the way down
to that exact point
where ice meets water
and everything is connected.

To the Clown Who Had His Eye Blown out by Flashlight Powder

Anne Hildenbrand

Chapter 7: The Poetry of the Anecdotal and Domestic

They laughed to see your face a cloud of smoke,
Its whiteness brightened by the bluish flame.
They clapped and shouted when you seemed to choke;
If they had known, they would have called your name.
They were so pleased to see the great red lips,
Streaked in coarse paint across your chalky face,
Tighten into a crooked line,
Your sloping eyebrows stretching to their tips,
Your hands hurled upward with a mindless grace—
And when you staggered backward, they could not contain
Their mirthful ecstasy. You seemed to catch their mood,
You groaned but once, and that was lost in shouts,
Then straightened up and clapped a hand upon your cheek—
It helped to stop the blood. The other hand you used
In boisterous bouts with members of the band.
At last while seeming to avoid the drummer's stick,
You stumbled through the rope;
Lay in the sawdust, trembling—sick;
Got up, pretended foolishly to grope,
And while they whistled with delight,
Found your way slowly, out into the night.

New Delhi Street

Linda Egenes

Chapter 7: The Poetry of the Anecdotal and Domestic

The saffron-saried woman sits
on the sidewalk
selling orange mangoes and yellow star fruits
with her eyes.

Chanukah Lights Tonight

Steven P. Schneider

Published in *Unexpected Guests*, by Steven P. Schneider.
Featured in Ted Kooser's column and website "American Life in Poetry".

Chapter 7: The Poetry of the Anecdotal and Domestic

Our annual prairie Chanukah party—
latkes, kugel, cherry blintzes.
Friends arrive from nearby towns
and dance the twist to "Chanukah Lights Tonight,"
spin like a dreidel to a klezmer hit.

The candles flicker in the window.
Outside, ponderosa pines are tied in red bows.
If you squint,
the neighbors' Christmas lights
look like the Omaha skyline.

The smell of oil is in the air.
We drift off to childhood
where we spent our gelt
on baseball cards and matinees,
cream sodas and potato knishes.

No delis in our neighborhood.
Only the wind howling over the crushed corn stalks.
Inside, we try to sweep the darkness out,
waiting for the Messiah to knock
wanting to know if he can join the party.

Blue Heron

Henry Robert Hau

Published in *For the Bird Sings,* by Henry Robert Hau.

Chapter 7: The Poetry of the Anecdotal and Domestic

A blue heron
crosses over our conversation

and the river is quieted
and the woods acquiesce
to the meaning of blue wings

my cambodian god

Tony Ellis

Published in *There is Wisdom in Walnuts*, by Tony Ellis.

CHAPTER 7: THE POETRY OF THE ANECDOTAL AND DOMESTIC

I have a cambodian god in my bedroom

I found him at T J Maxx,
black and alone on a shelf
in the household aisle
miserable between bright jugs and blue bowls

for $9.50 plus tax
I set him free
adorned him with rudraksh beads
tilacked him with sandal paste
washed him clean

now he sits
warm dark and silent
and watches over me while I sleep—
head and shoulders of an ancient culture
inexplicably at rest
                            in a Fairfield farmhouse

This Is How You Hang up Clothes

Judy Liese

Chapter 7: The Poetry of the Anecdotal and Domestic

The wind floats the wet clothes away from you.
Stiff, wooden clothespins,
worn smooth under your fingers,
give off the faint smell of pine.

They arrange themselves in patterns:
white clothing sun-bleached,
dark clothing, cool in shadiness.

Always you are reaching up,
sun-squinted towards Heaven,
mingled with the scents prairie grass,
fresh air, sunshine and clean, wet clothes.
And sometimes in the middle
of an Iowa winter,
you can shake out a sheet
from the bottom of the chest
and smell that sweetness.

House Painter Sitting on the Roof of a Queen Anne Victorian Looking over a Pear Orchard in Bloom

Charlie Hopkins

For Eli and Jeff

"Your love has given me wings."
From *"Volare"* sung by Bobby Rydell

At 52 with help from my sons
I place a 40 foot ladder and raise it to full extension
braced against the stump of a chinkapin oak.
With the ladder held and steadied by my sons
I climb to the roof of a rich man's house
and look over miles of Hood River Valley coming into bloom.
She is beautiful in spring as a Mexican girl dressed for her wedding.

Through her middle is a flow of water
continually drunk with gladness for itself.
From the head of the valley to where it empties in the Columbia
there is always this laughter!

Today I climb in fog and middle 50s, clouds with their arms all around me.
Above a certain height the knowledge I can fall
is balanced by an equal certainty I can fly.

Having fallen before I know the cost of coming suddenly to earth:

>   3 cracked vertebrae and sternum,
>   right fore finger broken at the knuckle,
>   nose in 4 places crushed and re-supported with steel,
>   collarbone snapped so I had to sleep sitting up
>   two months on the couch
>   peeing through a vacuum cleaner hose
>   into an empty bucket of bone white enamel.

From where I sit now I can choose the world I live in.
If I choose flight I will leave this world and land gracefully
in another.
If I fall from here the result will be the same.

I see pear blossoms weighted down with drops of rain
in the ashes of morning
before the heat of wheat deserts is drawn through the lung
of the river gorge.
I see the languid body of our Lord uncoil from sheets of sky
and I hear the river praising itself over rocks worn smooth with laughter.

This Enduring Gift

The shallower the water the louder is its praise.

I hear what the desert promises when she whispers in my hollow ear saying

There is no difference between falling and flying.

The wheat desert says that everything in this world is a door.
To fall is one door. To fly is another.
When a pear blossom the color of the risen moon is cut by wind
and carried up to me on the roof of a rich man's house
this is a third kind of door.

In the marrow of my breast bone that once was cracked but now is made whole
there is a staircase spiraling into quiet.
There is an emptiness inside the bone I have learned to walk through.

Now I can say I am completely alone or I can say I walk hand in hand with my Lord.
There is no difference between falling and flying as long as I will pay
the price this world insists upon.

The first step away from selfishness is a falling
that gives us wings.
When pride is exhausted it gives way to greater clarity
so the head may fall of its own weight
to rest over the beating heart.

What was lost is found not in the closed but in the open hand.
Then our faces shine like spoons full of water
and we are gathered into someone's arms
whose only name is silence.

From where I sit I see a silver blade of sky and the first blood of morning
but I don't look for meaning in this light.
I sit here counting the one syllable of the quiet.
Over and over the same syllable of the only name I answer to
the name that is yours alone in whom I am harvested in Fall.

Chapter 7: The Poetry of the Anecdotal and Domestic

I am flying!

I am climbing down this ladder to my sons!

The Poetry of Animals, Pets, and All of Us

CHAPTER 8

*Out of the earth
I sing for them,
A Horse nation
I sing for them.
Out of the earth
I sing for them,
The animals
I sing for them*

— Teton Sioux Indians

Contents

282	Simon	*Jeffrey Hedquist*
286	Ant Warrior	*Phoebe Carter*
288	An Animal of Ancient Ancestry	*Anne Hildenbrand*
290	Smallest Dog in the World	*Nancy Berg*
294	When Ninja Sits	*Carol Olicker*
296	Cleo	*Rustin Larson*
298	Night Heat	*Ann Du Bois*
300	The Whale's Song	*Andrea Dana Stevens*
302	The Love of Horses	*Megge Hill Fitz-Randolph*
304	Squirrel Brain	*Jeffrey Hedquist*
306	The New York City Zoo	*Freddy Niagara Fonseca*
312	The Gerbils	*Rustin Larson*
314	Mushikarati: The Mouse's Poem	*Angela Mailander*
316	So Say the Wise	*William Clair Godfrey*
318	On the Angels among Us	*Brother Ludovico*
326	Doin' What Comes Naturally	*Richard K. Wallarab*
328	The House Sparrow	*Henry Robert Hau*
330	How They Sometimes Show up	*Glenn Watt*

*Thou wast not born for death,
immortal Bird!*

— From *Ode to a Nightingale*, John Keats, British poet
(1795-1821)

Chapter 8

The Poetry of Animals, Pets, and All of Us

The word 'animal' derives from the Latin word *anima*, meaning *'soul.'*

This chapter is a veritable Noah's Ark. Just like great poets, animals are great souls and have much to teach us. What would you do if you had any of their superb qualities?

If you were like a lion, you would write with authority and power. Had you a nightingale's voice, you'd spread beauty and peace wherever you went. The graceful flamingo's every move would be your model for romance. Like an eagle, you'd surely soar to greater and greater heights.

Your zeal would equal the nonstop activity of ants. You'd be as loving and truthful to everyone as your dog is to you. The longevity of turtles, whales, and swans would be yours. You could be the greatest poet of all!

Every now and then some stray poets gain wonderful insights from the animal kingdom, and their poetry shares what they've learned. A rich and often quite hilarious inner world opens up, revealing to us much we never knew about ourselves.

Simon

Jeffrey Hedquist

Chapter 8: The Poetry of Animals, Pets, and All of Us

The ivory hunter relentlessly stalks my foot,
flops on his back and scans my eyes for attention.
Who is this soft, meaty fur ball who has captured my heart?

His Majesty.
Independent, imperious.
Disregarding requests not matching the feline agenda.
Selfish, disdainful, and then...

The commercial begins,
voice unrelenting.
It's time to eat, play, go out, come in, be massaged.

I comply. Under the thumb of an animal
without any.

This miniature white furnace with insubordinate claws
prepares my lap for nesting,
pink nose buried in my shirt.

I melt in the torrent of purrs.

My once-fantasy:
Train the beast. Ha!
Attempts at behavior modification were successful.
My behavior is now modified.

We've struck a deal, this cat and I.
I will feed, shelter and brush him,
provide healthcare, interior and exterior access, string chasing time.

He will just...be.
Seems fair.

Doing nothing,
he accomplishes everything.

Prostrate at his furry feet
I still have much to learn.

This moment is his only time.
His teaching —
by example.
If I could only be as quick to let go.
Forgive.
Be.

My apprenticeship continues
until I become the cat in my heart.

Would someone please scratch behind my ears?

Chapter 8: The Poetry of Animals, Pets, and All of Us

Ant Warrior

Phoebe Carter

Chapter 8: The Poetry of Animals, Pets, and All of Us

Armor-clad ants dart
in and out of the rocky maze of light and shadow.
They play hide-and-seek
creeping silently
on fragile legs in their silent world.
One pauses to gather his bearings.
Then he is off again
following a mission with a compass
unseen by man.

An Animal of Ancient Ancestry

Anne Hildenbrand

Sonnet #21 From *Sonnets to Iowa,* by Anne Hildenbrand.

Chapter 8: The Poetry of Animals, Pets, and All of Us

An animal of ancient ancestry,
A lowly salamander known as newt
Elected highway #7 as his route.
No other part would do, though he was free
To choose. So slowly, almost painfully
He crawled—thus causing passing cars acute
Discomfort, inconvenience, and to boot—
In spite of minutes lost—hilarity.

Now what to do? Unsolvable impasse.
Persuade the lowly newt to change his plan?
Put mighty evolution in reverse?
Far easier to shift the total mass
Of Everest! No, turn instead to man—
Move #7—oh, the problem could be worse!

Smallest Dog in the World

Nancy Berg

for Billie

Published in *Oracles for Night-Blooming Eccentrics,* by Nancy Berg.

Chapter 8: The Poetry of Animals, Pets, and All of Us

Seeking a soulmate, I bought a dog afraid of everything.
Hunched shoulders,
morbid shivering,
upper back pliable as a slab of oak;
people were always asking us if we were cold.

"That animal is almost too sensitive for life,"
says a friend.
I nod, blushing,
possibly even twitching,
stooping to paw at the stress-related hives on my leg.

I blanketed that dog
with a love so thick
it was far too gelatinous and rich
for any human.
Cooing incessantly,
I hovered, enveloped,
and watched her uncurl.
Now she bares her teeth at pit bulls
and flirts shamelessly with strangers.
So this is how you make a creature strong,
I see,
somewhat later than most
and yet still in this lifetime.

*"Doctor—help!
I can't stop singing to my dog."
"What could be more natural?," says the doctor.
"The heart yearns to praise."*

*"Doctor—help!
I can't stop kissing my dog
on the forehead."
"How could it be otherwise?," says the doctor.
"The heart yearns for beauty."*

The smallest dog in the world
shares my penchant for fanaticism.

This Enduring Gift

There we are, in the L.A. paper,
under "Poet Spreads the Word About Red Cross."
That's me in the beret, like some terrorist of mercy;
the sacred chihuahua's wrapped head to claw
in the international symbol for neutrality.
(I'm surprised I don't have Red Cross nipple piercings
and little Clara Barton-shaped decals on each tooth.)

"Doctor—help!
Hearing that 'Dog' is 'God' spelled backwards,
I have once again confused my priorities."
"Absolutely normal," says the doctor.
"The heart yearns for imaginary significance."
(Or did he say,
"The heart yearns for solace?")

The smallest dog in the world
scares away macho dudes
and emotional diabetics
who lack the blood sugar
for progressively saccharine terms of endearment.
This, I suspect, is a blessing.
That noise you hear is the pager,
the phone, the fax, and the door,
all of which we seem to be ignoring as usual.
Wrapped in fetal position
around the smallest dog in the world,
I have learned to form the perfect circle.

"Doctor—help!
I can't stop thinking about my dog;
when I'm out on a date,
when a man comes close,
when..."
"Impeccable choice," says the doctor,
waving snapshots of his beagle.
"A dog will give you more love in an hour
than a spouse can offer in a hundred years."

CHAPTER 8: THE POETRY OF ANIMALS, PETS, AND ALL OF US

The smallest dog in the world is more than
a mere fashion accessory.
There I am in velvet
at an elegant formal affair.
"I didn't recognize you without your other half,"
sneers a socialite.
At this the boundaries of selfhood evaporate,
as if they have attempted to pay by check
without a driver's license.

"Doctor—help!
I can't stop babytalking my dog."
"It's about time" says the doctor,
sounding suspiciously like my mother.
"Biology is destiny."

When Ninja Sits

Carol Olicker

This poem describes my experience when my cat Ninja rests on me. "Qualuuden" is a word I coined. It's a reference to the muscle-relaxer Quaalude which was widely abused in the 70s as a pleasure drug and is no longer available.

Chapter 8: The Poetry of Animals, Pets, and All of Us

When Ninja sits,
quaaluden,
on my chest
And melts on me, like butter into toast,
And when she kneads
(O gentle rhythm!)
Slightly clawed,
Then all the children I never bore
Wrap their little hands around my heart
And squeezing,
In her rhythm,
They forgive me.

Cleo

Rustin Larson

Cleo was a basset hound, overweight, lazy
and sad.
She had gastric distress often, produced
horrible smelling farts,
vomited in great gushes,
left her crap in Dairy Queen swirls near my swing set
and everywhere else.
She chewed pork chop bones
which she defended with low
barely audible growls, and
she would choke invariably
and stagger around the yard
making great rasping honks that nauseated me.
One day
a milk truck hit her
and broke her hip, and when she healed
she walked with her butt swinging sexily
like Susan Hayward in "I Want to Live!"
We kicked her away from our garbage
but she always returned, and since
she was not our dog
we could not kill her.

I want it to be clear
I harbored no love for this creature,
and when she died
I shed practically no tears at all.
It is only now
that I am middle-aged and ailing
that I think of her with some respect,
as I respect all of God's creatures,
including the unfortunate and broken.
If there is forgiveness
in memory,
let there be that and
all our bones dulled
by the teeth that erode,
the rains that come and
the sweet milk of the earth.

Night Heat

Ann Du Bois

Published In *Lyrical Iowa*.

Chapter 8: The Poetry of Animals, Pets, and All of Us

six o clock
snuck up on me
like a cat
stretching
slowly
to a slink

this cats gotta prowl
sniffing out
the motion
of you or perhaps just another
cat
scratch that urge
it's all the same

six fifteen
the artificial glow
of night melts
my shadow on concrete
me
strutting
tail tall

The Whale's Song

Andrea Dana Stevens

© Andrea D. Stevens (7/12/08)

Chapter 8: The Poetry of Animals, Pets, and All of Us

They tunnel the long distance sea
Calling out each other,
Fathers crying for their children
Riding out the last century
        for the grand connection.
Swollen sea horses and phantom cowboys,
Giant Chinese lanterns.
        In a night sea of ghost eyes,
        they love their lost children anyway.

This is the whale's song,
The great mammalian's cry.
        Leviathans crying out for love.
        Swollen lost water babies of God.

Earth Mother is gone.
The sky is bitter and bound.
We need to listen.
We are bigger than them in our dreams.
They travel the seamless seas and skies.
Ghost ships calling us to conscience
        calling us back to the sea.

They sing us lullabies
        that change our minds,
        turning the sky into sea blankets
        and rhythm riding pearl water's familiar lunacy.
They make the unicorns visible.
They make the unicorns sing.

Their invisible belly song, found only in wild seas,
They cry the long grey memory
        for lost fathering on earth,
        for the dead Indian nation,
        for forgotten grace,
        for all the honest crawling out of shells.

Look at their eyes!
Ring and crab nebula combined.
Even on land they make us listen,
They do not let us forget
We are in the great uterus of the sea.
These whales call us out all to bring us home.

The Love of Horses

Megge Hill Fitz-Randolph

First printed in *Yellow Silk*.
Published in *Yellow Silk: Erotic Arts and Letters*.

Chapter 8: The Poetry of Animals, Pets, and All of Us

On this pleasant brown afternoon, smudged
with February, by barns, I watch horses.
I watch the twelve dreaming girls astride them,
mud and snow, lapping up against each other. I watch
this strange kinship of opposites, girl and horse
stalled together in one closed motion.

The girls have grown more confident, though still shy,
as if they don't yet know what all this means—
the thick furred thing that lifts and flows beneath them
with a name. Each girl, I think, longs to ride up into
the woods alone, and close a leafy door.
So no matter how much she talks to you about horses,
she can never say exactly what she means.

Squirrel Brain

Jeffrey Hedquist

Chapter 8: The Poetry of Animals, Pets, and All of Us

A silent, unmoving horizon of white.

Then
a furry grey rocket
with orange plume
shoots across the snow
and stops

at invisible coordinates,
head down, burrowing
deep beneath the crust
his tail a waving flag
signals discovery:

Seconds later, up with a cheek-clenched meal.

How can this squirrel locate a hickory nut
buried 4 months ago
when I can't find the keys
I put on the counter last night?

The New York City Zoo

Freddy Niagara Fonseca

> *The creatures outside looked from pig to man, and from man to pig, and from pig to man again; but already it was impossible to say which was which.*
> — From *Animal Farm*, George Orwell

CHAPTER 8: THE POETRY OF ANIMALS, PETS, AND ALL OF US

Tell me, have you ever been to New York City?
Have you seen the rat race there and kept your wits?

    I have sailed the roughest seas and crossed the deserts—
    I have fought ferocious tigers in Bengal—
    Dangers of the Congo jungles do not scare me—
    I have climbed the steepest mountains in Nepal—
    I know the perils of Caracas, Rio, London, Cairo,
    But they're trifles when compared to New York City's.

Hell, there's nothing quite like New York City!
    Let me tell you, it's a testy, noisy jungle! Really!
        There is nothing, nothing like it.
            It's insane! It's a racket!
            Most unnerving
    And chaotic!
  It's a zoo!
It's a jungle, and a racket, and a total, total zoo!

Tell me, have you ever passed through New York City?
Have you joined the traffic jams and lived to tell?

    You take your chances when you cross Manhattan.
    You'll be lucky if you do not lose your cool.
    Savage tiger taxis leap through intersections.
    Buses scoot like horny rhinos by the curb.
    Motorized gorillas roar around the plazas.
    Twenty million legs and roaches hit the town.

        How they hurry, hurry, always hurry
        From one crowded corner to the next!
        Busy, busy, busy, always busy.
        Dammit, can they never once relax?

See, there's nothing quite like New York City!
    It's like rush hours always in this awful nutty den.
        There is nothing, nothing you can do
            About it ever.
            Oh, forget it.
    It's a madhouse
  And a racket.
It's intense—it's a jungle—no, a racket—nah, a zoo!

This Enduring Gift

So you want to come and live in New York City—
Have you lost your marbles somewhere on the way?

   Take the smelly subway if you really dare.
   Snakes, and panthers, and hyenas meet you there.
   Ambulances, cops, and bears compete on Second.
   Cheetahs sneak behind you, preying on your dough.
   Hordes of angry penguins stalk the zebra crossings.
   Wildebeests and sharks attack the crazy crowd!

      How they rush you, rush you, always rush you,
      Racing down the overcrowded streets!
      Faster, faster, faster, always faster—
      Faster than Arabian mares in heat.

Do you really want to work in New York City?
You are dreaming of big bucks and Wall Street stocks?

   Sure, we have the Empire State, fantastic Building.
   When you gaze below, you would not ever think
   That New York City was a jungle, den, or zoo—
   Yes, we have the Esplanade at Brooklyn Heights.
   When you watch the skyline there across the river,
   Really, New York City is a shining dream . . .

      But you cannot dream that dream forever.
      You must come down and cross the stream.
      Soon you act New Yorkian and you hurry,
      And so you lose your peaceful Sunday dream.

And every day more hopefuls want to join this place.
Are you crazy! What's your hurry? We don't have space!

Ah, there's nothing quite like New York City.
   Really, New York City is a busy, busy town,
      But I'll tell you what *I* am
         Doing about it.
         Oh I love it.
     It's a riot:
  I just relax
Now in my tranquil refuge at the New York City Zoo.

Chapter 8: The Poetry of Animals, Pets, and All of Us

To soothe my nerves, I used to cruise the New York City Zoo.
I'd cross Manhattan almost daily and really make it, too!

>Oh boy, the lions here are all so peaceful . . .
>Well sure, they roar like in the jungle,
>And yet . . . they don't attack you.
>All the wolves and jaguars look so docile . . .
>And if they growl, it's in their nature,
>But no . . . they won't harass you.
>
>The birds sing gorgeous tunes all day.
>Flamingos bow with grace and bend a leg.
>Placid camels nibble at a bale of hay.
>Gazelles approach the fence and simply beg.

But to get there, I had to cross Manhattan, too!
So I ran from zoo to Zoo, and Zoo to zoo!
Oh, my God, you really can't escape
The New York City vultures, bats, and apes.
They chase your ass around the block
All day all night around the clock.

Yeah, there's nothing quite like New York City,
   But there is something precious I have found
        In New York City at the Zoo.
            You know, I get to
              Feed the cutest
        Leopards at the
   New York City Zoo.
It is my job now—I'm so happy. *They* are happy, too!

>Here I can forget the hustle and bustle
>Of all that hectic, New York City life.
>Believe me, in the Zoo there is no hassle,
>And now I've got a much more quiet life.

Please come visit in my darling Zoo.
I'll let you hear my talking cockatoo.
My monkeys surely will endear you.
I've trained them so they'll pet you too.
All humans turn so peaceful in my zoo,
In my haven at the New York City Zoo.

How they love you, love you, always love you,
Often moving me to tears—
Yes, they simply love you, always love you,
Making you forget your fears.

See? There's nothing quite like New York City.
   Now, before you want to pack your stuff and move
      To New York City,
         Tell us please,
         Is it really you,
      Or the racket rather—
   Or the jungle,
Or the zoo in *you* that's calling *you* to the City?

Well, when you *do* come to New York City,
We will love you, love you, always love you,
'Cause we're all like humans and we love you—
Out in the Zoo, and here in the City.

Chapter 8: The Poetry of Animals, Pets, and All of Us

The Gerbils

Rustin Larson

First appeared in *Bryant Literary Review*.

Chapter 8: The Poetry of Animals, Pets, and All of Us

Happily busy in the middle of the night
Destroying their cardboard tube. To sleep
They make a hurricane of straw and declare
This is the middle of us—enough
Already. And their greatest achievement
Is destruction. I love these animals.
Happy enough with their cubes
Of unhappiness for dinner and beads
Of water from the metal tube. Cal
Spins the luck of his wheel and Reb
Files a song on the bars of their cage.
And Wil stuffs his nose in his haystack
And dreams of stuffing his nose in hay,
All while I worry my life away.

Mushikarati: The Mouse's Poem

Angela Mailander

A long time ago when
I was a very young mouse
I had a wild surmise

I wrote a poem about it
Feeling greatly pleased
With myself and clever.
I called it "Questions"
And it went something like this:

> QUESTIONS
>
> What is it
> That takes my life
> To learn

To tell the truth, in addition
To feeling pleased and clever,
I was uneasy in my fur,
Though I was too pleased
And clever to notice

And went on stealing and hoarding,
But often I felt glowing eyes on me.
And just outside my hole in the wall,
I felt the presence
Of electric fur.

This grew and I began to feel
Much less clever.
And slowly it dawned
On me that there is
Really
Only one question.

And it began to play with me:
    "Come out of that fur you little thief"
It said,
        "No use pretending
        I know you're in there
        I see your eyes sticking out
        Paws hanging down"

And with a shock I realized
My God I am
The cat.

So Say the Wise

William Clair Godfrey

Published in *Lyrical Iowa*.

Chapter 8: The Poetry of Animals, Pets, and All of Us

The caterpillar chews his way among the leaves and twigs each day.
Sometimes he takes a little snooze as on a twig a leaf he chews.
Sniffing whiffing as he goes following his squiggly nose
West to east and south to north, he scrunches up to sally forth.
Wise men say, "Out on a limb the universe exists in him."
He is there for little folks to find while climbing through the oaks.
Upon the branch on which he creeps an oak within the acorn sleeps.
"That is why", so say the wise, "there's more to you than meets the eyes."
He will climb upon your hand, showing off to beat the band.
He'll whirl and twirl and swirl and crawl and curl himself into a ball.
He chews the leaves to gooey soup; and leaves the leaves as bright green poop.
Where do you suppose he goes whenever he outgrows his clothes?
Along the limb and up the tree, where can this fuzzy fellow be?
Hunching munching through the trees in the balmy summer breeze
He does not worry that he may be breakfast for a baby jay.
That is why the wise men say, "We go on our appointed way."
When raindrops fall from out the sky he finds a tent to keep him dry.
Towards the middle of July he gets a sudden urge to fly.
In the fissures of the bark he finds a place that's safe and dark;
There he winds his snug cocoon, by the blessing of the moon.
For a while he rests therein, he toils not neither does he spin.
As the summer weather warms deep in sleep his form transforms.
From within him stirs a surge, an urgent urging to emerge.
While his guardian angel sings he forces out his wondrous wings.
No more munching leaves for you! It's sipping nectar drinking dew.
His solitary lifestyle ends to fly away and play with friends.
"That is why", so say the wise, "we must be like butterflies."

On the Angels among Us

Brother Ludovico

Seven Metaphorical Meditations On
The Winged Creatures God Has Given The Earth

Chapter 8: The Poetry of Animals, Pets, and All of Us

I

On Courtship

Upon Hearing Two Nightingales
Sing Nightly In A Lime Tree Grove,
Below An Italian Village

Nightingales: The beautiful, nocturnal warbler. When they return to central Italy in the Spring, for some reason they congregate on a certain island I know. Darkness never sang with so many beautiful voices to the ear of Man.

I LISTEN,
    and my heart with worship swoons!
  Two nightingales, two precious, star-crossed lovers,
Drunken with lime tree blossoms and the Moon,
    Echo their passionate arias to each other!
How sweetly, purely, uninhibitedly they sing!
    How rapturously, operatically *One!*
Their atoms humming the starry *Pulse* of *Being*,
    Hushing the centuries of toil to song!
To sing, to love, to wholly sing and love,
    And in *Love's* a cappella heartbeat find,
Life's treasure in the *Mansion of God*,
    Gone mad in a delirium *Divine!*
To sing, to love, to purely and ecstatically *Be!*
"Sweet, lovesick darlings, thy moment is Eternity!"

II

On Sublimity

Upon Watching A Seagull's Flights
High Above The Bay Of Katapala,
From Our Balcony
On The Greek Isle Of Amorgos

Seagulls: These master acrobats of breeze and wind-swell can only be truly appreciated with much time, to realize how varied and spectacular are their stunts. My writing desk was only a hundred feet from them, and I was their captivated audience for months.

ALL
    day I watched thee sweep from mightiest heights
  Of flights in steep breath-taking whims to skim
The bay's blue bosom without pause or fright;
  Then, up again! Upon up-drafting winds,
Mounting and mounting till mounted the mountainous air,
  But to repeat the dare of dizzying spells
In keen careens, and acrobatics rare,
  Trapezing on swings of the breezes' swells,
Stunts waged and staged, uncaged from *Unseen Hands!*
  Meseemed I deemed thy wing-tips gleam and glow
Like *Angels* performing for the *Child of Man,*
  Thy stints, the hints, of what *Omniscience Knows:*
The *Poetry* that sublimely, divinely through each thing sings,
The pulse, breath, balance; the very stones given *Love's wings!*

Chapter 8: The Poetry of Animals, Pets, and All of Us

III

On Reincarnation

A Meditation On A Swallow

Composed After Observing The Annual
Coming And Going Of Swallows,
From The Swallow Houses On The Shore Of A Lake.
September, 2007

Swallows: A personification of grace, and the precision of divine intelligence. The swallow and its progeny migrate back and forth thousands of miles to the same belfry, barn-loft, or tiny entrance to its man-made house. And yes, there are still homo sapiens that do not believe in God, and are convinced that all is left to chance.

O SWEET
    swift Swallow, gifted unto wings!
  Thy heart, a thimble, palatial with glad *Glory*,
A singing atom that suns' anthems sings,
    Scaling blue bluffs, and cumulus promontories
To sweep, glide, veer, make naked virgin *Grace*,
    To breathlessly stun the worshippers of eagles!
A *Pulse* beats boundless through thy tiny race,
    That may, that *must*, wing camels through eyes of needles!
Soul, my soul, Swallow borne by the *Hand of Heaven*,
    Resting here, in the brief Summer of this heart,
Made buoyant by some *universal leaven*,
    That bids dull dust to rise through cloud and lark;
Trust, soul, for like the tiny Swallow, voyaging through the seasons,
Ye weave through tombs and cradles, with the unseen thread of
Reason.

IV

On Worship

To A Mockingbird

Composed After Hearing
A Mockingbird Sing
High On Our Barn's Weathercock
On A Bright May Morning

Mockingbirds: This sprite jabber-mouth dumbfounds all human multi-linguists. Nothing like it, at least in North America. Can imitate hundreds of its feathered brethren with exactitude, and at the drop of a hat.

O THOU
    who sing'st with *Pentecostal* tongues!
  With voices come not from, but through thy heart,
Whose repertoire's all melodies sweetly sung
    From tree boughs, hedgerows, clouds, each dawn to dark!
Let no mere stuttering mortal thee accuse
    Of idle babble, or of mimicry!
Wren, thrush, lark, finch, all publish *Love's* glad news
    Through the miracle of thy ventriloquy!
Delirious Angel! That I might mimic thee!
    A linguist fluent with each voice of *Man*,
The poor, sick, caged, scorned, all races and all creeds,
    The dead, flooding hosannas through what I *Am!*
O! That *Spirit* might breathe through me, *Humanity's* every tongue,
Full-breasted, sweet-throated, as thou on yon weathercock in the sun!

V

On Eternity

To A Ruby-Throated Hummingbird
At A Window
At "La Casa Con Ventanas"
In Missouri

Hummingbirds: This little saint of the gardens freely exhibits its miracles, both to the amazements and endearment of its beholders. Among this one ounce darling's feats are its annual migrations across the Gulf of Mexico!

SWEET,
    humming, hovering haunter of foxgloves,
  Belled hollyhocks, and trellising tea-rose vines!
Brother of butterflies, sister of doves,
  O ruby-throated fairy feathered divine!
Thou tiny champion of *God's* mightiest *Being*,
  Whose thimble-hearted wing-beats feverishly span
Beyond this garden, to tumultuously sing
  The *alleluias* of an *all-giving Hand!*
To sparely sip, and not to drunkenly drink;
  To honor *Beauty,* not her throne defile;
Not to fall, but pause, victor on *Love's* brink;
  To harvest this *Earth* from *Heaven's* ethers mild;
Poised, balanced, buoyant; abstaining to abundantly *Be;*
Time's pulse, *Stilled* in thy Instant, humming *Eternity!*

VI

On Evil And Darkness

To A Great Horned Owl
Composed After Hearing Its Many Kills
In The Middles Of The Nights

Great Horned Owls: Seldom seen during the day, unless flushed by crows, this nocturnal predator is equipped with senses that would make the Einsteins of our race seem like bawling babes.

ANGEL
    of darkness, Drinker of night's blood,
    Gowned with horns, talons, beak primordial,
O Priest of night's primeval brotherhood,
    Performing obscene rituals predatorial,—
Thou, nearer to some ever-beating *Heart*,
    Seeing, hearing, knowing, what *Man* does not,
Probing the mysteries of death and dark,
    Stabbing shrew, rat, snake, in the *Light of God*;
Rapt in a rapture mortals may not fathom,
    Exulting in *Essence, Present,* day and night,
Thou know'st the Sun is but a golden atom,
    In a *kingdom of Transcendental Light.*
The swoop, the squeal, the kill; and in that kill, *Love's cry:*
The spanking of a babe's buttocks, in an *all-seeing Eye.*

Chapter 8: The Poetry of Animals, Pets, and All of Us

VII

On Death

To A Whippoorwill
Inspired By The Whippoorwill Heard Nightly
In The Dogwoods Outside Our Window
Missouri Farm, 2004

Whippoorwills: Seldom seen. It sings its lovely songs in the twilights of eve and dawn. For those who have never gone to sleep and woke up to songs of whippoorwills, my sincerest condolences.

AS
    lovely as the laughter of a child,
  These notes that trickle to me with their trill,
A planet reeling, bleeding, drunken wild,
  Nursed by the vespers of a whippoorwill.
Twilight is that hour of the *Timeless Soul*,
  Bringing balm, sup, and camphor gently glowing;
King, pauper, henchman, saint, on one pillow's folds,
  Paused, at day's end, forgetting to *new knowing*.
The living see death a dark ritual,
  Of veils, tears, shrouds, ashes and sackcloth and shrieks;
But to the departed, it is a carnival,
  Of drums, stilts, ribbons, burlesques and clowns and freaks;
Love, masked as death, come to elope at his *Sweetheart's* sill,
Meowing softly, with *"whippoorwill, whippoorwill, whippoorwill"*.

Doin' What Comes Naturally

Richard K. Wallarab

First published in *Lyrical Iowa* 2006.

Chapter 8: The Poetry of Animals, Pets, and All of Us

A hungry vulture
   casts a shadow
   on gray desert sand.
Beneath a cactus
   a dying cowboy
   sucks a swollen hand.
A tired sidewinder
   beneath a sandstone bridge
   yawns at the last breath.

The House Sparrow

Henry Robert Hau

Published in *For the Bird Sings,* by Henry Robert Hau.

Chapter 8: The Poetry of Animals, Pets, and All of Us

He sat on my windowsill
puffed up against the cold
February day
a small bright bard in the sunlight

I cherished his presence
and cheered his hearty chirping
so grateful for a real no frills song

How They Sometimes Show up

Glenn Watt

suddenly
   unexpectedly low
      and bursting

with a kind of joyful exuberance
   as if the voice
      of morning itself

tumbling
   in a broad jostling V
      over the bare shoulders of trees

a hundred and fifty,
   two hundred geese
      like a gaggle

of excited teenage schoolgirls
   yakking their way
      south for the winter.

The Poetry of Strife, Grief, and Conflict

Chapter 9

*Man is not the creature of circumstances.
Circumstances are the creatures of men.*

— Benjamin Disraeli,
British politician and writer (1804-1881)

CONTENTS

334	Caught Looking at the Moon	*Rolf Erickson*
338	The Black Hearse	*Bill Graeser*
340	The Terminal Temple	*Carole Lee Connet*
342	Statue of an Enraged Lion	*Freddy Niagara Fonseca*
344	One Moment	*Tony Ellis*
346	Mumbling	*Bill Graeser*
348	Dying	*Karen Karns*
350	What Will Never Dry	*Robin Lim*
352	Ice	*Glenn Watt*
354	How Many?	*Michael Hock*
356	Tornado	*Judy Liese*
358	After the End After the Beginning	*Margo Berdeshevsky*
360	My Hands	*Tom Le May*
362	Sole of the Shoe	*Matthew A. Bovard*

Many do not know that we are here in this world to live in harmony.

Dhammapada

Chapter 9

The Poetry of Strife, Grief, and Conflict

When our hearts are being torn apart by upsetting events, we want to forcefully spit out our words and sentences to ease our pain. At such times, one doesn't mince words. Neither can one be cryptic or vague, or the impact of what is said is diminished or even lost.

To be effective and enduring, all poetry needs to adhere to certain criteria regardless of topic, style, or era. Each word counts. Any shade of meaning has to be succinct. The poem can be sophisticated and even intricate, but its metaphorical make-up and imagery need to be fully functional and persevered through its entirety. Ideas and word choices want to be universally accessible so that they may be appreciated by literary minds as well as the proverbial man in the street.

In the end, what we learn is that no matter how poignant the angst or deep the hurt, the poem reflecting our inner chaos must contain integrity and harmony. As Shelley (1792-1892) phrased in his *A Defence of Poetry*, "Poetry is a mirror which makes beautiful that which is distorted."

Caught Looking at the Moon

Rolf Erickson

Chapter 9: The Poetry of Strife, Grief, and Conflict

There was supposed
to be a war
somewhere

I was on my way

an alarm rang
off in the distance
as two children
played in a puddle
after the rain

the moon rose
round and hard
over fresh plowed fields

my bicycle skittered
left and right
on the soft gravel

by the time I got to the pine forest
it was already dark inside

I had to find my way by smell

the trees were damp
and dripping fresh hints
everywhere

when I got to the lake
they had already left

or maybe they never came
or it was the wrong lake
or the wrong war

I pedaled on bravely
pretending I didn't really
want to go anyway

once
I stopped to rest
and got caught looking at the moon

it seemed like almost forever

so round and pink
then orange
gold and finally
pure pure white

wisps of clouds
I couldn't even see
softened its edges

and reached out to ignite the stars

heading home in the dark
I saw the lights
before the house

climbing the porch steps
cracking open the door
all the right smells were there

that's when
I remembered
the war

but I'd forgotten who
I was supposed to be
mad at

it was too late

I went in

Chapter 9: The Poetry of Strife, Grief, and Conflict

The Black Hearse

Bill Graeser

Chapter 9: The Poetry of Strife, Grief, and Conflict

would gladly
give its black away
for the yellow of the taxi,
the red of the fire-engine,
the ringing bell of the ice-cream truck.

And would be relieved to take
a load of lumber on its back
like the old Mack flatbed
or diesel of eighteen wheels.

But how then would the dead
get where they're going—flowers
tender as hearts by their side?

No the hearse must be as it is—black
as the blackest fur of the blackest cat,
a car without a radio,
purposeful as a shovel
in the one thing it knows to do.

The Terminal Temple

Carole Lee Connet

Iowa Poetry Society General Adult Honorable Mention 2000, published in *Lyrical Iowa*.

Chapter 9: The Poetry of Strife, Grief, and Conflict

She squats on a piece of cardboard
just inside the door
of the white marble
lavatory
in New Delhi International Airport.

Her job—
handing three squares of toilet paper
to the foreigner who doesn't know how
to use her left hand
and a cup of water.

I rush in clutching a packet of tissues.
Her dark eyes follow me silently
into the sit-down stall.
At the sink I feel her eyes watch as I wave my hands dry.
No paper, no tip.

I avoid her eyes following me to the door.
A small voice stops me: "What country?"
I turn, expecting an outstretched palm,
and look into the eyes of a child
cradling a roll of pink toilet paper.

"Ah-may-ree-ka."
She savors the word.
"India hard. Work all day. Five children."
My right hand fumbles for my last two-rupee coin.
She touches my small offering to her forehead.

Statue of an Enraged Lion

Freddy Niagara Fonseca

> *I saw the angel in the marble and carved until I set him free.*
> — Michelangelo

Published in *The Eclectic Muse*, Richmond, B.C., Canada in 2004.

Chapter 9: The Poetry of Strife, Grief, and Conflict

Who condemned your savage spirit to stone
and chiseled your features—then left you alone?
He squashed your pride and though you hardly age,
inside this stony hide you burst with rage,
but hell, you won't give up—you'd rather die!
Your mighty roar is now a marble cry:
For many centuries you've wished him hell.
To hell he'll go—your bulging eyes can tell!

He sculpted all the anger in your eye,
but if you can't unleash your wrath and try
to tear this hulking shape apart and rise
triumphant from your bitter years in stone,
how will you shred his arrogant renown
and grasp what lions would consider wise?

one moment

Tony Ellis

Published in *There is Wisdom in Walnuts,* by Tony Ellis.

Chapter 9: The Poetry of Strife, Grief, and Conflict

a language of eyes
meets across a frozen room

a moment in time
is stolen and devoured

a long reverie
cast in seconds

then the noise of life suspended
returns
and a lifetime of maybes
is glimpsed
and is gone

Mumbling

Bill Graeser

*The date of John F. Kennedy's assassination

It almost rained in Dallas
November 22, 1963*
but the sky can only do
so much...

so the limousine went
forth as planned
without the bulletproof
glass roof.

Today we tie a flag to a bush
and call it patriotism—
lost
in a war more a lie

than Vietnam ever was,

and what can the sky do?
Or the quiet earth that
opens for the dead,
or a poet (or almost poet)

writing with upraised hand
on clouds

that drift away mumbling
with the wind.

Dying

Karen Karns

Chapter 9: The Poetry of Strife, Grief, and Conflict

My mother, pinned beneath ninety years of gravity,
can not move. Her body, a tiny bundle of bones
girded with diaper tape, lies on its good side, one
leg tossed across the other like kindling for the fire.

Blue tweed eyes, cobwebbed at the corners with
crust, scan the room for my father, landing like
sparks on his pale damp face. My lungs catch
on the bedrail. He does not see how palm and
eye turn upward now toward the gathering smoke.

What Will Never Dry

Robin Lim

From *Tsunami Notebook*, poems washed up from the sea of tears. Robin Lim 2005 - 2009.

On the beach at Meulabouh,
54 days after the tsunami,
I found a seaman's hat
just coming ashore, home without the sailor.
Two twisted tricycles,
plastic torn from soup packages,
a little bit of hand crocheted shawl,
a boy's shoe, size seven, with no sole.
A hermit crab, living in a perfect shell.
A rusty, broken, military tower, looking west.
The sun is setting upon a peaceful glass table top green and silver sea.

Behind me is a mass grave and a Mosque still standing.
God, what does that mean? In nearly every village,
and broken seaside city, the arched Mosques
with onion shaped copper crowns, still gleam in the day,
stand proud and mostly white.
The Indian Ocean tenderly sprays my face with his salty spit.
I am aroused by his breath in my ears, and so I walk forward a step
until I am wet.
He is warm, the temperature of tears.

Ice

Glenn Watt

Chapter 9: The Poetry of Strife, Grief, and Conflict

And as he listens he begins to feel
it is always winter in this room
where everybody brings the frozen pond
of their week, and one by one,
crusted or windblown, rife with slush
or blinded by glare,
fractured and fissured
with hidden thin spots, patches
of lapping black water, they begin to talk,
often after long silences,
in quick spurts or sudden flurries,
rambling drifts or stutters pocked
with snatches of phrase and meaning,
bold or reticent, as if an invisible fist
pressing against their chest or forcing them
farther out, how each day they managed
or didn't manage, bruised and mending,
the ice, cracked tailbone, skinned elbow,
busted skull, strategies of footwork and footwear,
tricks to test and probe for support,
one moment happy to trace thick shore slabs,
the next out skirting scalloped edges,
someone occasionally broken through, wild
or teary eyed, flailing at the crumbling lip,
he himself more than once cut off, frantic,
his world collapsing beneath him,
the sodden bone-numbing weight of it
dragging him down, reaching for a hand,
any hand, so it isn't a game anymore,
he can no longer fool himself,
still wakes up every morning on treacherous footing,
and as he listens he begins to lean
against their words, begins to navigate the ice.

how many?

Michael Hock

Dedicated to Sri Gary Olsen, current Living Master, and founder of the MasterPath.

© 2008 Michael Hock.

A billion times we've told ourselves to wait
cheating self with the lie that this or that will occur
when the time is right.
Like this: Do It Now!
right or wrong, you tell yourself to wait
or you set your whole being on fire.
God is not waiting! You are!
galaxies hooked-up and blossomed in rapture in the time
we've already spent waiting.
Shake it loose!
Make love with Truth!
Bliss Now Or Bust!

Tornado

Judy Liese

Chapter 9: The Poetry of Strife, Grief, and Conflict

I am haunted by the way
the house sits thirty feet from its foundation,
like Dorothy's house in the land of Oz.

There are no Munchkins here,
no good witch to lead the way home.
The trees along the road do not shout at us in anger,
but lie broken in half,
or tossed, roots and all,
into cornfields no scarecrow can protect.

My cowardly eyes turn
towards boiling, yellow clouds in the far sky.
My joints creak in rebellion
against sitting at my new job for too long.
Where is the magic oil can?
What red shoes will dance away this image
of a long finger spiraling down
to pluck some one's home from its foundations?
Nothing feels secure
and the wicked witch never really died.

After the End After the Beginning

Margo Berdeshevsky

> *Tears in the eyes of fishes*
> — Basho

© Margo Berdeshevsky
Previously published in *But a Passage in Wilderness* (Sheep Meadow Press, 2007). Also previously published in *Poetry International*, #10, (2006).

After the end of the world, the dragon flies are the first,
returning. Frogs in chorus in a lead-weight rain, the bones
of buffalo, pissing.

After the end of the world, a shredded page, uprooted
monster trees. A blue jacket, a lace head cloth, a black
boot on a wheelchair stem, a mudded page of the floating
Koran.

After the end of the world, flooded rice fields, a blind
child seeing ghosts of ghosts, stabs his forefingers in his
eyes, screaming.

After the end of the world, Ayesha is chopping chiles to
spice our gruel—I was crazy but now I sing for the world,
she says and says and says again. After the end of the world,
a crazy woman who loves God, singing ahead of the heat.
After the end of the world, a woman who sings that the bad
ones perished,   Allehu   Akbar   in the next hot dawn again
and again, ever after.

After the end of the world, over and over—I lost, I lost, I lost,
and God is great, the mosquito ballet meeting the dragon flies,
circling.

This is not a dream, this is a tragedy, a boy making his words
a sing-song, spindle-shins, kicking. After red words on the broken
columns: this is not a dream, this was tragedy, fresh fish who may
have wedding rings in their bellies.

After the end, a new market. After the end, what kind of town had
it been?   yellow velvet, and minarets.   a shredded boot.   blue
china, broken.   a baby's rubber thong, not screaming.

After the finale, smiles left that say, I lived.   I dream of
corpses drowned in the noonday heat. What time is it now?

After the end of the world, the taro plant blooms in another
language, its flood-root, fetid emerald in the mud. After the end
of the world   bruised   dirty   determined Sisyphus —who
ever breathes—rebuilds.

— Aceh, December 26, 2004 —

My Hands

Tom Le May

Published in *Lyrical Iowa 2006.*

Hard working hands, blunted fingers
suffering industrial mortification of the flesh.
My hands, I stare at them
constantly as if they were shooting stars.
Handsome hands balled in fists,
fingers curled in like a nautilus shell.
Red knuckles and calluses
In ridges and rows, the fruits of my garden of life.

Tool-using hands that hold hammers,
wrenches of chromium steel
earning a living in usefulness.
Fingernails cut close to the quick
for strumming the guitar.

Mine are tall story hands:
historic hands, geographic hands.
I have a palm like the Great Plains:
Broad and square.
I've got a lifeline like the Mississippi:
Long, deep.

Sole of the Shoe

Matthew A. Bovard

Chapter 9: The Poetry of Strife, Grief, and Conflict

I once looked into the sole of a shoe.
It was worn and paper thin
from traveling around the world.
Treading among holy shrines,
leaving behind a piece here and a piece there.
Seeking out a resting place.
Only to find more dirt and stone.
Wearing it down little by little
but remaining strong,
the sole protects the soft flesh.

The Poetry of Erotica, the Body, and True Love

Chapter 10

*We are born for love.
It is the principle of existence,
and its only end.*

— Benjamin Disraeli,
British politician and writer (1804-1881)

CONTENTS

366	I Lie Down	*Libbett Rich*
368	My Body	*Leah Marie Waller*
370	Photograph from Okinawa	*Diane Frank*
374	Carnival in Rio!	*Freddy Niagara Fonseca*
376	Advent of Autumn	*Susie Niedermeyer*
378	The Feminine Mystique, and the Chains that…	*Brother Ludovico*
388	Song	*Megan Robinson*
390	Chinese Ghost Wedding	*Nancy Berg*
394	In the Herb Garden	*Rustin Larson*
396	Sparks Flying	*Patricia Wood*
398	Wild Woman	*Barry Rosen*
400	The Sixth Day of Creation	*Viktor Tichy*
402	We Are Drunk	*Nynke Passi*
404	The Raptors	*Thomas Centolella*
408	You're the Most	*Paul Johan Stokstad*
410	Seed Time in Fairfield, Iowa	*Charlie Hopkins*
412	To a Young Waiter	*Sharalyn Pliler*
414	Tenth Anniversary Prayer	*Charlie Hopkins*
416	The Master's Gift	*Michael Hock*

Age does not protect you from love.
But love, to some extent, protects you from age.

— Anaïs Nin, French author (1903-1977)

Chapter 10

The Poetry of Erotica, the Body, and True Love

We know that some readers can be shocked when reading erotic poetry. But there are always poets who don't seem to mind spilling the beans. In many early civilizations, as well as modern non-western cultures, there are examples of love poetry that voice strong overtures as well as deep erotic undertones.

In recent times, Neruda's *100 Love Sonnets* look lush and romantic on the page, but his deft metaphors also create a subtle, alluring aura of mystique surrounding sex. In Elizabeth Barrett Browning's *Sonnets from the Portuguese*, the sensual imagery is less overt. One anonymous American poet covers a whole range of erotica, shining like a sublime romantic through the most lurid carnality in his *Meditations of a Carnal Poet*.

Even those who write to shock feel a desire to share the stirrings of Love with the rest of us. So even if some readers take offense at the exultation of physical love in poetry, it won't keep poets from revealing and celebrating the universality of all aspects of Love.

I Lie Down

Libbett Rich

I lie down
my body is raised
my back creates ground
breasts rise to mountains
sweeping hair becomes rivers
arms are roadways
leading to feet who make lakes
fingers who form tributaries

I envelope the world
my body creates it
It gives form back to me
I create light
to permeate my insides

You press through me
to my inside world

a pole of light moves
through my body
swiveling up and down
around
and through us

My Body

Leah Marie Waller

Published in *Under the Cedar Tree*, by Leah Marie Waller.

Chapter 10: The Poetry of Erotica, the Body, and True Love

Body
I strive to balance you
between obedient and wild.
I trip you, skin you and bleed you,
make you an outcast and tease you to tears.
I run you through finish lines
against the wind to steal fourth place.
I've plumped and dieted you
curled you, healed you, made you up
and with a corsage and a velvet dress I took you to prom.

Now I walk you around parks
in long mysterious strides
and demand the secrets of life
on a small playground swing.
I dirty you with days of sleeping in
and bleach you with lavender bubble baths.
I sail you across Lake Rathbun,
pole you up and stake you down for a shelter wherever I choose.
I spend thirty dollars on your sushi, but won't spare quarters to do your laundry.
I swim you in the wavy salty potato chip ocean
and fry you like a toasted cheese on the beach.

And when you get older, body,
I will plow you and rake you and put seeds in you.
I'll mock you brown haired and blue eyed
into a James or a Rebecca.
I'll pluck you into music and dip you into dance.
I'll nurse you, educate you and love you even when you break the rules.

And my body when you are complete
with money and fame and a next generation
I'll retire you in a house rectangular and purple.
Then as you rest there finished, three-storied and sea stormed,
I'll crash on the beach next to you
dance in the air around you
and never care to live in you.

Photograph from Okinawa

Diane Frank

Published in *The All Night Yemenite Café*, by Diane Frank. © 1993 by Diane Frank.

Chapter 10: The Poetry of Erotica, the Body, and True Love

In the photograph
she is coming down the stairs
from the bath house where she lives.
You are the 19-year-old Marine
from North Carolina
whose words flow into her ears
like an exotic song
from the other side of a mystery.

You are tall, handsome
and the wide muscles of your arms
push into the seams of your shirt
before you scatter your uniform
on her tatami floor.

She is lost in the cornflower blue
of your eyes as you rock
her narrow bed
and fill the halls of the bath house
with cat sounds.

And in the geisha curves
of her perfect island body
you are trying to forget the daylight
of the military base
where you don't have a voice.

When you ask her to smile
for the photograph
you don't notice the way
her eyes are glazing over the pain
she feels every time she remembers
the soldier who went to Viet Nam
and exploded one afternoon
in the middle of the jungle
in a cloud of orange fire.

This Enduring Gift

And you are unaware
that moments before you leave this island
for the last time
she will try to fold herself
in your suitcase.

A week later
two of your friends will tell you
that they found her at midnight
running naked down the street.

When they bring her back
to the bath house
she will dream she is eight years old
trying to dig a tunnel to North Carolina
with a silver spoon.

She has no idea
that twenty years later
after your round-eye wife
breaks all of your dishes
and walks out of your house
for the last time,
after your next girlfriend
is dragged out of her apartment in Manhattan,
tied up, and thrown into a suitcase,
after five pilgrimage journeys
to holy places in the Himalayas
at altitudes beyond where
the people you've left behind can breathe,
and the other woman you have finally come to love
walks out of your house for the last time
and won't even answer your phone calls,
you will find her photograph.

CHAPTER 10: THE POETRY OF EROTICA, THE BODY, AND TRUE LOVE

She doesn't know
that you worship her now
inside a golden frame
beside your paintings of bodhisattvas
and holy stones from the Ganges River.

She has no idea
how much you loved her,
and you didn't either
at the time.

Carnival in Rio!

Freddy Niagara Fonseca

From *Three South-American Dances*

Chapter 10: The Poetry of Erotica, the Body, and True Love

Row after row of color, costumes, glitter galore—
Wave after wave of thundering feet and droning, deafening voices—
Billow on billow of prancing, advancing masses of dancers—
    We're dancing the samba, the samba, the samba in
    Rio—Rio de Janeiro, Brazil!
We shake our shoulders, bottoms, and bellies to the beat . . .
Of *the bongos!—the bongos!—the bongos!*

Hours and hours of dancing, singing, laughing, and fun—
Day after day of cheer in the fiery heat of roasting Rio—
Night after night of feverish lust and great, fantastic vices—
    We know no worries whenever we dance in the streets of
    Rio—Rio de Janeiro, Brazil!
We twist and turn and stamp, and thus we succumb . . .
To *the rhythm!—the rhythm!—the rhythm!*

Beat after beat of raging blood and rising desire—
Song after song of attraction and lure of the sexes—
Dance after dance of reveling, heaving *oceans* of bodies—
    We're dancing the samba, the samba, the samba in
    Rio—Rio de Janeiro, Brazil!
We gasp and groan like all our ancestors did . . .
In *the Congo!—the Congo!—the Congo!*

Stream after stream of dark, irresistible rhythms—
Wave after wave of hot, tremendous, African forces—
Billow on billow of burning, baking, boiling catharsis—
    We're back in *the Congo!—the Congo!—the Congo!*—and
    Not in Rio de Janeiro, Brazil!
We join our fathers and mothers, and shake and mate to the beat . . .
Deep in the *womb* of *the rhythm!—the rhythm!!—the rhythm!!!*

Advent of Autumn

Susie Niedermeyer

Published in *Under a Prairie Moon,* by Susie Niedermeyer.

Chapter 10: The Poetry of Erotica, the Body, and True Love

All at once, from the mature green everywhere,
a knowing has come. Soft as wine
on a woman's breath
it seeped in under the door,
climbed in the window like a thief.
Gone are the warm transparent afternoons,
the fruits and thousand fragrances.
Let me savor the cool breeze,
the shadows of clouds, and remember
how the trees reached for the apricot sky
like the lines on the palm of your hand.

From all our moments something
must remain, though my eyes see
only the empty seat beside me.
You are intangible now,
yet in our season breathed in gladly
like the fragrant, damp earth.

Ah, but it's warm inside, the fire burns bright.
Why should I grieve when your presence
falls ever so gently over me, now and then,
and weighs no more than a feather.
So come inside, bring the last pink rose,
and we will share the silence.

The Feminine Mystique, and the Chains that Bind

Brother Ludovico

For Lovers, Paramours, Harlots, Brides of Christ, One Night Flings, Wives, Daughters, And The Mother of Moons And Stars

CHAPTER 10: THE POETRY OF EROTICA, THE BODY, AND TRUE LOVE

ALONE:
LISTENING TO GORDON LIGHTFOOT
ON A SNOWY NIGHT

JUST
      when I think you've vanished from my mind,
   Absolving in a blessed blizzard of God,
Leaving me un-bereaving, deaf and blind,
   To your ghost rattling chains of lust and love;
Then, off guard, I hear Lightfoot's buttery croon,
   The twelve-string, sleigh bells, the angst of simpler times,
I see you standing in your lamp-lit room:
   Pink, flannel nightgown, the smile that was mine.
Each time I hear Salvation Army bells—
   In book stores, junk stores, or street markets see
A teal-green coat, or Spanish tresses swell
   Cascading down a Pandora-sweet physique,
I pause, lean forth, about to tap a stranger's shoulder;
To whisper: *"O my Love, never have you looked lovelier"*.

IL MORSO
(The Bite)

MY
    heart's been bitten by a tarantula!
  Yea, by the sly tarantula of Love!
Poisoned, with melancholies and manias,
  The stillest well-spring of my deepest blood!
Now, in both waking, and my slumber's dreams,
  Rage fevers of exultation and doom,
A little spider, up and down a string,
  Taunting and teasing a mummy from a tomb!
These deadened veins are now drunken with Love's venom,
  With bacchanalian wails, whines, dance!
Kindled by hell's furies, blisses of Heaven,
  Tormented to tantrums by one shy glance,
Stung by a sweet tarantula meek as a dove,
O Lady! 'Tis for thee I whirl in th' *Tarantella of Love!*

ON FINDING AN OLD PHOTOGRAPH OF REGINA

AMIDST
    a clutter of half-discarded things,
      I found your photo, and, pausing awhile,
    Hearing your young heart's lark-sweet carolings;
      I bent to kiss your Audrey Hepburn smile.
You, and I, arm in arm, paused on some path,
      That ribboned through these Tuscan olive trees,
Love's throne, crumpl'd to a dog-eared photograph,
      Our moment, drowned, in a whisp'ring sea of leaves.
Yet one leaf's whisper may haunt us to the grave:
      With *"what if, should have, or how it might have been"*,
Youth, the Unknown, making us metaphysical slaves,
      Teasing tired flesh, to play the fool again.
A scrap of paper: mothballed, seared, doomed to the slough of Time:
    Pressed to my heart, my Lady, it sparkles a diamond divine.

THE CARNAL LOVER

I HAVE
    unveiled the *Feminine* on Her pedestal,
      To find cadaverous Her divine mystique,
Licking this *Angel's* toady throat, and the galls
      Left by Her vipers in Her pits; Her reek
In fetid public nests, and acrid musk
      Of thigh-squeezed juices; fondling haggish breasts,
Nuzzling gourd-like goiters, whipped by taskmaster *Lust*
      To clench fistfuls of sagging butt grotesque.
I have raped Her blossom's scarlet-sweet illusion,
      To kiss the wicked thorns of Her afflictions:
Swastikas, jeweled clits, silicon infusions,
      The butchered veins of *Beauty's* vain addictions.
Then, *Love's* omnific *Eye*, glaring through a pretty peony,
Commanding saints and Caesars to kneel, and worship on bended knee.

CHAPTER 10: THE POETRY OF EROTICA, THE BODY, AND TRUE LOVE

TO A MOONFLOWER
(Translated From The Italian)

NOT
    in the arena of *Day's* glaring hours,
  Dost thou bring forth a spectacle of bloom,
But in *Life's* midnight *Heart*, ye coyly flower
  Thy naked glory, to an Angel-banded Moon.
Thy beauty was not meant for the world's parade,
  Not plumed and painted with gauds of vanity,
It pales the rose's scarlet rich display,
  Smiling the fairest smile of rare-most *Modesty*.
O Lady, from what dark and primal depth
  Has such a simple sweetness trellised *Life's* vine,
To breathe to candled heaven, such a virgin breath?
  Through what ages, kingdoms, tombs and cradles climbed,
Till these hands hold the blossomed *Miracle* of thy face?
Until my lips kiss, petals of pure *Light* and *Grace?*

UPON SEEING THEE RAISE THY HOLY VEIL
ON THE COURTYARD BALCONY
AT THE CLOISTER OF THE POOR CLARISSAS

WHEN,
      from thy face, ye lift'd thy holy veil,
  Then in my heart, I felt thy fingers raise
A gloomier veil, inviting Spring-sweet gales
  To kiss awake my soul with Heaven's praise.
When Angels lower their star-sequined wings,
  Their naked loveliness must mortals blind,
So I, with wondrous vision of thy being,
  Forsook my worldly sight, to see *Divine*.
The finest veil, say saints with sacred stares,
  Trembles between this kingdom and the next,
Sweet Lady, Bride of Christ, Sister of Poor Clare,
  This one, meek gesture, slew my dread of death.
Thou gazed into my eyes a *Smile* of deathless *Love*,
Lifting that rare-most veil, dividing *Man* from *God*.

ON A LADY'S SMILE
The Allure

BLINDING
      keen vision with a rarer sight,
    Stilling the hammering heart to purring pangs,
In alleys of hell, a candelabra of light,
    A dish of truffles, thrust into death's fangs;
Cleaving through ramparts that no army mounts,
    Trembling *Doubt's* valleys with the flute of *Faith*,
Earned with a gift, no moneylender counts,
    It in a world of darkness, a morning breaks.
Searing through snowdrifts, with Summer's scarlet lips,
    Melting cannons' throats with fern-green fire,
An Angel of God, breaking the bread of flesh,
    A promise to men, that *Man* is something higher:
All pilgrimages, through all purgatories, reconciled,
By dropping this hanky, Lady, of Heaven's sparkling smile.

THE BLUSH
(On Truth's False Idolatry)

UNTO
      these delicate, blue-blooded threads,
    That fret the porcelain of thy fair white feet,
I, like a mendicant, kneel, bend, bow, beg
    To give what the wretched give the saintly meek.
And lo! What miracle my kiss enkindles!
    To stir thy dormancy with the fires of Spring!
Fevering *Modesty*, until it tingles
    A pallid milkmaid to a damasked queen!
My lips thaw a divinity from thy toes,
    A sap that swells to thy snow-shrouded heart,
That it might bleed the ruby of its rose,
    Quickening with *Love's* dye, thy every part!
Feet, thighs, breasts, cheeks, smile; all flushed with this heady wine;
    An Angel, crimsoned, with its flesh-stuff blushed *Divine*.

CHAPTER 10: THE POETRY OF EROTICA, THE BODY, AND TRUE LOVE

TO THE ANGEL IN A BAKER'S WINDOW
From The Play
"The Gypsy Poet, And The Princess Celestina"

COME,
      dark-eyed maiden with the raven hair,
  O wild rose blooming midst ovens, sieves, loaves, flour,
The wind of the South, headily perfumes the air,
  Smiles through chill Autumn, one last Summer hour.
Come, Princess, from thy drudgeries and sighs,
  Pour in my mouth, the red wine on thy lips,
Come, be my lady; I, thy minstrel blithe,
  Let be this fleeting moment, our *Timeless* tryst.
And deep in golden wheat and blue corn-flowers,
  Let us sip nectars given to our Youth,
Oblivious to age, death, hunger, sorrows dour,
  Let us share the secrets of our naked *Truth*.
Ere Winter's shroud, or the Reaper's scythe, while our blood still sings,
  Let me adore thy altar, Lady, and worship thee with my dreams.

THESE TEARS THAT FROM THE MADONNA'S WOUNDED HEART

  Upon Seeing The Icon
  Of The Virgin Mary Weep Tears
  At The St. Nicholas Albanian
  Greek Orthodox Church in Chicago, February, 1987

THESE
      tears, that from the Madonna's wounded Heart,
  Trickle forth from Her idols' and frescoes' eyes,
Weep from Her Angels floundering in the dark
  Of crack and whorehouse, now dehumanized,
Polluted of their precious pristine meaning,
  Tears pooling at the feet of each slain child,
Whose throat was slit, midst their a cappella singing
  Of Innocence; by an age warped and wild
With the sterility of sodomizing greed,
  Tears of the Angels, turned to acid rains,
Smearing on mirrors lipstick notes of serial deeds,
  Squeezed through syringes of saints gone insane;
These same tears, blinding stone eyes waking to death's dark dole,
Falling like sparkling manna, on the kingdom of Man's soul.

UPON THY DISFIGUREMENT

*A Sonnet Written
After Making Love To Celestina*

*From The Play
"The Gypsy Poet And The Princess Celestina"*

THOU
    dost not limp in the vista of my eye,
      But float as with an *Angel's* buoyancy;
  Thy step, the footfall of a virgin bride,
      Who humbles *Heaven* with *Earth's* poetry.
As imperfection magnifies *Perfection*,
      Man's tragic flaws, *God's Deity* defines,
So this that seems dame *Nature's* indiscretion,
      Drowned by thy sweetness, becomes a pearl *divine*.
E'en as a beggar girl, by an artist hired,
      Doffs rags to pose before his daring brush,
Whose urchin body, blinds with goddess fires,
      Granting poor flesh, a rare celestial blush;
So is *God's Glory* cameo-ed on thy cheated hip,
A rose of rare-most *Beauty*, to which I bring adoring lips.

LOVE'S RENDEZVOUS

I HEARKENED
    to *Thy* blushes, believed *Thy* sighs,
  Scourged weak my lusty loins, fasted from dreams,
Forswore ambition's kingdoms till I die,
  Each breeze and flower, *Thy* holy thunders deemed.
I left my ancestry, forsook *Truth's* reasons,
  Vowing to brand my kiss on *Thy* rare smile,—
Into the droughts and tempests of the seasons,
  I pledged a pilgrimage of untold miles.
But reaching this shore, as the clock-tower chimed,
  I found *Love's* wreckage glutted by *Time's* tides,
Not my *Beloved*, whom I so yearned to find.
  Then lo! Despair turned prayer in a cloudless sky!
Thy *Smile!* Weeping through every star, unveiled of all ado—
O Fool, my soul! *Eternity*, not *Time*, was our secret rendezvous!

CHAPTER 10: THE POETRY OF EROTICA, THE BODY, AND TRUE LOVE

SOUL OF MY SOUL

SOUL
    of my Soul, and *flower* of my flesh,
  With whom I wake to conscious being from dust,
God's Hand, but now, brought us from primal rest,
    Spun *Still*, here, from *His Fist's* first swirling gust.
It was a dream, *Beloved*, that marred our sleep,
    We from long banishment have been recalled,
No serpent thee beguiled with glozing speech,
    We did not pluck the *Fruit*, we did not *fall*.
The sinful plague and wrath of history
    God bade us dream lest we should disobey,
'Twas *Life's* first moment, not antiquity,
    Wherein we dreamed all *men* were but bondslaves.
In us, fair *Eve, Man's* sweet *Beginning* lies,
The Kingdom of Heaven smiles within our eyes.

MY MOTHER GAZES
THROUGH A MILLION MAIDENS

    MY
        Mother gazes through a million maidens,
    Upon Her sons not more not less than Adam,
Her Song, sung in turtledoves, as in ravens,
    Love's *Mystery*, Love's lovers never fathom.
My Mother smiles through planets' each last flower,
    Her Bosom pillowing each brow that's bled,
Laughing the cosmos into clovered hours,
    Embracing each heart living, each heart dead.
My Mother whispers through each fevered dream
    With Heavenly seductions to believe,
Within Man's ribs, a bird with painted wings,
    An orchid blossoming from nettled weeds.
My Mother favors no child; not the lion, nor the lark,
Our Mother kisses, blesses, each seed sown in Her Heart.

FAREWELL, SWEET ROSE

*Composed After Walking Through
A Flower Garden At Twilight,
Hours Before The First Killing Frost*

FAREWELL,
    sweet Rose, goodnight my lovely one,
  Tonight thou shalt be cheated of thy Beauty,
A strange new dram, this night thy blood shall numb,
  Claiming, crimson Angel, thee as its booty.
That sun thou swear'st thy god, shall prove a craven,
  Paling in ardor that so ravished thee,
This garden's bounty, harbors no sweet haven,
  Safe from that scythe that mows the last least weed.
I see thy face, blossomed in maiden prime:
  Gazelle-like eyes, peony mouth, cascading chestnut strands,
That shift, that lift'd, made naked the divine,
  Commanding, like a vision, me first be a man.
But no; I ruffle up my collar, turn to a frosty setting sun,
Farewell, sweet Rose, goodnight my lovely, my only *one*.

LOVE'S SACRIFICE

YOU
    burn my poems in your candle-flames,
  Thinking to kill the will that gave them birth,
And yet such vows are fruitless, vowing in vain,
  To hush the heartbeat of the Universe.
True love may not be burned into an ash,
  For 'tis an *Essence* bearing th' test of fire,
When you burn my words, you but burn *Love's* chaff,
  That falls from Heav'n, with what's supremely *higher*.
My poems are but softly humming moths
  Hatched from the tombs cocooned deep in my heart,
Angels, that have their earthly fleshes doffed,
  Bearing light's mission into this kingdom's dark.
Love is not covetous, *sweet Lady*, it is a sacrifice,
My poems are moths, that perish adoring thy true *Light*.

CHAPTER 10: THE POETRY OF EROTICA, THE BODY, AND TRUE LOVE

RETURNING TO MY MISTRESS

VOICE
    of my *Heart*, *Sister* of my *Soul*,
      How could I ever have forsaken *thee?*
Abhorring *thee* as cadaverously cold,
    A reechy witch, seducing my divinity
With courtesan wiles; cursing *thee* as a whore
    Of shameless follies, hideous as a boil,
Viperous, gargoylish, a henchman's sword,
    At which I spat for all my damning foils.
And yet, patient as one who tirelessly weaves,
    Thou hast been my invisible handmaiden,
Thy breath, perfuming warm the bitterest breeze,
    Enfolding me when I was sorrow-laden.
True *helpmeet*, again I kneel; ask *thee* to be my *bride;*
O sweetest, fairest *Poesy*, forgive my foolish pride!

OVER MERLITA'S CRADLE

MERLITA
    sleeps, and in her countenance
    Personifies *Man's* birthright of *Divinity;*
No Michelangelo, chipping and pumicing
    Carraran marble for a century,
Could master such celestial lineaments;
    An infant Angel, her curls jeweled with stars,
Swaddled in the manger of *Innocence*,
    Chiseling from flesh, what we invisibly *Are.*
Ah, *Something* far more exquisitely kind
    Than we have sensibilities to know,
Has sculpted this masterpiece sublime,
    Infusing rarest *Light* in cheeks, brow, and pugged nose.
Yes, oh yes, we are more than what we know or seem;
Merlita sleeps; her eyelids veiling the treasure of all men's *dreams.*

Song

Megan Robinson

You sing to me
as my heart sings within me
of the hills of my body.
I look
and indeed, there are hills and valleys,
mountains and meadows,
places where light and dark
dance in shadow.

My heart blooms.
I stand hip deep
amid roses and lilies,
gardenias and violets twined
in my hair,
and I sing of the hills
of my body
to you.

Chinese Ghost Wedding

Nancy Berg

> *"A few of the guests allow as how, yes, one might think that marrying dead people is bizarre. But as an occasional feature of life in these parts for longer than anyone can remember, ghost marriages are just another relic of ancient China."*
> — Michael Kramer, *TIME Magazine*

Published in *Oracles for Night-Blooming Eccentrics,* by Nancy Berg.

Chapter 10: The Poetry of Erotica, the Body, and True Love

You could say they wouldn't have loved each other
in the flesh,
she being obsessed,
somehow,
with the inner life of Margaret Thatcher,
he being obsessed
with the same jet black Yamaha 650
that found its final home
halfway embedded in a wall
in a village not far from Beijing.
Now five days later
the new refrigerator and color TV
go to the bride's parents.
The groom's family,
once again in the wrong place at the wrong time,
walk away with only a lecture—
some state-sponsored cremation man
angry about wasting precious land
on bodies instead of crops.
But then of course there's the reassurance
of a son
and a daughter
so sated with connubial bliss
they have little time
or inclination
for uninvited appearances
in kitchens
or even in dreams.
And of course, when the two were alive,
you could say
there were too many questions,
everybody asking Who, What, When, Where, How
and especially *Why* do you love,
as if the mind could embrace such shadows,
as if the half-formed currents of the heart
could stand any more confusion.
How when the cancer took her,
she thought she was being taken by a lover,
her last inhale touched,

somehow,
by the breath
of peach blossoms
and the quiet singularity of death itself.
You could say she
melted off waiting,
unaware of her brothers and sisters
kneeling awkwardly
by the door;
just as you could say he roared off growling,
thinking only of the twisted chrome
and wasted fuel,
but in both cases
you could just as easily be wrong as right.
There's how the two families together
lost four nieces
and two nephews
in Tianenman Square,
with very little to show for it...
Still, the point is,
it may have taken only three dollars
to exhume the bride,
but they waited five months
for the right opportunity.
All the thickness of factory air
swept away by the latest typhoon;
the last transistor radio
placed carefully inside the double grave—
there was never a prettier day for a wedding.

Chapter 10: The Poetry of Erotica, the Body, and True Love

In the Herb Garden

Rustin Larson

Published in *The Albany Review*.

Picking the ones that heal, the ones to eat,
to brew, to hang for fragrance, I walk
with my new wife, her moist palm
in mine. The herbs fountain
from the ground: sunlovers,
shadelovers, those finding it hard.
Unnerved by the stranger we married,
we search for the right plant to solve us.
I discover one, gold and dried, hanging
from the ceiling of the herb cottage.
We should brew this as tea, bathe in it:
its essences clearing our blood,
synchronizing heartbeats, and breath.
She uncovers a cluster of green, holds it
like a bride's bouquet, saying we should both
hold on until we trust its fragility
in the different seasons: her
early spring, my autumn.

Sparks Flying

Patricia Wood

When my parents first met

Chapter 10: The Poetry of Erotica, the Body, and True Love

I saw him in the dark...
We were dancing, talking...
Meeting before we met
Sitting before we sat...

Speaking before we spoke
Laughing before we laughed
We knew one another
Right from the very beginning!

Wild Woman

Barry Rosen

Chapter 10: The Poetry of Erotica, the Body, and True Love

You wait devotedly at my door every night—
sometimes breaking it down to satisfy your wild cravings for love.
If I let you in, your nibbling love bites dent my skin.
I ponder why you are such an aggressive woman.
Was it my Jovan aftershave that turned you into a beast?

When I come home,
you seduce me with your saucy stretches
showing off your latest purchase from Victoria's Secret,
orange and white,
licked clean in preparation for my arrival.
If I ignore you,
you sulk as if I had pulled the plug on your Mastercard.
Do you ever have a hot dinner or massage ready for me?

The voyeur in you cannot leave me alone.
You push your way into the bathroom
to join me in the bathtub.
But you run away when I splash you with love drops.
Why do you squirm and twist when I pick you up?
You act like I am the latest masher in town.

I pamper you with salmon feasts and tender tuna.
But when we only have Walmart to eat,
you frown and complain as if I just took you out to that dive on Hwy 66.
You crawl into my bed at night
muzzling my red paisley bedspread,
but when I throw you out at ten
you act like a rejected tramp.

I anguish over the thought that someday
you will be a cat woman and not a cuddly wild kitten.
But you have opened my heart to love
and even if you leave me for some stray Tom,
I will always be grateful for how much you
have taught me about women
and how much love we have shared
under the covers, behind closed doors.

The Sixth Day of Creation

Viktor Tichy

First prize *Ohio Poetry Day*.

Chapter 10: The Poetry of Erotica, the Body, and True Love

A modeling tool, shaped like the rib of a child,
transforms a lump of clay
into nostrils that quiver inhaling.

A trace of eyelashes
betrays the grateful words
she whispers to her Creator
raising her eyebrows
in the demure curves of a cyclamen.

Her wavy hair, turned into flowing locks
is still wet with amniotic fluid.
The dome of her forehead
parts the waves of soft clay,
like the morning when our daughter's crowning head
spread your thighs further apart
than I ever dreamed possible.

Her shoulders and neck
swoop in the curve of the flying gazelle
I adore in your arched body.

I peel off the rubber mold for a wax shell
the way you remove diapers.
Next week I will cast her in molten bronze.
I have only fingers and heart
to accomplish what you have done
with every cell of the blood in your veins.

In the courtyard of short shadows
your voice sang Eve's lullaby
the instant I knew
our daughter had chosen us for parents
under waving date palms and blooming papayas.

Perhaps I can be your equal,
for she, who is born out of my hands,
wants to be divine as the child
that emerged out of the life-giving orchid
I have been worshiping for seven years of mortal time.

We Are Drunk

Nynke Passi

Chapter 10: The Poetry of Erotica, the Body, and True Love

Are our tongues birds
that first perch on moist lips,

then fly deep into a familiar,
foreign heart, singing?

Morning and night rub cheeks
like lovers.

Clouds accent the chants of the waves,
the arias of gulls.

Trees reach up like hands, wanting
to touch heaven.

Stars pierce the night, leaving holes
in God's skin.

We pick stars like daisies,
make our own chains.

Dressed in sunlight,
we smear the wine of time

across God's cheek
so we can lick it off.

The Raptors

Thomas Centolella

Published in *Lights & Mysteries*, by Thomas Centolella.

CHAPTER 10: THE POETRY OF EROTICA, THE BODY, AND TRUE LOVE

I've seen them all over the city. After midnight
near the consulate, closer to the streetlight
than you might expect: a parked car, windows misted,
wings for a trademark. And the muffled urgencies
from the back seat—someone about to die, perhaps,
or be delivered—the sleek silhouette of a woman's legs
lifted and spread behind the fogged glass,
and between her legs, a slow moving, a denser kind
of fog . . . Or outside the bus terminal late in the day,
at commuter peak, the sedan that sat illicitly
by the crosswalk, the jowly man in the driver's seat
going nowhere for now: head back, eyes closed, mouth
open like a slaughtered pig's, while his companion worked
her blond head over his lap, and a thousand people off work
too intent on getting home even to notice.

But we never took that route, that strange craving
to be caught in the act, have others confirm our willingness
to trust reasons that reason itself could never explain.
When she came to me it was for moments
she couldn't claim well enough on her own to keep,
and I took her to where the world endured, the elements
held sway. The small town a temblor had ruined,
blocks of exposed foundations that went deep.
A houseboat where, twice a day, high tide kept us buoyant.
And the coastal road with its blind turns that ended in air
and dared us to keep going, to live that vista.
Whatever we were looking for seemed to find us,
and the only ones to bear witness were a solitary
egret, a yellow moon, the stripped-naked limbs of eucalyptus.

And once, off a high trail, after a warm rain,
her face gleaming, eyes intent, nipples showing
through her soaked blouse, she pressed me against a tree,
said, "I like holding it in my hand," before she took me
into her mouth, one rapt creature at fullest power, feeding
on another. And the pale mountain flowers, barely-there
pinks and blues, like colors for the unborn children
we'd only dream about—these are what she drew
all over her letters later, like another language
altogether, as if words alone couldn't be trusted,

couldn't do justice to that kind of need.
While above us that day, as above us now, lazing
on their massive, recurring thermals: the raptors,
seemingly at play, but raking the valley floor
for anything alive and there for the taking,
anything worth killing for.

Chapter 10: The Poetry of Erotica, the Body, and True Love

You're the Most

Paul Johan Stokstad

CHAPTER 10: THE POETRY OF EROTICA, THE BODY, AND TRUE LOVE

You're the most
beautiful thing I've ever seen,

which is saying a lot
because I've seen

a single rose
in a silver vase

the sun
illuminating the underside
of fifty clouds

two chickadees
pecking for dinner, alone
outside a lecture hall

and a flower petal
purple, against a
white sink

Seed Time in Fairfield, Iowa

Charlie Hopkins

> *"Pursue agriculture."*
> — The Rig Veda
>
> *"Replenish the Earth."*
> — The Bible

Chapter 10: The Poetry of Erotica, the Body, and True Love

In red dusk a door opens.
A man jumps out of his tractor
pulls down his overalls and lies deep
    with furrows he has made.

For 10 minutes he doesn't mind his wife
or what his sons will say when they know.
Only the woman lying in the fields matters.
Long black furrows braided over her shoulders
and the sky painted red with desire for him.

The woman in the fields is making him do
    what must be done and the farmer knows it.
Black dirt takes the perfect shape of his hands
    and of his belly
so corn will come up stiff and green from his seed.

And when he gets up from his labor
there is the wise tractor silently approving.
    There is the sky with no end to it!

To a Young Waiter

Sharalyn Pliler

Chapter 10: The Poetry of Erotica, the Body, and True Love

To your well-dressed table
I come, a tired crone,

my mind full of lists,
costs, the ticking clock;

but your eyes twinkle
at the timeless She.

I sigh, smiling, startled awake,
eyes downcast seeing that you know

what, worn with cares,
I have forgotten, that

shy as maidens, eternal virgins,
Venus breathes us ever new.

The clock has not stopped, but now,
your round cups of tea and soup

fit into my palms
like warming stones.

Tenth Anniversary Prayer

Charlie Hopkins

Chapter 10: The Poetry of Erotica, the Body, and True Love

Forget me when I'm gone.
Leave me in the long rich furrow of your heart
and cover me with your hand
your hand full of eyes.

The one I thought I was who followed the river
limping with nails in his feet singing about the moon
has entered the water and been carried in a spiral
to your heart.

Whether I sit whether I stand whether I kneel
I am swimming naked with your nakedness
following the curve of your blood through the hollow of your hand
your hand full of eyes.

the Master's gift

Michael Hock

Dedicated to Sri Gary Olsen, current Living Master, and founder of the MasterPath.

© 2008 Michael Hock.

Chapter 10: The Poetry of Erotica, the Body, and True Love

my darling, i woke up late today
so i catch-up with myself more slowly,
but just so you know,
just to say it so it's clear,
in this early monsoon morning,
i love you. my whole self
has become a garden blossoming,
scent of all those flowers mingled,
and you have blessed me such
that it is all you.
even though i still roam, jumpy,
between roots in the rich desert dirt,
and your scent drifting into absence.
i am yours endlessly.
my being a sweetness approaching
the unbearable, a joy that mind
cannot hold and finally i am free,
my world, my creation
a present i have been shaping
for endless ages, where
this body, these emotions, this mind
are just hand crafted
and sublime wrapping paper
holding the gift i give,
forever, to you.

The Poetry of Abundance and Times Well Spent

Chapter

II

Poetry ennobles the heart and eyes, and unveils the meaning of all things upon which the heart and eyes dwell. It discovers the secret rays of the universe, and restores us to forgotten paradise.

— Dame Edith Sitwell, British poet and critic (1887-1964)

Contents

420	Samoset	*Meredith Briggs Skeath*
422	Maine Song #4	*Allen Cobb*
424	Platte River Liftoff	*Steven P. Schneider*
426	The Fool	*Glenn Watt*
428	Sometimes	*Tony Ellis*
430	Middle-Aged Man	*Charlie Hopkins*
434	Father in His Coffin	*Bill Graeser*
436	To a Cumulus Cloud	*Brother Ludovico*
442	Lines of Force	*Thomas Centolella*
444	Michelle Kwan	*Jason Walls*
446	One Hundred Years	*Elizabeth McIsaac*
450	Drug Books	*Matthew A. Bovard*
452	Hammock	*Linda Egenes*
454	Teacher	*Rustin Larson*
456	Someday I Will Have a Mountain Cabin	*Christopher Seid*
458	Three Non-Haiku	*Brian Stains*
460	"A Fossil, Dad!"	*Viktor Tichy*
462	Morning	*Allen Cobb*
464	Always a Good Time to Grow up	*Meredith Briggs Skeath*

Never say there is nothing beautiful in the world anymore. There is always something to make you wonder, in the shape of a leaf, the trembling of a tree.

— Albert Schweitzer, Alsatian theologian, musician, philosopher, physician (1875-1965)

Chapter 11

The Poetry of Abundance and Times Well Spent

Chinese Zen master Yunmen (ca. 864-949) addressed the assembly and said, "I am not asking you about the days before the fifteenth of the month. But what about after the fifteenth? Come and give me a word about those days." And he himself gave the answer for them. "Every day is a good day."

I must confess I harbor a guilty pleasure. One of my many favorite ways of having a really good time is to loaf around an entire Sunday doing nothing important at all. Not even writing poems. Ah, the abundance of having just *Nothing* on my mind!

To simply forget I'm a poet...no magical new lines to come up to haunt me all day long...no more frustrations. To be totally blank and sleep like a newborn baby....

Then to wake up the next morning with a most uplifting idea for a poem. A poem that will appeal to all people on earth, other worlds, stars, even the black holes, the Universe, all the way to *The Throne Of God,* so to transform the world at last! Ah, mañana, domani, mañana, zzzzzz.

Samoset

Meredith Briggs Skeath

> Samoset was the first Native American to come forward to greet and guide the Pilgrims.

Published in the *Ideal Bulletin*, 1984.

Chapter 11: The Poetry of Abundance and Times Well Spent

For a planet poised between fire and ice,
tentative, green, in parfait swirls of white;
for corn and soy gathered in narrowing light,
all give thanks, and all are right.

But greater than the planet is the path
it takes—unseen, life-giving, an ellipse
(just large enough) of space.

And greater than the path is the pointer
north: the knowledge by which we steer.
And greater still is the pilot who puts

the compass in our hand. He stands nearby
as we adjust our course, he watches
the heavens clear.

It's hard, though, to praise great men—
they pass thanks on to their source—
so this day is for more than praise
(though praise is due). It is to picture

a stranger wading ashore with a few,
hungry for freedom. The native inside
his misting breath saw the alien
and felt, "I see myself in you,"

and gave unasked more than enough
to see a winter through.
That was the start of America, a hand
extended between strangers.

That is the union we build, stage by stage,
each year we make Thanksgiving
less a day, and more an *age*.

Maine Song #4

Allen Cobb

Published in *Cave Paintings,* by Allen Cobb.

Chapter 11: The Poetry of Abundance and Times Well Spent

I want to see those shattered rocks again
where sea and sky in seeming torment
batter the land
where the spume scent drags the heart
to the far horizon
and the wind hides choruses of
ancestral sea-captains.
I want to see the bent Scotch pine
knitting the tips of cliffs together against the wind
even when there is no wind
and the sun shines on gold-black sea grass tresses
that mold the sinews of low tide terrain.
I want to step through the cabin door
into the morning merriment of gulls
the honk and throb of lobster boats
and the buoy bells
where the salt smell sharpens the spring air
and soft shell crabs emerge from their sandy lair
to sidle across miniature rock-encrusted beaches.
I will take refuge inside that cabin
while gusts of unimaginable rain assault the walls and roof
amid glimpsed veins of far-off ocean lightning
and remember then the crews of storm-thrown
thrumming merchant ships
climbing swells and smashing the waves
wind-blown in perilous management
of forces far beyond the control of men.
I want to see the shattered cliffs
on those convoluted coastlines
where land and sea meander intertwined
two worlds enmeshed
in the dance of time.

Platte River Liftoff

Steven P. Schneider

Published in *Unexpected Guests*, by Steven P. Schneider.

Chapter 11: The Poetry of Abundance and Times Well Spent

My son and I watch
the sandhill cranes lift off the Platte River
on a chilly Nebraska morning.
One island after another, beating their wings,
making the crane call from deep
within
their long throats,
the sound that calls us back a million years.
We have taken so many treks together,
listening to the roar the melting glaciers make,
the winds in the firs,
and now this, by the river, hand in hand
we see them fill the sky:
a sea of locusts, a tornado, a blizzard of cranes.

Moments after liftoff, the cranes fly east and west,
in two directions simultaneously
crisscrossing the morning sky
getting lighter,
the sun peeling away the lavender cloud cover.
The cranes land in the cornfields next to the river.
Their sound moves from one end of the field to another,
and deep within us the joy cells
of the body
light up just like the pink on the horizon.
The cranes bend their long necks to the ground,
digging their beaks into the dirt
between and beneath the brown stubble of last year's corn,
sifting through the matted hay-like stalks,
digging for the bones of mammoth elephants
who roamed this area thousands of years ago.
We soak up the natural music of the scene,
composing in our heads the geometry of flight,
their takeoff and landing on the river.

The Fool

Glenn Watt

Chapter 11: The Poetry of Abundance and Times Well Spent

This evening,
I take my tea to the back step
and sit against the house.
My sitting rock beneath me —
like a large loaf of bread
fresh from the oven —
is still warm from the afternoon sun.
I look out at the garden
and at the afterglow of the sunset
and begin to re-build
the castle of love and joy
within me.
This time, it comes easily,
the spires and minarets soon reach
all the way to the heavens,
the foundation dug deep into the ground,
and I know my time has come.
And soon I get up
and begin to dance around the garden.
I hope no one is watching,
but I don't really care.
My arms are up,
the moon, almost full,
is shining through the neighbor's trees,
and our cat, white as the moon,
is catching bugs at my feet
as I turn, bow and spin
quietly as a fool
around and around among the flowers.

sometimes

Tony Ellis

Published in *There is Wisdom in Walnuts,* by Tony Ellis.

Chapter 11: The Poetry of Abundance and Times Well Spent

sometimes
a light like molten fire
rushes through my veins
and a grin splits my face
so certain
that I must know everything

sometimes
there is nothing so fulfilling
as the white tassel of a carpet
seen through the eyes of everything
or a simple green pot
sitting clean
on a perfect surface

Middle-Aged Man

Charlie Hopkins

Chapter 11: The Poetry of Abundance and Times Well Spent

I am not young.

I am the color of winter grass
gray on the backside, golden on the belly.
I watch a hawk circle a mesmerized field rat
going round him like an eye with the rat as its pupil
to teach him death.

I know the coyote
hunting in grass up to his testicles
lies to the rabbit and the mouse saying

"I am grass. These blades can't cut you."

But on a good day
while the mouse himself is stalking wild celery seeds
that click against each other like teeth,
the coyote goes with the eloquence of blood
to the heart of the mouse.

I am not young.

I have seen the beginning and the end.
Now the middle swells around me like a waste of water.
Cold mornings I get up and make my own fire,
stand naked in my shaving mirror and recognize the cold
that looks for emptiness to fill.

There are rooms in me round as the astonished eye of a mouse
where children have been sacrificed,
where jars of human hair and teeth and human fingertips are stored.
There are dark corners in every lighted room
and the shadow thrown on hard wood floors like a carcass.

But on a good night
when the heart is beating on his skin drum,
blood stumbles drunk through the hallways of the body
waking up the dead and the half dead.

I go out and look at stars.
I raise my hands to whoever comes to save me or destroy me.
I say

Thank you
for this chance to see and hear and feel myself
in this deep water where life begins,
where fish of joy swim with fish of madness and disgust.
I can't tell the difference sometimes.
I fight with myself in the night, fight with my love.
I can't tell where shadow ends and darkness begins.
When even a rainbow is a twisting of the light
how can I know myself apart from darkness
know myself from apart from light?

I listen to this heart
to this blood beating and I am saved.

Chapter 11: The Poetry of Abundance and Times Well Spent

Father in His Coffin

Bill Graeser

Chapter 11: The Poetry of Abundance and Times Well Spent

The first thing he did was put up shelves
and a workbench for his projects

and a window to watch the worms burrow by
and a chair to sit and do his crossword puzzle—

asking himself out loud for the elusive word.
If he could have fixed death like a broken toaster

he'd be here now—looking for leftovers
in the refrigerator, but the worst death does

is relocates us, the spirit so tenacious,
so luminous in the dark.

To a Cumulus Cloud

Brother Ludovico

*Composed After Seeing A Single Cumulus Cloud
Drifting In A Blue October Sky,
From The Stone Tower At "Pilot Knob",
One Of The Highest Hills In Iowa,
Near This Poet's Birthplace,
October, 1999.*

Chapter 11: The Poetry of Abundance and Times Well Spent

I

SWEET
    Breath perfumed with cumulus loveliness!
   White mountainous *Wave*, buoyed on a bluest *Sea!*
  O gale-swelled *Sail*, bloomy with *Deathlessness!*
   Child-Angel, fluttering through eternity
With scudding glee, yea, over these harvest fields,
  Gold-leafed and coppery with frothing grains,
   Drifting o'er barns and farmsteads with plumed keel,
Over steeple and churchyard, beneath whose stones,
  Richer than the richest granary yields,
   My fathers lie, giving like *Biblical* rains,
Their dreams bleached princely from their peasant bones!
O beauteous *Maiden*, made coquettish with *Illusion*,
Must men's hearts hope with Promise, or know the dagger of *delusion?*

II

WHERE
    is thy *Maker*, O whimsical, lyrical *One?*
   That rascal *Shepherd*, tending as *He* lazes,
  Each flock and herd that nibble beneath the Sun,
   Hearing each bleat and buzz, knowing lovers' mazes?
Dallies *He* on the very verge of things?
  Hammocked in breezes blue, buried in barleys gold?
   Inhaling from *Life's* hookah, into *Love's* lungs,
To breathe a flute-song making dumb stones sing,
  Dazed with that *Cosmically Conscious* opium,
   That winds the last lost lamb back to its fold,
While ticking Time's ages like a pendulum?
Where's *He* who watches men's dreams with a somnambulant *Eye*,
Dreams with which I, fair *Cloud*, thee dreaming now personify?

III

FOR
    I first spied *thee* as a little child,
      Sail just so, through my lambing time of days,
    Over high cottonwoods, swan-proud and wind-wild,
      A fairy frigate gilded with dawn's rays,
    Riggings and masts, torched with celestial fire!
      Hull and poop, burnished with the Sun's beginning,
      Its mainsail bellied blessed with *Eternity!*
As I, made hopeless thrall with Youth's desires,
    Mounted my pony free of this world's sinning,
      To chase *thy* shadow splashing giddily,
Thy mariners shantying windier, sweeter, higher,
As I upon my stallion, a godling lording o'er day's things,
Galloped the farm's green fields, first losing the race of dreams.

IV

AND
    with the coming of Time's storm of seasons,
      I saw *thee* through the eyes of errant days,
    My heart, stabbed, my mind tricked with idle reasons,
      I saw *thee* drift the sky a sottish knave,
    A bacchanal, polluted with heady wines,
      Wayward and blusterous with rakish course,
      Impregnating virgin lovers with cold rains,
    With lightning laughing, only to damn *The Divine!*
      Mustering Angels, but to beat like whores!
        Enshrining savage *War*, with rainbows vain,
    Sweet zephyrs, whipped to slaves and concubines!
Winds, thunders, hails, ransacking with hellish holocausts,
The sacred-most of temples, that a boy with manhood lost!

Chapter 11: The Poetry of Abundance and Times Well Spent

V

ONCE
    more, sweet *Cloud*, beclouded blind with need,
  I woke from slumbers leaden with dull sorrows,
Ashamed of my dreams! Of *Lust*, *Fame*, and *Greed*,
  Lost in a gypsy's crystal ball of morrows!
I found *thee* next, a *mistress* of the Moon,
  A *damsel* draped with shimmering veil and gown,
  A moonlight silver, only moonlight rare,
So rare I with a naked *goddess* swooned,
  Charmed of will, vowing *Beauty's* charms to own,
Her *Venus* breasts, sweet roses that soft-bloomed
  With promise to unyoke each yoke of *Care*;
And yet, struggling from sated sheets, to mascaras on her sill,
I saw *thy* face unveiled, a *murderess* giggling o'er her kill.

VI

THEN
    in the country-sides and marketplaces,
  At forges and anvils, with scythe and with flail,
Blinded by itching palms and leering faces,
  My laughter changed to groans, my songs to wails,
Believing *thy* each mood my every need,
  Becoming for *thee* a curser, brawler, sot,
  A lover of alleys, debauch, and drink,
Stung with a wanderlust that shirked staid deeds,
  Seduced by *thee*, whose whims I thought my lot;
I, baited by an Angel's harlotry,
  A drunken moth that danced to candles' brinks;
The pony, pastures, cloud, all faded to a fiddler's dream,
That could not have e'er been, that could have only seemed.

VII

AND
    yet now, fairest most *illusionist*,
  I see *thee* from both pinnacle of age,
And this stone tower, sublime with saintliness,
    Adrift o'er flocks and buttery cocks of hay,
More lovely than Man's heart could ever dream,
    A snowy *cloistress*, a *bride* who keeps each vow,
      Gentle as breath, modest as violets,
A *smile* that crowns this earthly realm of being;
    Dear God! With wearied bones, and jaded brow,
I rattle chains who could have fluttered wings,
      Wincing with *Hope's* lost angst, which is *Guilt's* found regret!
'Twas me, *Cloud*, not *thou*, who enchanted my soul with mirrors,
Who, fickle as weather, did not hold *Truth's Treasure* dearer!

VIII

O! THAT
    I might believe, yes! Dear God yes!
    Bow my brow to *thy* glory, and believe
My chains are not chains, death is not death,
    That what these bones are, is a tiniest seed
Sown in an ever fallow Fertility,
    A garden of Earth, Sun, and Stars that conspire
      In muddiest mulches, under snowiest shrouds,
To swell the kernel with *Divinity*,
    To grant each flower a wild lion of *Desire!*
O weep sweet *Angel*, on this dust I leave!
      Rain! Snow! Sleet! Parch! Burn!
          Knead these dreams fair *Cloud!*
Like a yeast, let them leaven Man's mind to what *thou art*,
Until Man lifts from flesh, with a pure and simple *Heart!*

Chapter 11: The Poetry of Abundance and Times Well Spent

IX

ADIEU,
    my *Angel!* Adieu, my truest *Love!*
  The sunset's fires, now make revelatory,
 Heaven in Earth's soils, Heaven in Man's blood,
    Wheat lit like matchsticks! Clotheslines billowing *Glory!*
The barns, like kings! The homesteads, regal queens!
  Silo and chimney burnished unto cupolas!
    Each weathercock, *God's* trumpet blaring *Grace!*
All burning, fading, drowning like a dream,-
    The pony, hedgerows and haycocks, the heyday
 Between *Spring's Hope*, and *Autumn's nostalgia*,
A seed sown in the furrow of a churchyard's grave:
Man, Earth, and *Cloud*, mists dissolving with death's *delusion*,
To seas of stars, *smiling*, beyond parades of *Love's Illusion!*

Lines of Force

Thomas Centolella

Published in *Terra Firma*, By Thomas Centolella.

Chapter 11: The Poetry of Abundance and Times Well Spent

The pleasure of walking a long time on the mountain
without seeing a human being, much less speaking to one.

And the pleasure of speaking when one is suddenly there.
The upgrade from wary to tolerant to convivial,
so unlike two brisk bodies on a busy street
for whom a sudden magnetic attraction
is a mistake, awkwardness, something to be sorry for.

But to loiter, however briefly, in a clearing
where two paths intersect in the matrix of chance.
To stop here speaking the few words that come to mind.
A greeting. Some earnest talk of weather.
A little history of the day.

To stand there then and say nothing.
To slowly look around and past each other.
Notice the green tang pines exude in the heat
and the denser sweat of human effort.

To have nothing left to say
but not wanting just yet to move on.
The tension between you, a gossamer thread.
It trembles in the breeze, holding
the thin light it transmits.

To be held in that
line of force, however briefly,
as if it were all that mattered.

And then to move on.
With equal energy, with equal pleasure.

Michelle Kwan

Jason Walls

Michelle Kwan: Olympic Champion Figure Skater

Chapter 11: The Poetry of Abundance and Times Well Spent

With vase, she figures curling

Triple Lutz in twisted vague water

Adheres to curve to Salchow, land opposite:

    Scatter glassy rim

Hilly buds of star-matter

Mounds of earth, circled brier: thicket formed sharp

With

Eyes colored news-filler

Hands shaped China circle ice in country dream-like

Double   Toeloop   bloom

    And her flowers

One Hundred Years

Elizabeth McIsaac

Published in *A Sun Palette of Song'ans"* Book II, by Elizabeth McIsaac.

Chapter 11: The Poetry of Abundance and Times Well Spent

A Buddha sat, in silence,
under a bodhi tree — one hundred years.

Then, one day, a leaf
floated, touched
the Buddha.

A Buddha sat, in silence,
under a bodhi tree — one hundred years.

Then, one day, the tree sighed
three
leaves —
one, on his head
one, on his shoulder
one, scratched his nose.

A Buddha sat, in silence,
under a bodhi tree — one hundred years.

Then, one day, as breeze tickled the tree,
it sneezed
— a twig
spiralling, tap — into his lap.

A Buddha sat, in silence,
under a bodhi tree — one hundred years.

Then, one day, the tree frowned, snorted —
a small branch
airing, falling — at his feet
with a crash.

Then, the Buddha opened
One eye
and said: "Oh Tree, you are telling me
something?"
And Tree said: "Oh great buddha, I am earthed.
You are walker. Why don't you smell other-land
rains, see other-sky sides of the earth." And the

Buddha said:
"I Am earth.
I have no —
where to go."

*A Buddha sat, in silence,
under a bodhi tree — one hundred years.*

Then, one day, birds —
branched, sang, chirped, argued, ate, fluttered
— leaves, twigs, feathers, eggs
down.

Then Buddha opened
the Other eye
and said: "Oh Tree, you are telling me
something?"
Then Tree said: "Great Buddha.
My silent heart
branches shelter to singers.
Your heart
can Voice. Why do you sit here?"

Then the Buddha said:
"I branch the universe.
Songless ones
cannot hear me."

*A Buddha sat, in silence,
under a bodhi tree — one hundred years.*

Then, one day, the bodhi tree was very old,
branches
weighting, falling, piling, faggoting
— down.

Then, the Buddha
opened Both eyes and said: "Oh Tree you are
telling me something?"
And Tree said: "My branches are fire, potash,

dust. Oh great buddha,
You,
are Source. Why do you sit here?"
Then the Buddha said:
"Those who can be warmed
will arrive without coming."

*A Buddha sat, in silence,
under a bodhi tree — one hundred years.*

Then, one day, the ground shook —
cracking, rending, and Tree
leaning
low
almost ...
... then, the Buddha opened his Third eye
and said: "Tree you are telling me something!"

Then Tree said:
"Large with knowledge,
heavy with desire,
hard with resolution,
splintering with surrender —
may I
touch
your feet?"

Then the Buddha said: "I am gone!"

From that day on,
the Buddha walked legs,
voiced wisdom,
smiled heart,

*but never again sat
— one hundred years
under any one tree.*

Drug Books

Matthew A. Bovard

Chapter 11: The Poetry of Abundance and Times Well Spent

My own mad mind keeping it self company.
Perhaps just the diary of a mad man.
Spouting drivel upon the page.
Attempting to contort into something vaguely resembling art.
Feigning talent and saying strange things
calling them profound.
Perhaps just an absurdist
caught in a real world.
Hoping that one day it will join
him in absurdity.
But what do they need absurdity for?
They have each other.
Out there working away.
Passing time through business.
While I am here in my room
looking into my own mind.
Reading and discovering great minds
that have come before.
Diving into a book and swimming
deep in its pages.
Looking at a new world.
Transported to the other side
of the universe.
No chemicals. No herbs. No liquid courage.
Just words twisting deep in your mind.
Like a double helix of thought.
Tripping out the self and into expanded being.

Hammock

Linda Egenes

Chapter 11: The Poetry of Abundance and Times Well Spent

A garden room,
waxen white gardenia in a pot,
cool, sweet relief from summer's heat.

A whiff of rosemary
and the hammock suspended on a wooden frame.

I lie down and
drift into a reverie
of cloud and leaf
bird and flit
shadow sunshine sky.

Distant shouts,
children laughing.
A bicycle passing
on the path below

and then stillness.

A sudden sadness
for the rush of life—
when all we ever wanted
was to be cradled by air.

Teacher

Rustin Larson

— To David Wojahn

First appeared in *POEM Magazine*.

Chapter 11: The Poetry of Abundance and Times Well Spent

Your words were conscience to me: Keats singing
how delicately time flowers
to accomplish the impossible: the songs
of spring budded in the future.

I worked ambition,
curving its bony fingers
around the curse:
meditating a single icy bloom.

If it was all failure, perhaps you knew
it would be: verses reincarnating,
opening like violets
in a graveyard, without violence,

without breath. This is all I have
to pay you:
their subtle fragrance,
their half-remembered blend of red and blue.

Someday I Will Have a Mountain Cabin

Christopher Seid

Chapter 11: The Poetry of Abundance and Times Well Spent

Someday I will have a mountain cabin at the end of a long dirt road.
I will live simply there, alone, and entertain very few guests—silence being my favorite companion.

Someday, my son will get to do what he wants.
It may take him awhile to find something he likes and settle into, but eventually he will, and he will be happy.

I will greet him at the front door of my cabin when he comes to visit with his wife and children.
I will be surrounded by books, musical instruments and broken dreams.

My son will think: *The poor old man. Look at him. What a mess.*
And I will make coffee on an old cook stove, serve fruit and bread.
After he leaves, I will retire to meditation.

I will sit cross-legged on a pillow on the floor until the sun goes down—perfectly still, barely breathing, until the end of my life.

Three Non-Haiku

Brian Stains

Chapter 11: The Poetry of Abundance and Times Well Spent

ONE

A brief wind in an empty place.
Stillness,
Long before,
Long afterward.

TWO

Hot day.
No sound but the wind in distant trees.
I could slip past it all now.

THREE

It is subtler than starlight.
It is why I laugh without a reason.

"A Fossil, Dad!"

Viktor Tichy

First prize in *National Federation of State Poetry Societies.*

Chapter 11: The Poetry of Abundance and Times Well Spent

He squats to a black slab of slate
where a lace of gray calcite
replaced the veins of a leaf;
a sarcophagus from times
when the Earth was so young,
even birds had teeth.

The Adam of my Eden,
the clay I have given eyes to,
becomes a paleontologist
deciphering the cuneiform of life
from ancient mud
that refused to learn new facts.

Awed by the passionate curiosity
in his androgynous face,
I glimpse the bas-relief
he will one day cast
from the imprint I am leaving
in his yielding heart.

Morning

Allen Cobb

Published in *Cave Paintings,* by Allen Cobb.

Chapter 11: The Poetry of Abundance and Times Well Spent

This morning's breeze
sends sunrise leaf-shadows
dancing on the bedroom wall.

Always a Good Time to Grow up

Meredith Briggs Skeath

Chapter 11: The Poetry of Abundance and Times Well Spent

'cause God isn't done with us,
it's not a one or seven-
night stand.

It's a dance.
Take a step
see what happens,

see if you can take a hint,
follow a lead,
regroup.

The heart opens
closes like an anemone
or a house that's shut.

We're cautious even when
we don't need to be.
The music's playing.

It's always a good time
to grow up.

The Poetry of the Mildly Nutty (Humor Included)

Chapter

12

"We may live without poetry, music and art;
We may live without conscience, and live without heart;
We may live without friends; we may live without books;
But civilized man cannot live without cooks."

— Edward Bulwer-Lytton, English politician, poet,
playwright, and novelist (1831-1891)

CONTENTS

468	The Gray Dress	*Raven Garland*
472	The Trees Striptease	*William Clair Godfrey*
474	I Could Have Danced All Night if I Hadn't…	*Nancy Berg*
480	Junk Pile	*Bill Graeser*
482	Buildings	*Allen Cobb*
484	Some Really Nonsense Poems	*Elizabeth McIsaac*
486	Fishy Doggerel	*Angela Mailander*
488	Louie the 14th	*Tom Le May*
490	High Coos and Buddhist Leanings	*Ann Du Bois*
492	Toad to My Gray Hairs	*Ruthie Hutchings*
496	Beauty Hard to Believe	*Henry Robert Hau*
498	Bareback English	*Viktor Tichy*
500	If You Want to Drop Your Body	*William Clair Godfrey*
502	My Elephant	*Gale Park*
504	The Love Song of J. Alfred Frog Prince	*Angela Mailander*
508	Laughing Leaves Retreat	*Barry Rosen*

*There is nothing left to you at this moment
but to have a good laugh.*

— Zen master

Chapter 12

The Poetry of the Mildly Nutty (Humor Included)

Time for jokes, outrageousness, and to catch the reader off guard. Some poets have a knack for the absurd, sometimes taking pleasure in writing just plain hodgepodge.

Most of them would choose the freedom of writing over writer's block anytime. No particular style needed, no conventions of society, no pesky restrictions anywhere.

Under normal circumstances, no poem in this chapter would make much sense. But who wants to be stuck in ordinary life forever? Why not take a chance and twist and shape the language, break open giddy repositories of quirkiness for a while, and find unexpected opportunities in made-up sentences as well as totally bizarre scenarios.

Then serve all that nonsense to unsuspecting readers, and there you have it. We'll share the joy — ours to reveal ourselves as the whacky concocters of this thing called poetry, yours to revel in the joy of reading it and having a cool chuckle or two.

The Gray Dress

Raven Garland

Chapter 12: The Poetry of the Mildly Nutty (Humor Included)

Obedient pleats.
Capped sleeves.
From the neck—
Starched and stretched—
Plaid ribbons
Tied in a bow
Pinned to the waist for show.

Birthday Girl goes for a whirl,
Unfastens the stiffened bow.
Jumps with a flair
From stair to stair
And descends to the Life Below.

Breezes and cousins
Ice cream and laughter
Eight straight candles-
But then The Day After:

Formal Sunday Dinner
Aunts and Uncles with sad sagging faces
Food and forks all set in their places
Hint of oregano
Scent of red anger
Orange words roiling with whispers of danger.
Spit conversations, enflamed words of fury

Auntie's Eyes crack bright lightning, striking and igniting the air-
Catapulted commotion a plate full of roast beef mashed potatoes sweet delicata all steaming with gravy and salt is flung towards two uncles who duck and bend and where does it end but with a crash to my chest gluing gooey the ribbons on the gray dress the whole front of my dress is saturated and too warm now and it is seeping through to the skin and bones and heart the sweet heart and my mother wipes with a sponge and tells me in the loudest silence not to notice what is happening and so the sponge is damper than my eyes.

We sit.
We serve.
We eat.
We depart.

In my quiet cave I conceive my new wardrobe. There'll be no more muted gray.

From now on I wear hot pink pants
yellow silk sashes
polka dot purses
bells on my ankles
lime green skirts
and lavender hats.

And Mars always tempts me
to say this or that
and I do.
I speak
I talk
I tell tall tales
I tell tales true.
I gossip
I gab
I open my mouth
I blab.

May 2007

Chapter 12: The Poetry of the Mildly Nutty (Humor Included)

The Trees Striptease

William Clair Godfrey

Published in *Lyrical Iowa*.

Chapter 12: The Poetry of the Mildly Nutty (Humor Included)

It's time to see the trees striptease.
To see them losing all their leaves.
Oaks and maples drop their dress
Exhibiting their nakedness.
Soon they'll to the closet go
To wake up in a coat of snow.

I Could Have Danced All Night if I Hadn't Spontaneously Combusted

Nancy Berg

Published in *Oracles for Night-Blooming Eccentrics,* by Nancy Berg.

Chapter 12: The Poetry of the Mildly Nutty (Humor Included)

When it was still there in August,
my landlady threatened to call the fire department.
The pine needles were already so thick and dry
and sharp on the carpet,
even with socks on,
you couldn't walk without drawing blood.
But I was in love
and it was bigger than anything they'd ever shown on television.
My Christmas tree had become a Magnificent Obsession.
It was more than the red, black, fuschia, and turquoise lace
draped around it,
or the *Rudraksha*, crystal, and angelskin coral.
It was more than the gracefully curved plastic corkscrew drinking straw
and the brass pennywhistle all the way from Ireland
balanced skillfully in the nether branches.
It was more than the paper boats made of theatre programs
or the ecumenical touches—
luminous postcards of St. Anne and the Virgin,
Krishna neatly shellacked on a maple leaf,
the copper ornament that spelled *Shalom* in English and Hebrew.
It was more than every piece of cheap, miraculous jewelry
I ever used to turn *myself* into a Christmas tree.
It was more than the fact that they never let me have one
when I was a kid
because I was Jewish.
It was more even than the most spectacular neon star
you ever saw
wearing a long striped hawk feather
at exactly the same jaunty angle
Maurice Chevalier wore his perfect straw hat.
(The package said
"DO NOT MAKE THIS STAR STEADY BURNING"
but I did it anyway and burnt out all the miniature bulbs,
wanting, as always, too much at once.)
But God, it was more than all that.

There was something that made me keep that tree
through Valentine's Day
and hang little pastel hearts all over it.

This Enduring Gift

There was something, on Easter,
that made me hang all those hollow eggs
I decorated myself with Day-Glo paint and macaroni.
I had to stop letting people over—they didn't understand.
My Christmas tree and I celebrated the Fourth of July together.
I wore a red, white, and blue jumpsuit.
The tree wore at least 100 tiny American flags.

You see, when they said my Christmas tree had become
a fire hazard,
I knew they didn't mean somebody would strike a match nearby.
It was a fire hazard
because someday it would spontaneously combust
from the intense heat of its own unbearable beauty.
And I was waiting,
ready to see at least one of us go out
in a supremely self-sufficient blaze of glory.

It was right there on page 433 in the Book of Lists
between the brain radiation levels of 60 celebrated persons
and a collection of 10 people who had Stigmata.
There it was in glorious black and white:
"Eight Cases of Spontaneous Combustion."
And while I realized I might never develop holy wounds
on my hands and feet,
and the only person who knew how to measure brain radiation
died in 1952,
deep inside I knew that some day,
with the flawless timing of a fine Swiss watch,
I had as good a chance as anybody to spontaneously combust.

Just like Euphemia Johnson, age 68,
who spontaneously blazed one rainy day in England
while drinking her afternoon tea.

Or Mr. and Mrs. Patrick Rooney
who crossed over together one Christmas Eve
during the second chorus of "Silent Night"
when Mrs. Rooney suddenly turned into a pillar of fire
and Mr. Rooney died from the smoke in the air.

Chapter 12: The Poetry of the Mildly Nutty (Humor Included)

That one went deep.
Now I know when people say
"Do you love me?"
they really mean
"If I spontaneously combusted, would you inhale the smoke?"

But best by far,
Miss Phyllis Newcombe,
age 22,
who probably spent 3 or 4 months
perfecting a pink organdy gown
with pearl buttons, a polka dot sash,
and baby blue lace at the collar and cuffs,
just to wear to the dance hall that night on August 7th
when she waltzed with the prettiest man there—
the one with the strongest arms
and the wisest eyes
and the prettiest white teeth.
The music was like satin and velvet;
like those luscious chocolate caramels
she once got for Valentine's Day.
She was so radiant everyone was staring;
even the people waltzing kept craning their necks to look at her.
Something was becoming more and more curiously alive
about the room.
It seemed the air itself was waltzing
1-2-3... 1-2-3... 1-2-3... 1-2-3...
It must have been on a 2
that Miss Newcombe smiled exquisitely
and happily burst into flames.

Neither Miss Newcombe's partner
nor the pink organdy gown
were as much as singed.
For a split second the gown hovered in mid-air,
as if confused.
Then, with nothing left to cover,
it dropped delicately to the floor
like a rose petal.

This Enduring Gift

I like to imagine Miss Newcombe's partner understood.
That he picked up the dress
and quietly left the hall
while everyone else went crazy.

People and Christmas trees who spontaneously combust
go to a secret place
where everything is switched on and awake.
Those little golden particles
you see when you're excited
are constantly vibrating in the air.

Miss Newcombe *had* to combust.
She'd never be 22 again
in that gown
on that night
with that man
with those teeth.
Here, she moves in a state of constant consummation
with the dazzling uniqueness of an albino giraffe.
All the trees are Christmas trees
with silver garlands and sequins
and those electric glass ornaments
with bubbling water.
Every moment is always, always, always enough.

Chapter 12: The Poetry of the Mildly Nutty (Humor Included)

Junk Pile

Bill Graeser

Chapter 12: The Poetry of the Mildly Nutty (Humor Included)

This
is the
Junk Pile
of words. The
"fart" and "stinky"
words we first giggled
with. The "I don't know"
and "I did not" words we fibbed
with. The "fatso" and "retard" words
we fought with till we bled. The "dick"
and "tits" words that proclaimed our know-
ledge of sexuality, and all the family of four-
letter-words we hurled like stone through glass.
The "drink-till-you-drop" and "drug" words that
again we giggled, saw double and passed-out. All
the out-grown, worn-out words that only a desperate
poet would rummage through, or gather like tin can for
pop-art, or assembly as museum for how we used to think.

Buildings

Allen Cobb

Published in *Cave Paintings,* by Allen Cobb.

Chapter 12: The Poetry of the Mildly Nutty (Humor Included)

all too tall
too too terribly tall
swinging and swaying and dropping like birds
drunk on evening wine
all much much far far too tall
the buildings are too tall
they arch and stretch and tip
up
toward the moon and the rolling sun
they vibrate and hum shrilly in the early light
they vibrate and hum
vibrate and hum
deep inside
machinery lifts elevators
phloem in cellular trunks of cement
lifts and turns and times and lights of the low sky
for miles
the sky is so hushly lighted up
so on into the night
after day they glow
and sing to the distant ceiling
they grow so slowly as the ground sinks down
they are all too tall
all too tall and high
standing and groping with silent minds
but with hearts that hum
too tall
all

Some Really Nonsense Poems

Elizabeth McIsaac

Published in *A Sun Palette of Song'ans, Book II*, by Elizabeth McIsaac.

Chapter 12: The Poetry of the Mildly Nutty (Humor Included)

I had a hat,
The dog bit off the ribbon,
My cat
pulled out the threads.
I had,
a hat.

The phone is ringing out,
the toast is burning up,
the tea is boiling over
and my pants are falling down,
but, but,
there's butter on my hands.

Bright-eyed Susan
swaying in the bhajan breeze,
child-flower in Mother's garden
giggling over blueberry cornbread
with her friend Harry Krishna
for Sue

Fishy Doggerel

Angela Mailander

*Any of various fishes of the order Coelacanthiformes, known only in fossil form dating back as much as 80 million years, until a living species, Latimeria chalumnae, of African marine waters, was identified in 1938.

(From New Latin *coelacanthus*, "hollow-spined").

Chapter 12: The Poetry of the Mildly Nutty (Humor Included)

The Coelacanth* is hollow-spined;
Thus, if he's so inclined,
He disappears within himself,
Whilst, fossilized upon a shelf,
His body sits for 80 million years.
But shed no tears,

He reappears in 1938.
And in returning sees it's not too late
To know his form as virginal,
And all that stands implied, vestigial
Forevermore in every cell and atom,
Expands in greater depth than he can fathom.

Louie the 14th

Tom Le May

Chapter 12: The Poetry of the Mildly Nutty (Humor Included)

Louie the 14th played his guitar
Deep in his palace, under the stars.
He made it cry, he made it moan
He played like an angel, he played like a Stone.

Louie the 14th sure loved his dog.
He sure loved his chain saw, he sure loved his log.
But although he truly loved all these things,
He couldn't deny the pain they would bring.

Louie the 14th was raised in the woods.
Ma ran off with the circus, Pa ran off with the goods.
Louie survived by thinking fast on his feet,
His bamboozle bodacious, his flimflam was fleet.

Louie the 14th was singin' the blues,
Workin' his mojo and payin' his dues.
The Devil himself came to pay his respects,
Make love to his woman and embezzle his checks.

Louie the 14th had a powerful thirst.
He was dry to the bone and then a thunderhead burst.
They say that he died with a smile on his face,
His dog by his side and a cop on his case.

High Coos and Buddhist Leanings

Ann Du Bois

Published in *Lyrical Iowa*.

Chapter 12: The Poetry of the Mildly Nutty (Humor Included)

When i think of you
undifferentiated
i really mean me

When i think of me
undifferentiated
i really mean you

Toad to My Gray Hairs

Ruthie Hutchings

Published in *The MacGuffin,* Humor and Parody Issue, 1995.

Chapter 12: The Poetry of the Mildly Nutty (Humor Included)

Coarser than my brown
and yellow hairs, whose fineness
never grew up past second grade,
you'd think I'd be thankful.

In the morning, all hairs homogenize,
regardless of color,
coerced and glued;
but by afternoon, the gray ones
bend and cork,
creating the exiting echo
of a ghosting hair-do.

The gray hairs fly out
like bobbing apples that won't be bit,
kids who jump up in a bus,
eager to be noticed.
As though after 40 vanity works
in reverse.

I believe each gray hair propels
from its coiled trajectory
an old wise thought
to some silver world
where wax figures
are sculpted of insights.

Jerry says she's keeping
her gray—a nod to nature,
or perhaps a prostrate
face-on-the-floorboards smooch.

She can represent that sanguine,
"it's just a phase of life" side of me,
so I can keep using the dye.

Yes, I'll keep covering those
gray daddy long legs—
at least until a grocery boy stifles a shriek
when he thinks he's relishing

the back of a blonde,
and I turn and crush him with
a wizened smile.

But I plan to grow old gracefully:
my teeth will wear toe shoes
when they glide to the water glass.

And my mind, once peopled
with trees that could be named and
    leaned against,
with knotted and whorled leaves that
    were known,
will be filled with nothing
but soft fields of wheat,
and a tangerine-streaked
    gray sky.

Chapter 12: The Poetry of the Mildly Nutty (Humor Included)

Beauty Hard to Believe

Henry Robert Hau

Published in *For the Bird Sings,* by Henry Robert Hau.

Chapter 12: The Poetry of the Mildly Nutty (Humor Included)

December, first snowfall,
Wet stuff, won't stick
Till late afternoon I surmise

Then birdsong!

Beauty hard to believe
In this weather

Insufferable starling I suppose
I tilt my ear happily

To discover the lyrical beak
Is my own stuffed-up nose

Bareback English

Viktor Tichy

Published in *Utah State Poetry Society.*

Chapter 12: The Poetry of the Mildly Nutty (Humor Included)

A black stallion mounts an amber mare
against a burgundy sky;
his mane, a banner of smoke,
an accented vowel at the end of the line.

The foliage drapes redundant adjectives,
as the bleeding slices of a leftover sun
sculpt the fluid contours
of your kneeling body.

As the image of mating horses
dilates your pupils,
with the neigh of a filly,
you slide all the way down.

Your every muscle resonates
with a different syllable,
kneading my senses
with hooves of galloping verbs.

Having no sins but each other,
I buck in mid-stanza as you start to write.
To finish your twenty line poem,
we open Kama Sutra.

If You Want to Drop Your Body

William Clair Godfrey

Tune: *Humoresque*

Chapter 12: The Poetry of the Mildly Nutty (Humor Included)

If you want to drop your body,
Drop instead into samadhi.
You'll be glad you did when you come to.

If you think that life is folly,
Turn from pot to Patanjali.
He will make you happy when you're blue.

You're in for some great surprises
When your kundalini rises,
And the purple flames envelope you.

Transcendental Meditation
Will eliminate frustration.
Love and peace and joy will come to you.

My Elephant

Gale Park

© Gale Park, 2005.

Chapter 12: The Poetry of the Mildly Nutty (Humor Included)

An elephant in the backyard can sure ruin the garden
And the neighbors' barn, when you have a jumping elephant like mine.
He is lonesome for the neighbors' elephants.
It's hard to keep him corralled.
And when he gets away, it's hard to get him back home.
He argues.
We have to trick him.
I'd like to tell people about him,
But nobody would believe me.

The Love Song of J. Alfred Frog Prince

Angela Mailander

In Norse mythology, *Yggdrasil is the name of the "World Tree" (an ash tree, to be exact). While the name means "World Ash," it also means "Odyn's horse" as "Yggr" is one of the many names of Odyn, the chief of the gods. Because of the etymological identity of the two names, the horse is said to be bound upon the world tree. Yggdrasil is thus a profound as well as complex symbol, which includes the full range of the meanings implicit in the Christian cross (often dubbed a "tree"). We may reasonably ask why the horse is bound to the tree, rather than the god himself, as is the case in Christian mythology. The horse is a symbol of the god's "vehicular form," the form (or body) that is needed to be manifest and active in this world.

Chapter 12: The Poetry of the Mildly Nutty (Humor Included)

Your Highness,
No doubt you've heard
of the frog
On a log
In the hole
In the bottom
Of the ocean?
Well, I'm the one.

I live in the Sargasso Sea.
Usually, I float just beneath the surface
And only my eyes,
Eminently suited to the purpose
Through a long evolutionary process
Stick out:
Jewels among the crap—
Yet all of it is here by design.
I am a collector
And everything's connected
To everything else.

Mostly I just look around,
Waiting for flies. But sometimes
I do crawl out, pearly belly exposed,
Wreathed with whatever happens
To be floating above me:
Sea weed, strings
of words, old shoes, inner tubes,
and, inflating myself, I sit
on something that will hope-
fully support my weight
to bask in the sun and croak.

But there is a word, a sound
That will take me down
Like a diver's bell
Past rags of thought, scuttle fish,
And a thousand silvery sardines,
Till sound is changed
Into the opening and closing

Of sea anemones, down past
Where day and night can reach.

And there's the hole all right
In the bottom of the ocean.
But the part about the log,
The log as big as the world ash Yggdrasill*
Is a common mis-
under
standing.

In fact, Your Highness, you can swim
right through that hole in the bottom of the ocean,
And then you'll see no reason
Not to kiss me—for I am a Prince and we
Have the world in common.

Chapter 12: The Poetry of the Mildly Nutty (Humor Included)

Laughing Leaves Retreat

Barry Rosen

Chapter 12: The Poetry of the Mildly Nutty (Humor Included)

I

The snow is melting.
Whispering pines
gossip with excited maples
about the new arrivals.

II

Smells of citronella
sweep past
sweaty noses
inhaling the Divine.
Are they aware of their nostrils?

III

Silence
beckons Mindfulness
like the lake breeze
cajoling sleepy pines
to awaken.

IV

In between thoughts
awareness flickers
like a candle
caught between two breezes
searching for Itself.

V

Desireless,
the mind expands
into evening breezes.
They rustle with laughter.

VI

Silent mosquitoes
sting
silent meditators
in an uncontrollable
moment of Desire.

VII

Between the waves
of a cosmic voice
universes are merging and emptying
into the silent stillness
of Consciousness awakening
to Itself.

VIII

A leaf floats by
red, yellow, with
tiny black dots.
Like a half moon face,
it smiles at the sky
glad to reach the earth.

IX

Whispers of
Vedic mantras
ripple In ponds of
consciousness.
All is well.

7-15-2005

Chapter 12: The Poetry of the Mildly Nutty (Humor Included)

The Poetry of the Arts, Poems, and Books

Chapter 13

I cannot live without books.

— Thomas Jefferson, American President and
Founding Father
(1743-1826)

CONTENTS

514	Birth of a Poem	*Leah Marie Waller*
518	Tag Sale	*Bill Graeser*
520	Poetry Dances, Olé!	*Freddy Niagara Fonseca*
524	Iowa Omen	*Diane Frank*
526	These Words Are Wounds	*Brother Ludovico*
528	Lady with an Ermine	*James Tipton*
530	Poetry: The Art of the Voice	*Ken Chawkin*
532	Somebody Has to Play Mozart	*Silvine Farnell*
534	Paper Music	*Elizabeth McIsaac*
536	If I Could Write	*Jasmine Bartolovic*
538	Elvin Ray	*James Moore*
540	Open Readings on Other Planets	*Bill Graeser*
542	Advisement	*Patricia Regan Argiro*
544	Poet as Art	*Matthew A. Bovard*
546	Books	*Freddy Niagara Fonseca*

*Far away, there in the sunshine are my
highest aspirations. I may not reach them,
but I can look up and see their beauty,
believe in them, and
try to follow where they lead.*

— Louisa May Alcott, American novelist
(1832-1888)

Chapter 13

The Poetry of the Arts, Poems, and Books

When asked to comment on his art, Italian sculptor, painter, architect, and poet Michelangelo (1475-1564) replied, *"I saw the angel in the marble and carved until I set him free."*

A search for cultural identity is found in all expressions of art, but art as its own exploration was rare until the beginning of the 20th century. With urban expansion and changes in how man saw himself, adherence to form and tradition began to fade. Artists started turning inward and looking at the origins, workings, and expressions of their own art forms. Poetry about Nature and the natural world continues to hold our attention, but the added focus on the artist and his medium is a welcome expansion of its repertoire.

We gladly recognize musicality in a painting, drama in a sculpture, and poetry in dance. A cathedral may sing the glory of God. Interconnectedness of all the arts has become quite evident.

In this chapter we find poems about books, dance, painting, music, words, calligraphy, poetry, language, the muse, and 'the poet himself', all seen through the poet's eyes.

Birth of a Poem

Leah Marie Waller

Published in *Under the Cedar Tree*, by Leah Marie Waller.

Poetry met me
under a willow tree
on the cuffs of an Iowa river.
I was scarred
but he kissed my wrists
and told me that everything
would be all right.
He removed my clothes
slowly,
a sock,
then a sleeve.
So smooth I didn't know
I was naked
until the March breeze
laughed across my back.

I reached for something
to cover myself
but everything I grabbed
was just more and more
of him.
I had no choice
but to embrace him,
lest I expose my nakedness
any longer.

He was warm,
light, tender, and romantic.
So many kinds of delicious
I thought I should explode.
I spun, ran, ducked and dipped
in and out of reality.
Kissing the bends and joints
of my sudden desire.
Then I opened my eyes
and he was gone.

My mother told me I was foolish
to lie with a lover
who held thousands of hearts.

This Enduring Gift

"Did you think he would stop for you?"
she asked.

My soul began to grow round and plump
over the next nine mouths.
I had decided
to put it up for adoption
when it was born.
I had no job
and no house
after all,
I could never support
such a thing.

It was a rainy morning
when the writing contractions began.
Closer and closer together,
shorter and shorter lines.
I felt pain
but I would not take drugs.
Pleasure,
though I screamed.
Suddenly the tiny thing burst out
caught by the gloved white hands
of the page.

My small bloody poem,
coughing and gasping desperately
for life.
I stared down at it.
Into the large blue eyes
of poetry
and I knew
in every batten
of my being
that this scroll
this flesh
of my flesh
was the answer
to life.

Chapter 13: The Poetry of the Arts, Poems, and Books

Tag Sale

Bill Graeser

Published in *Long Island Quarterly*.

Chapter 13: The Poetry of the Arts, Poems, and Books

in the old house
where lived the
white-haired lady
I never saw
but through the window
of her kitchen
as I walked the meadow
behind.

Where we now stand
going through her things
like seagulls through clamshells
though she's not here—some
ridiculous price on her sleeve.

Heaven being what it is
she will never know
how little it sold for, how
claws clutched her china
and carried her curtains away.

And me with her book
of Wordsworth poems
dated 1898
looking out the kitchen window
to the meadow—grass rising
for nothing but light.

Poetry Dances, Olé!

Freddy Niagara Fonseca

> *Discourse on virtue and they pass by in droves. Whistle and dance the shimmy, and you've got an audience.*
> — Diogenes

Chapter 13: The Poetry of the Arts, Poems, and Books

Poetry Dances, Olé!
Yes, she really does.
Literary she isn't—*Dancing* is her thing!
She has burst on the scene like a *Rock Star*,
and to get a
pert *Calypso* going or a pompous *Waltz*,
all she needs
is her knack for *Dancing*, a quick
    hip *Swinging* wide a mile and legs like wow! —
    There . . .
    she's already *Shuffling* up a storm on the *Page!*
I'm taking my Muse *Poetry* to *Party* tonight.
She insisted on
tackling all of the latest *Salsas* and *Tangos* —
anything goes.
No time for *Grammar* — too much fun at the *Dance!*
    Quite formal in *Sonnets* and
    well-*Versed* in *Ballads* she
    can be at times, but nah, not tonight!
The *Classics, Nonfiction,* and *Romance* are
quite eager to meet her.
Their *Chapters* won't *Jive* like her *Haiku*, but hey,
all they want is to
revel in *Rhythm* a little and join her in *Print!*
    Stepping slowly or fast,
    or all debonair,
    she's always the life of the party!
Wouldn't she love to *Break-Dance* with
hot *Punctuation*, or
Slow-Dance some grave *Saraband* with
old-fashioned *Spelling?*
You bet! She adapts to all *Styles* in a flash, and
    once she has licked a *Can-can*,
    she lives it and
    can up the ante to a *Tap-Dancing* frenzy!
A while ago, she would hang and *Jig*
with the *Bards* and *Homer;*
take to the *Stage* to romp with *Shakespeare;*
or *Dance* to *Dante,*
raising all *Hell* with her dynamite *Feet* and *Rhyme!*

> All of her *Blank Verses*
> have been rehearsing for
> ages and now turn to *Merengue* at last.
> See? — she's never been a wallflower — she'll
> *Prance* like a pro!
> You give her a *Subject*, a *Theme*, and in less than a
> second, *She'll*
> be wiggling her *Syntax* to share with the crowd
>> what a *Sentence* of zest,
>> a *Turn* of a *Phrase*,
>> and a body to *Shake* can do.
> *Dancing* back to back and belly to belly,
> she's so good at tempting
> *Language*, *Diction*, and *Slang* with her chutzpah.
> Look how those guys are
> scrambling to touch butt with her *Couplets*
>> as all of her *Stanzas*
>> get wilder when *Dancing*
>> all those seductive *Boleros* she knows!
> Hey, *Commas* and *Verbs*, you make room for this gal —
> her *Syllables Rock!*
> Knee-high and in trance, she's *Dancing* the
> *Limbo* with *Fiction* right now,
> while *Scribbling Ideas* with her toe.
>> Archly sensual and with
>> sly innuendo, she
>> kicks up her heels — she never holds back.
> You know her legendary *Poetic License*: She's
> been found to be nocturnally
> *Shimmying* naked with errant *Prose*
> and *even Free Verses*,
> luring you to *Reel* to her *Beat* and mystique through the night.
>> Whatever you may be *Reading*
>> between her *Lines*,
>> *Hers* is the joy to play with *Words* that are willing!
> Knowing her *Measure*; unveiling her *Meaning*,
> she gladly engages her *Fancy*
> while rapt in the *Dance*. She has *oomph*, oh yes! —
> she kicks butt, *Olé!* —
> she's having a *Ball* while taking the floor, and

all heads turn, bodies *Twist*, and
everyone cheers
as we're *Waltzing* away to be *Read* in a *Book!*

Iowa Omen

Diane Frank

To be published in *Swan Light*, by Diane Frank. © 2009 by Diane Frank.

Chapter 13: The Poetry of the Arts, Poems, and Books

Three hawks fly south
   as your voice trembles
      across the great plains.

Fields of sleeping cows
   a gentleness in the land.

Here is the omen:
   Sky splashed with aurora,
      blue stars, curtains of light.

The letters are gold
   on red silk —
      Japanese calligraphy.

If I had the right kind of ink
   I'd write them
      on your skin.

These Words Are Wounds

Brother Ludovico

Chapter 13: The Poetry of the Arts, Poems, and Books

THESE
>   words are wounds whose blood bleeds through these pages,
>   Granting keen sight signs of an unseen pain,
>   An *Angel*, that with devils, hemorrhages,
>   Whose writhing ecstasies, leaves abiding stains.
>   Let none who trace these tracks of ink-black tears
>   To dens of darkness led through blinding snows,
>   Lusting for the kill, with sugared or venomed spears,
>   With hunters' prides presume this prey to know.
>   For 'tis a beast of myth, waked from *Man's* dreams,
>   That gnashes for *Light* midst its savage dark,
>   Stricken to the *Quick* of its *deathless Being*,
>   Quarried in the *mystery* of its own *Heart*.
> These words, a dying beast, oozing a *Spirit* deep,
> *Man's* crucifying stigmata; indelibly, ineffably sweet.

Lady with an Ermine

James Tipton

Based on the painting by Leonardo da Vinci

Chapter 13: The Poetry of the Arts, Poems, and Books

She holds an ermine in her arms
And looks away—or, I should say,
Looks to the side. The light is full
On her face. The ermine is looking at me.
Her long fingers wrapping him may take
My attention, his smooth white coat, her
Puffy dark blue and red sleeves—but they
Are nothing. It is her face, calm in the light,
More specifically, her eyes—her eyes
That know a peace that stretches from her
Time into mine. For Leonardo painted her
Over four hundred years ago. It doesn't matter.
She looks through the turmoil in
That darkness of time. There's
The placidity of her gaze and me. Nothing
Between us. That's how Leonardo painted her.
Brown eyes looking away into darkness and
Finding yours, if you're lucky. I feel
Privileged, as if I'm in an intimate moment
That no one else knows, reading their museum notes
Or the writing to the side of the painting or
Listening to a learned guide explain the painting
On headphones. They don't know about the mystery
That Leonardo puts into the eyes. The mystery
That time is a joke.

Poetry - The Art of the Voice

Ken Chawkin

Chapter 13: The Poetry of the Arts, Poems, and Books

How fine will your breath become
from listening to these words?
How soft will they seem to be
as they settle through the mind
like silent snowflakes falling
from a windless winter sky?

I often marvel at the mystery—
how words can work
on a listener's heart and mind,
upon hearing a poet's thoughts,
a poet's breath, flowing
from an inner voice—
a windless wind, speaking
through a voiceless voice.

Somebody Has to Play Mozart

Silvine Farnell

On being asked for a poem of my own, when I offered to say one by someone else

Chapter 13: The Poetry of the Arts, Poems, and Books

But you know, I don't write poetry
so many great poems in the world already

What I love is the sound of them, their taste in my mouth
crispness of consonants
fullness of vowels
to say them, sing them, dance them, sound them out
to people like you

to feel the silence
words sounding in silence
sculpted in silence—your silence

To teach people like you to taste them, sound them, dance them
until no one is left in the whole world to say
   I hate poetry—I never understand it
because everyone's felt it singing inside them

That's what I love
not writing my own
but for you I make an exception.

Paper Music

Elizabeth McIsaac

Published in *A Sun Palette of Song'ans, Book I*, by Elizabeth McIsaac.

Chapter 13: The Poetry of the Arts, Poems, and Books

At first I'm drawn:
   The sight, the touch, the smell —
        the *Paper;*
a mastercraft of love
from sun-extruded fibers,
and water, pure and cool;
its edges easy, deckled,
like fingers, free and live.
And then with brush or pen:
   effect an elemental point,
   and nudge it with a vision
   to watch it grow —
        the *Line.*
The final choices flow,
and raise that plane
to match the facets of my mind, and so
the conjuring of light transformed —
        the *Color.*
These three
   in dialogue
   will realize —
        the *Form.*
And when the four
   refer themselves as one,
   they take on life —
        in *Motion.*
and move my eye and heart to hear —
        the *Music*
that makes me want to draw.

If I Could Write

Jasmine Bartolovic

Chapter 13: The Poetry of the Arts, Poems, and Books

If i could write anything I would write songs — like Leonard Cohen. It would be something like the primal longing for Self or God or connections that I often — always — confuse with sex.

Or I would write poetry that empties out the longing, leaving me open and transparent and thin as a reed. Or of children's stories that disguise an ancient truth — such as Beauty and the Beast — and the transformational power of unconditional love.

I would write of heroes and heroines — everyday people — men who work the mines or build the power plants along the Ohio River to feed their children.

I would write of women who dig deep within and say "no, thank you" to unequal alliances.

I would write of Camelot and handsome men and beautiful women and children who do not die and beds that rock us to sleep.

I would *not* write of wars, rumors of wars — leave that to the Bible.

I would write of bodies that do not age or wrinkle or sag and could drink Pepsi and marguerites and Jim Beam and Southern Comfort and still awake with clarity and ease.

I would write of the veil being so thin that I could visit my mother and Aunt Nan and return nurtured.

I would write of my first love — Chip — 2 year old — 4 year old awesome, and we would dance and sing and laugh into eternity and I would sing the song the deer sang as they came to visit my father at the start of his last ride.

I would sing and write songs of eternal love and eternal unity and light — on Both sides of the veil.

I would write songs of remembering forever without the pain of separation.

I would write poems of inspiration to leave for my grandchildren's grandchildren so the roads I've traveled have not been in vain. Maybe we could propel each other forward. Maybe we *do* stand on the shoulders of giants and yet I always and also believe we each stand alone.

I would write lullabies for old ladies sleeping alone with memories of hot juicy hard snuggling nights, and memories of sensuous little bodies of mine and Lee's children's bodies flapping and snuggling and kicking and animal contentment.

I would write songs of stories of baby smells — Johnson's Baby Powder and fresh clean pee.

Elvin Ray

James Moore

Tribute to Elvin Jones 1927-2004

Published in *Modern Drummer* and *The Iowa Source*, 2004.

Indianapolis, summer, jazz fest 2000,
Jones in his 70s, hot day, me hugging the stage.
A frail cat with a million-dollar smile
climbs behind the trap set
like an African king ascending the throne.
He's playing with young cats.
It's afternoon, picnic-style seating.
He seems too old to wail,
but wail he does. Such syncopation!
Rolling fills, offbeat staccato, behind the beat,
around the beat, under it, through it,
defying gravity, toying with tempo,
crackle sway roll cymbal crash!
Smile bursting but struggling, too.
At one point, an old foot cramps up,
stops playing bass drum altogether,
arms soldiering on.
It is a thing of beauty watching him.
A lifetime spent in the driver's seat,
doing time behind Coltrane and Miles,
Parker and Ellington and Mingus.
I saw Buddy Rich in his prime back in the late 60s,
a powerhouse display of mesmerizing mastery
and explosive command.
But Elvin, he just dishes it out like an ice cream vendor,
having fun, working it, but working, too.
You can feel his joy, his pain, his intensity,
his smack-dab outta time in-time thwackery.
Cadence pulse stroke pound splash!
Skeletal elemental elegance.
Life Magazine called him
"the world's greatest rhythmic drummer."
"He's happy. No more suffering,"
said Keiko Jones, wife of 38 years.
"He's been fighting for so long."
Ah, the sweet darshan sitting so close
to one so close to God's heartbeat,
so loose, so superfluid,
the looser, the tighter, even for a brief afternoon set,
even so late in the game.
Rest well, elastic innovator of the golden wrists.
Swing low, sweet chariot—
Saint Peter's truly in heaven now.

Open Readings on Other Planets

Bill Graeser

Chapter 13: The Poetry of the Arts, Poems, and Books

There's always a sad poem about desolation in space,
the itchiness of spacesuits, the dreariness of the Dark
Side of the Moon. A giddy poem about weightlessness
and the joy of seeing the smiling face of one's home
planet, of touching down, opening the hatch and breath-
ing those familiar fumes, and there'll be at least one poem
about sex on the "Moon's of Poombiss," where the woman
have twelve breasts—six in front and six on their backs,
a poem that goes round and round not wanting to end.

When it's my turn to read someone will comment how on Earth
we only recently discovered poetry need not rhyme, that if Whitman
hadn't visited the "Flexstar Region" as a teenager earthlings might
yet be in the narrow courtyard of a sonnet with a feather in our cap.

And though I can't write metaphor like a "Mirror-headed Garvinian,"
or recite like a "Seven-throated-Shlaba," as when any poem is read
it no longer matters how many noses we have, whether we exhale
a purple mist or if we had moon rocks for breakfast, we are if but
briefly buckled in and blasting off to the same place in a spaceship
called Poetry.

Advisement

Patricia Regan Argiro

Published in *Writers on the Avenue*, 2000.

Chapter 13: The Poetry of the Arts, Poems, and Books

Take words. Seriously. But take
care that such seriously taken
words do not turn, glancing like
scimitars that, cared too much for,
can kill you with your own hand.

Take rhythm, rhyme. Act verbs.
Count syllables as they, dancing,
move across your mind, spilling
onto your tongue and falling
outside you into the earless air.

Care carefully, maintaining
mundane concerns for food and
drink: clean rooms, feed cats,
protect your sanity.
Still, above all, take words'
arrangements seriously.
But not so seriously as to
exclude the living word.

Poet as Art

Matthew A. Bovard

Published in *Knew rEvolution*. © Matthew A. Bovard, 2009.

Chapter 13: The Poetry of the Arts, Poems, and Books

Leave space to see if something
new comes to finish it off.
Sit on the moment. Wait for it
to fill you. Then when you feel
filled, open the flood gates.
Let it all pour out of you.
Hold none of it back.
Peel back your flesh
to show your bones.
Bleached white
from penetrating rays of life.
Crack the bone open and
let the audience suck
on the marrow. Feed
yourself to your audience.
Serve up your shit and guts
upon a silver platter.
Reflect in their eyes after you
have infected their being.
Spreading a virus of
expression to lead them
to the edge and
jump to freedom.

Books

Freddy Niagara Fonseca

Published in *The Neovictorian/Cochlea*, 2006, and *winningwriters.com*, 2006. The poem has been on permanent display at Revelations Cafe & Bookstore, Fairfield, Iowa since December 2004. It's available as a bookmark and a broadside.

Chapter 13: The Poetry of the Arts, Poems, and Books

Sometimes, when I think of the vast
wisdom ever contained in books—

countless scriptures of all creeds; scrolls in
indecipherable languages; tomes of science;

the great Library of Alexandria destroyed by
fire centuries ago, priceless knowledge gone;

thousands of books burned by the Third Reich;
books still held secret at the Vatican;

hieroglyphs in Egypt and whatever Atlantis
must have contributed to the written word;

books simply lost and never retrieved;
others molded, fallen apart, discarded,

and all the many books I'll never be able to read in a
life-time even if I lived a thousand years;

and when I think of all these while browsing
at garage sales, used bookstores—(o, the good

feel of an old book and the sense of care for
books you surmise some previous owner had;

to see his or her name written on the title page,
sometimes with the date of purchase or gift)—

yes, then I tend to hold a book in my hands a little long
sometimes, deliberating whether I'll buy,

and I read again what's on the flap; scan a
few more pages; find a keen phrase here and there;

ponder on the title, the design, the author's
name, weighing it all in my hand . . . And

This Enduring Gift

page after page of long-forgotten lore, myth, and
adventure slowly take shape and mingle with

my own memory of myth in the back of
my mind, passing through my skin, stealing

into my bones, my heart, holding me spellbound
for a life-time it seems, and somehow beneath

my feet the deeper caves and mysteries of the earth
open wide where I glimpse that which

I cannot name but know that it exists;
and I'm feeling so strangely rooted and connected

to all cultures, beliefs, poetry, romance, peace,
Wars, and history . . . and I *may* take the book home,

maybe not—it doesn't matter, for as I'm
standing here, simply lost in time for a while,

some power is reclaiming everything I thought
was lost to man one time, and I see the

Great Communicator of it all in all these
many chapters, paragraphs, sentences, words

working their way with a purpose, meaning,
and conviction across so many ages,

and suddenly it seems that everything is all here now,
and really never was gone at all, as long as

books have ever existed, and readers found them,
and as I close the book, walking out to get some fresh air,

there's all the magic in the air as of old still, and
I can live with that, and be an open book to all.

Chapter 13: The Poetry of the Arts, Poems, and Books

The Poetry of the Wilderness We Harbor

CHAPTER 14

*History is a nightmare from which I
am trying to awake.*

— James Joyce, Irish writer and poet (1882-1941)

CONTENTS

552	Radio City Hall	*Laurie Sewall*
554	I Turn My Back	*Paul Johan Stokstad*
556	The Deer	*Susie Niedermeyer*
558	Night Birds	*Andrea Dana Stevens*
560	You Left Me	*Sharalyn Harris*
562	Untitled	*Tom Le May*
564	Blackberries All Dried up Now	*Carole Lee Connet*
566	Territorial Waters	*Viktor Tichy*
568	Creatures Nobody Recognizes	*Rustin Larson*
570	And if It Happens	*Susie Niedermeyer*
572	Retreat from Kandahar	*Carole Lee Connet*
574	Where They Hung a Crucifix	*Robin Lim*
576	We Seep into This World	*Brother Ludovico*
578	The Sandbox	*Richard K. Wallarab*
580	Window Decoration	*Susan Klauber*
582	Three Poems out of Southeast Iowa	*Charlie Hopkins*
584	The Forgiven	*Glenn Watt*

*If you're going through hell,
keep going.*

Winston Churchill, British politician
(1874-1965)

Chapter 14

The Poetry Of The Wilderness We Harbor

Contemporary poets are witnessing violent tensions between our spiritual aspirations and the realities of the modern world. Unlike personal and tender themes, which usually evoke a more lyrical language, some poems express feelings and ideas in strident eruptions and harsh speech. To capture such feelings as directly as possible, some poets quickly forsake any semblance of predictable language patterns and shoot from the hip.

It is often argued that modern poetry is mostly prose because of its absence of a yet universally accepted form. But when a poem is molded directly from a deep feeling level into the rhythm of the spoken word, a tangible emotional undertone becomes discernible which is key to the poem.

Particularly when poems are passionately written, an unexpected and variable 'something', different from prose, emerges, which actually manifests in a recognizable form — the emotive force of the poem itself.

Radio City Music Hall

Laurie Sewall

Chapter 14: The Poetry of the Wilderness We Harbor

Rows upon rows of strange feathers and hats —
legs upon legs of knees, marching a jerky beat.
My father and I on the train, then Hayden Planetarium.
Dark, except sparkles of holes, whole constellations, under a glassy dome.
I loved none of this — mysterious dancers, the sprawling exhibit of lights —
as much as I loved my father
taking me into the city — the lilt of his head
as he dozed into sleep, planets traversing the ceiling above.
I remember a world of glittery things, electric —
a wild cadenza inside, the conductor waving fine sticks
while millions of wings appeared in a fury of leaves, disappeared
like migrating birds over ponds that would outlast it all.

I Turn My Back

Paul Johan Stokstad

*Je tourne mon dos
aujourdhui,
quand je pense
au drapeau
de mon pays,
il a tourné au gris
et blanc et noir,
et il vole au vent renversé.*

*Dans mon rêve, ce soir,
quand la limousine
du président passe
devant les foules,
ce ne sont plus les gestes
d'accueil et de joie,
si pourtant on lève les yeux
pour le regarder...*

*Maintenant, j'écris
en français,
honteux de ce
qui se passe
en anglais,
et en honneur
de ce qui a été dit
en France*

*Un Américain seul,
sans public,
sans voix,
sans microphone,
je tourne mon dos
à Washington
et regarde au loin...*

Chapter 14: The Poetry of the Wilderness We Harbor

When I think
of the American Flag, today
it has changed to black,
white and gray
and it is flying upside down

In my dream, tonight
when the president's
motorcade passes
the crowd doesn't wave,
or cheer, or even watch

Tomorrow, I write my
imaginary poem
in French,
in shame for
what's happening
in English,
and in honor of
what's been said
in France

Right now, sitting alone,
just one American,
with no public
no voice, and
no microphone
I turn my back
on Washington
and look away

The Deer

Susie Niedermeyer

Published in *Under a Prairie Moon,* by Susie Niedermeyer.

Chapter 14: The Poetry of the Wilderness We Harbor

By now the bones are but sloppy shorthand
for a life. The mouth is slurred with silt,
ribs protrude like long curved fingers
and the pelvis is riddled with buckshot.
The tongue that used to sing is gone
and water eddies through the teeth,
loose in their sockets.

Walking the banks of the river
that splits the land like a scar,
I scan for driftwood, river glass,
and consider my life, my ties to a place,
to a man. Married more than half my life,
the thought of leaving is almost inconceivable.
I stand twisting the end of my scarf,
looking down at the stripped apparition
anchored by the sand and sense a white tail
flashing through the trees.

A breeze ripples the surrendered water.
This creature surely knew love,
for what is running but the body in love
with its marriage to the wind?
And what these arching ribs
but the fierce embrace of sun and scent—
what these perfect hooves but anchors to the sky?

Night Birds

Andrea Dana Stevens

Chapter 14: The Poetry of the Wilderness We Harbor

Unimportant   muttering a single word
You uttered   some fantastic   secret
Misbegotten and very far away
Across the bare dining table.

There's nothing but a hollow ending sky.
I never saw you and went your charming way
Without harming anyone but me.
It was your shadow I could no longer see
On our misplaced forgotten floor.

You eased your way out of the sky
I was left over from your day
Clumped shoelaces   cracked lampshades
Missing landscapes.
You put out the cat with my heart.

After long gray indifferent sighs
You cut yourself a piece of cake
Then climbed the stairs
And took the stairway with you.

I am left like some old owl
Standing on one foot
Dreaming she's a bird
With head under wing
Looking out the window
Hurt   Stained.

There are night birds
Outside my window pane
Not trying to make me listen.

You Left Me

Sharalyn Pliler

Chapter 14: The Poetry of the Wilderness We Harbor

You left me.

Yes, I was unbearable,
But weren't you unbearable too?
Who do you imagine yourself to be,
To believe you should be above trouble,
Above tears and anger and frustration
In the struggle to become whole —
Man and woman, like steel against stone,
like gold in the fire
that burns off the dross,
both win or both lose —
Wasn't that why we swore, "'till death"
To see imperfection to its end?
Men dream of strength, but
Women dream of love and
Even shrews, I tell you,
Are but bitter goddesses crying for perfection,
Their inner softness measured by the hardness of the shell.
Foolish man,
If you are not strong enough to bear
My passion's struggle to emerge,
Did you think there is for you
Someone waiting who is more holy?

Untitled

Tom Le May

Chapter 14: The Poetry of the Wilderness We Harbor

> Every day I become
> More like an Indian
> After the Trail of Tears
> With a life inside
> No white man can see.

Blackberries All Dried up Now

Carole Lee Connet

National Foundation of State Poetry Societies Power of Woman Award 1st prize 2000.
Published in *National Foundation of State Poetry Societies Review*.

Chapter 14: The Poetry of the Wilderness We Harbor

Elderberries lift purple paws
to the pregnant sun, bending on brittle bones.
I cut the hollow stems, pluck shiny seeds
the size of glass beads on a Blackfoot dress.
Below the navel, an inverted red triangle,
sign to men at a distance—
I am woman.

I walk the medicine path.
I am warrior of the unseen.
I have no fear of forms.

Wandering through a harem hung with gauze,
invisible threads stick to my face.
A belly dancer with eight legs
winds her silk scarf around a stunned monarch.
Each web stitched with white lightning,
sign to men at a distance—
I am woman.

I am spirit catcher.
I spin the invisible.
I leave no loose ends.

Two riddled trees still bearing a few pippins
sag against an apple-peel moon.
When I reach up for the scarred fruit,
a speckled snake wriggles from under the dry grass.
Gold sequins on her skin-tight sheath,
sign to men at a distance—
I am woman.

I am a line drawn on air.
I walk with my belly.
I taste with split tongue.

Stripped to the sweat
I eat the remains of initiation.
But I am no longer fertile—shriveled apples
on a scarred tree sagging with a handful of riddles.
The serpent sheds below my navel,
sign to men at a distance—
I am woman.

I will ascend to mountains, to temples.
I will find my way back
to the world unseen.

Territorial Waters

Viktor Tichy

First Prize in National Foundation of State Poetry Societies.

Chapter 14: The Poetry of the Wilderness We Harbor

Frigid waves boil granite knuckles
of the Old World.
Embraced by her thighs stretching the skin
of a kayak, I slide through
the Baltic surf,
four-year-old shoulders
wedged between the knees of my mother.

Again I taste the salty panic of my birth,
inches from my first home,
but miles from the amber and lead
dotting the skeletons under the sand.

Lost in the amniotic waters of Europe,
I am choking in separate existence.
I am learning to be a man,
to be horrified,
yet yearning for the rest of my life
to drown in the lap of a woman.

Creatures Nobody Recognizes

Rustin Larson

First appeared in *Loonfeather*. Published in *Crazy Star,* by Rustin Larson.

Chapter 14: The Poetry of the Wilderness We Harbor

In the evening, alone together,
we eat our pauper soup.
On the radio, the music
of bowling balls rumbling
down a dark set of stairs
accompanies the excited cicadas. They rattle
until their skins burst, becoming
creatures nobody recognizes.
As the music falls asleep
into its black space, I think
of those creatures arriving into emptiness
the way a woman sings her way under
cool sheets.

I could spill my voice and burst
above your hurt glance which says
there's not enough money,
above your lips closed in a pout around the spoon,
above your eyes stubbornly holding back
their reservoir of starlight.
If I could burst through this shell
and be a boy again, I'd listen
to the rattle of cicadas. I'd pick their crisp
larval shells from the bark
of an elm. I'd ask those dried, split bodies:
what does the heart become
when it opens, and how will we
know it again?

And if It Happens

Susie Niedermeyer

Published in *Under a Prairie Moon,* by Susie Niedermeyer.

Chapter 14: The Poetry of the Wilderness We Harbor

If it happens that you carry
your heavy-plumed sorrow
into the sea, turn back before the swells
lift you like a lover and subsume you,
limbs curved in aqueous silence.
Remember, it is not your time.

Or when you find the world collapsed
down to your pale curled form
on the bed, sheets bruised
by wine and spilled fire, smoke
in the halo of your hair,
open the window and let the cool vector
of moonlight run down your face.
Know that the fragile monochrome body
you see in the mirror
is your home only for now.

Cup a breast in your hand,
pass a finger across your lips
and go to the garden beyond the peonies
crushed by wind, into the starlight and fireflies
and brandish the tender scalpel
of your longing. Dance abandoned,
knee deep in clover until your eyes shine
with dawn. There is no light like yours.

Retreat from Kandahar

Carole Lee Connet

Iowa Poetry Association 1st Place World Events.
Published in *Lyrical Iowa*.

Chapter 14: The Poetry of the Wilderness We Harbor

Holed up in the honeycomb
caves and *kezar* tunnels of Tora Bora,
land of black dust, barren knees
of the White Mountains
above the black forests of Spin Ghar.

White turbans, bearded faces muffled
with dust the color of their wives' burkas,
they will fight in the riddled labyrinth
for honor, for the promise of
paradise.

They will fight to the last
Kalashnikov bullet, until the colossal
pressure and rush of heat from the daisy cutters
dropped at their man-shaped doors
blasts them to ashes.

In the catacombs of Tora Bora,
they will leave behind empty white boxes of
dates, dumbbells, cluster bombs,
a few fingers and a horde
of black widows.

Where They Hung a Crucifix

Robin Lim

Chapter 14: The Poetry of the Wilderness We Harbor

A daughter is valuable.
She can someday weave.

The sky is full of electric cables,
cement towers reinforced with steel.
The hair on my arms rises
when I walk under such a night.
Sparks of lightning ricochet
between glass insulators crackling,
scolding, unzipping the sky.

This is the Indonesian power station slum
where the children of Sumba
live under leaking asbestos
like animals in stalls.
Here is the dirt floor
where women lean away
and weave blankets
dyed with dark roots,
on bamboo back strap looms.

Ibu Rica in labor, is unwinding all the indigo
threads of her life with Samuel,
and the harsh man before him.
Samuel picks lice from the head of
his smallest daughter.

Three walking children
go to school without rice.
There are no tourists
to buy their cloth.

Some of the men in the clan
come home with busted faces,
to watch television.

Christ was born in such a manger.
Christ was born in such a manger.

Bali, 2003

We Seep into this World

Brother Ludovico

From *Whispers in a Dark Alley*

Chapter 14: The Poetry of the Wilderness We Harbor

WE
    seep into this world a carnal wraith;
  Arthritic, nauseous, choleric with greed,
Perpetually seeking out some grave
    Which cradles a primitive Divinity.
Flesh wades through gores of decadent spirit,
    Stealing from tangled bodies in fouled sheets,
Shrewish, or swinish, sly vixen or coy ferret,
    With whom we wrestled deep in jungled heats.
We step on pickles, condoms, pizza crusts,
    The table-scraps of dream; this toil, this toll.
We paid a corpse to eke forth drops of lust,
    Only to stoop, and retch into a toilet bowl.
We pull the lightbulb string, staring in a cracked mirror,
Unshaven, paunched and balding, hysterical with childhood's tears.

The Sandbox

Richard K. Wallarab

First published in *Lyrical Iowa* 2008.

Chapter 14: The Poetry of the Wilderness We Harbor

Tin tanks immobile lie
beneath the tumbled fort.
Plastic soldiers scattered
across the desert sand
await the general's call
to stand and fight again.
One broken warrior
rests outside the box
no longer needed
soon to be forgotten.

It is lunch time.
The next war begins
this afternoon.

Window Decoration

Susan Klauber

Chapter 14: The Poetry of the Wilderness We Harbor

Their bodies were left by the sudden freeze,
two perfectly preserved dead flies
screened and framed in my bedroom window,
one heading north, the other south, my window west,
like a statement of existential life
caught in the mesh between flight and liberation.

I wonder if their souls slipped through quietly
after a long and happy life.
Or was there a big scene recounting all the stupid things they did
freaking out frothing moronic at their stunned spouse
over a simple misunderstanding that melted
into stinky provolone on white silk.
Soup bones trapped in their wings
to lug around everywhere they went.

And as they squished through the screen,
they saw the sign "Mary's Polishville Cemetery"
that they had reverently dipped their wings to every day
when they flew the dirt road to Pleasant Plain.

Now, they meet the Virgin Mary face to face,
and find out it was not that Mary
but some immigrant farm lady
who had a thing for dead bodies
and needed some cash to pay the mortgage.
Maybe they found out it wasn't a joke after all,
that the Madonna always looked sad holding baby Jesus
because she really did want a girl.

But there must be a God! I feel it in my bones,
bones that will one day no longer be mine,
dismounted on the screen,
leaving only air and memories
for other eyes looking at the endless prairie
over a dead carcass.

I hope I won't have been just a pest
buzzing when everyone needed silence.

Three Poems out of Southeast Iowa

Charlie Hopkins

Chapter 14: The Poetry of the Wilderness We Harbor

Where I Live

Wind gutted fields.
Poplars bent over and fucked by the wind.
Wind raped barns, howl of a wind blind dog.
Generations of corn stalk knocked to the ground
plowed under.

Wind peeled houses the color of shuck
fallen on their backs in hay
bleached blond as a woman's hair.

From where I am I can smell the river.

.

The Banker

I love the shape of your mouth
as you lie.

Your tongue a curved and rusted sickle.

Your harvest lips drawn back like competing messiahs
before a congregation of teeth.

.

You Say My Heart Is a Church House

You say my heart is a church house
with seven windows facing a soybean field.

You say the million stars over my rooftop
are a million reasons to live.

But I say I would take God by the throat
and never let go of him till I was
chosen.

The Forgiven

Glenn Watt

Published in *The Contemporary Review*.

Chapter 14: The Poetry of the Wilderness We Harbor

Naked, crown of thorns,
spikes driven through both palms and feet,
what if we could take
everything that has ever been done to us
into the furnace of ourselves
and burn with it —
the wound festering, the fever,
the flames leaping higher and higher —
until it is burned away...

and then give back the only thing left,
the stone turned,
the rising out of the ashes,
our love.

The Poetry of the Exalted and Transcendent

Chapter

15

*Earthly things must be known to be loved.
Divine things must be loved to be known.*

— Blaise Pascal, French mathematician
and philosopher (1623-1662)

Contents

588	This Lamplight Falling on My Child's Face	*Brother Ludovico*
590	These Highest Dreams	*Allen Cobb*
592	The Divine Abode of My Own Buddha-Nature	*Leslie Gentry*
594	This Balloon of Joy	*Graham de Freitas*
596	Hymn of Praise to the Divine Mother in…	*Charlie Hopkins*
600	Metamorphosis	*Megan Robinson*
602	To the River Is a Place I Go	*Henry Robert Hau*
604	A Vision	*Gale Park*
606	Giant Sequoia - A Hymn	*Freddy Niagara Fonseca*
610	Delphi	*Allen Cobb*
612	The Temple	*Catherine Castle*
614	Seeking to Hide	*Angela Mailander*
616	Lament for Lost Silence	*Allen Cobb*
620	The Egrets	*Henry Robert Hau*
622	A Hymn to the Moon-Mother	*Brother Ludovico*
632	Gates of Dawn	*James Tipton*
634	Poem Written Dream-Side (Qin Guan)	*tr. Angela Mailander*
636	Unexpected Call	*Meredith Briggs Skeath*
638	Brother Sun Sister Moon	*Matthew A. Bovard*
640	At the Speed of God	*Michael Hock*

My religion is kindness.

— The 14th Dalai Lama (born 1935)

Chapter 15: The Poetry of the Exalted and Transcendent

*If the Sun and Moon should doubt,
they'd immediately go out.*
— William Blake, English poet, painter and printmaker (1757-1827)

I decided to add an extra chapter on the topic of matters cosmic and divine. With the steady expansion of world consciousness, more and more people report genuine experiences of advanced states of consciousness in daily life.

Poets, always sensitive to change, find much of value about this to ponder and write. Typically, once inspiration strikes, they tend to quickly "disappear" into a different solar system. They'll stare at you with a most glazed look if you dare talk to them during their flights or as they sit down to express what is beyond words.

Not every modern poet seems to be enthralled by this topic, but fortunately a few poetic daredevils will take off to the spiritual stratospheres whenever they can to return with immeasurable treasures from echelons far beyond our world.

This Lamplight Falling on My Child's Face

Brother Ludovico

Chapter 15: The Poetry of the Exalted and Transcendent

THIS
    lamplight falling on my child's face,
   Falls on a flower bloomed to *Light's* pure *Essence*,
Earth's orphan, adopted, by a deathless race,
   A sister, made brother, in one *Father's Presence*.
Here the murderer is as the lover,
   Blood, expiated by its own pure *Truth*,
Each soul's a soldier, seeking midst war, Life's *Mother*,
   To grant rebellious dreams a lasting truce.
Each lamplight falling on a midnight cradle,
   Falls on a sun that does not rise or set,
Sweeter than lullabies, truer than fables,
   A blush, enkindled with *Everlastingness*.
Arms, tucking in armies, with an inexhaustible embrace,
This lamplight falling on my child's sleeping, smiling face.

These Highest Dreams

Allen Cobb

Prologue to a book of praise and jubilation
in celebration of the Vishnu Schist*

*One of the oldest geological strata: *e.g.*, the bottommost layer of the Grand Canyon. Remnants of the original crust that formed when the planet first cooled from a molten ball.

Published in *Cave Paintings*, by Allen Cobb.

Chapter 15: The Poetry of the Exalted and Transcendent

welcome to today
to the day of the earth, proud mother
to the solidity of her rock
to the elusive altitude of her sky
to the mollusks moving in her seas
    and the novas in her midnight hair

welcome to her destiny
to the magnificence of her growth
her gardens, her expansion, and her laws

welcome to her progeny
her sons and daughters of outrageous youth
and welcome, all, her kings and princes
    knights and martyrs, saints and presidents
    traditions, faiths, and fears

this is the station
this day
this state, this page
and all the travelers press upon the carriages
    and limousines
in eclectic expectation
all in a rush to consummate their journeys

and while yet some grave children
run to tumble down their playmates' colored towers
the innocence is ultimate
    of the hour
the fine curtains of each tiny window
billow gently onto heaven

within us all
is the station that we seek
and the innocence to take us there
    is indestructible

this is the station
the journeys all entwine
each tiny window opens to a growing majesty

the premise clear
this welcome is complete
and here begins a trail
of smiles of many flavors
with infinite pretensions
and some unmitigated measure
    of delight

The Divine Abode of My Own Buddha-Nature

Leslie Gentry

Published in *Lyrical Iowa* 2006.

Chapter 15: The Poetry of the Exalted and Transcendent

A shaft of sunlight slides through the patio door,
    soft and soporific as the
        sonorous bubble of aquarium filters
            and refrigerator's hum.

I have not chopped wood nor carried water
    nor become awakened in the midst of
        mendicant chores,
But in mindfulness I fold each towel
    warm from the dryer
        and sidestep the cricket
            on the sunlit floor.

This Balloon of Joy

Graham de Freitas

Published in *These Flames That I Speak: Experiences Reading Vedic Literature,* by Graham de Freitas.

Chapter 15: The Poetry of the Exalted and Transcendent

My Lord!
It is hard to button my coat
or even pull my skin about this balloon of joy and everything,
that swells with every heartbeat.

I walk lightly
(held up by its lightness),
an ant to Your mountain,
a little witness to the slow volcanic surge
of Your grand unfolding.

All I want to do is smile
as I feel You smile
and love You as I feel You love me.

I have You wrapped tight in my skin
where You belong
and I will embrace You forever.

Hymn of Praise to the Divine Mother in Her Role as Queen of Nature

Charlie Hopkins

Carol

Chapter 15: The Poetry of the Exalted and Transcendent

In September I walk in spirals through Chicago
on curved streets elegant as a rattler's back.
Stepping over rainbows in oil gutters I see my reflection
standing with well dressed mannequins
in department store windows.

But I am older than Chicago, older than the prairies.
In my chest springs seep water into tanks
where milk cows gather at dusk to drink the sky.
Wild dogs howl up and down my spine!

In October I stand by an open window in Fairfield, Iowa
contemplating the Fall.
Leaves like Puerto Rican brides
red and gold are falling and flying.
And I am flying with them as a bridegroom
over cities swollen with the blood of people
cut off from the sea.

I fly over solitary farm boys courting domesticated animals
forbidden by the Bible,
see my own body below me making love to deer and antelope
in New Mexico.
I put on antlers and wade with cows into water
the color of heaven!

I want to spread my arms wide as prairies!
I want to kiss everything alive!
I will lie in fields plowed black as Ethiopian women
and pull the sky down on top of us!

Because I am awake in the love that makes leaves bud in the highest branches
of an ash tree!
Because every cell of my body is dancing in African circles
like one hundred thousand ash leaves in a wind!

This love I offer to the Mother.
You with your prayer voice, your prayer smoke rising.

This Enduring Gift

You with your prayer teeth, your prayer skull throbbing with rivers!
There are no roads higher than your hipbones.
Your face is a cliff of fiddle fern with no trail to the top.
So come down to me because I can't climb high enough
to reach you.

I have built altars to myself in high places
and I have fallen.
I have climbed on ladders made of breath
and I have fallen.
But your breath is a wave swelling in the Gulf.
Your breath folds into itself and breaks in sudden laughter
on the beach!

Mother, if I stand before you in a rain of galvanized nails
and tell you I am Jesus,
if I limp with bullet holes in my hands and feet,
or come to you with an atom bomb,
lift me in your arms and heal me!

Let your breath come from the four corners of the sky!
Come like dawn through my open window
and lay your hands upon me!
Lift me up and enter me!
Make my belly swell with a new earth,
a new sky with a new moon in it!

When I walk in the streets of Chicago there is a lamb's heart
in my heart.
Light enters through the wound in my side.
I welcome strangers who stand on corners like ash trees
giving back breath.
I welcome meadowlarks with flowers in their beaks
and gray winged gulls come from the Lakes
who follow rivers inland to live with drunk men under bridges.
I welcome the Mother who has no place to go
where she has not always been.

Chapter 15: The Poetry of the Exalted and Transcendent

Once I carried heavy burdens,
crazy women with hair the color of drained oil.
I walked in circles gathering the dust
that falls from wings of sparrows
and collects in creases of our eyes.
I carried the skull of the moon between my shoulder blades
where wings used to be.

Then one night the moon rose off of me.
Stars fell and there were rivers in my hands!
There was water falling over me,
water seeping through hillsides into springs!
There were oceans inside me and my heart full of waves!

Tonight in Fairfield, Iowa,
there is a fine light falling from the wings of meadowlarks
that can fill the trenches of embattled faces.
December now, the sky is full of white flakes of fire.
I stand in a grove of oak trees naked after the Fall.
Trees grown so close together they touch each other like children.

I praise the thousand genitals of an oak tree!
Praise the open face of the sky.
God's breasts round and full, I praise!
I praise your belly covered with moss roses.
Praise your long arms embracing six billion men and women,
embracing everything that breathes and does not breathe.
I drink your voice seeping through me, Mother!
I kiss your red mouth!

Metamorphosis

Megan Robinson

Published in *MIU Student Magazine,* Act One, in the 1990s.

Chapter 15: The Poetry of the Exalted and Transcendent

Silken strands of hair
fall to my feet,
the sound of breaking glass echoes
in my ears.
Bald as a newborn,
my past swept into newspapers
and thrown out with the trash,
I wait in bridal splendor
for my initiation.

To the River Is a Place I Go

Henry Robert Hau

Published in *For the Bird Sings,* by Henry Robert Hau.

Chapter 15: The Poetry of the Exalted and Transcendent

To the river is a place I go
to sort myself out.
O it helps me to see
what I have become
and what I need to lose.

It's the place in the city
away from the city,
vaccination against insanity.

The river is a silvery hymn
of filial words and eternal sounds.

My river, an ecstatic aphorist
of birds and trout, carp and salmon,
shopping carts and Firestone retreads.

Neon damselflies zither in the summer air...

A goldfinch reaches down a thirsty kiss
tethered uttermost to a willow wisp.

Here the river dreams caudal fin,
whispers insects, herons ... gulls;
O the light in August, uplifting wings.

A Vision

Gale Park

© Gale Park, 1998.

Chapter 15: The Poetry of the Exalted and Transcendent

Chain me to a vision of

a thousand suns,

To watch gorgeous gardens dress

and light petals fall in languid symphony.

Delicate purple.

Giant Sequoia - A Hymn

Freddy Niagara Fonseca

> . . . the venerable aboriginal Sequoia, ancient of other days, keeps you at a distance, taking no notice of you, speaking only to the winds, thinking only of the sky . . .
> — John Muir

CHAPTER 15: THE POETRY OF THE EXALTED AND TRANSCENDENT

I

O *Sequoiadendron giganteum!*
Oldest and grandest of beings;
Noblest of souls in the world.
You've long been present in my timeless thoughts,
And I am hearing your higher silence waving over all.

II

Heaven seems to be your foremost ideal—
For ages have I seen you grow,
Largest of trees in the world.
A tiny seed contained your kingly race,
And deep in my heart I feel your countless roots, deep in my breast.

III

Is there anywhere anyone like you?
Prior to Buddha and Christ,
Your grandeur graced the world,
And since you've entered the plane of the greats
Your lofty span has linked the times of old to those of today.

IV

Generations have lived, passed, and returned.
Who has *not* admired your crown?
From your crest you view the world.
Straight and proud, but oh, so tender are you,
My *Sequoiadendron giganteum*, beloved being.

V

Forests like yours are tall cathedrals—
Quietness among your groves is whole.
Born within that pristine world,
Where sunbeams break through mist and early dawn,
Your day is like an age in bright surroundings—your nights are light.

VI

On the slopes of the Sierra Nevada
Gather and rise my sequoias.
Their being in my world
Is one of more than peace and harmony.
With outstretched arms and lifted face, they live, and live, and live!

VII

Fires, nor floods, nor storms subdue them.
They clutch the earth and touch the sky,
Strongest of trees in the world!
Though man tried hard once to destroy their kind,
They'll never be conquered, and where they dwell, they share their
      domain.

VIII

As gigantic as their presence is,
So immensely full and high is
Their love for all in the world.
Oh, when the wind is wafting over you,
Your voice is carried round the listening globe, o my sequoia.

IX

Indestructible giant sequoia!
Visible token of goodness,
Compassion, and care for the world...
Deep in my heart I'm being moved today,
For I've been hearing your whispers of greatness, wisdom, and truth.

X

O *Sequoiadendron giganteum!*
Noblest and fondest of beings.
Your soul is loved in the world,
And in my life you'll always grow higher,
For I am hearing your soaring divinity uplifting us all!

Chapter 15: The Poetry of the Exalted and Transcendent

Delphi

Allen Cobb

Published in *Cave Paintings,* by Allen Cobb.

Chapter 15: The Poetry of the Exalted and Transcendent

    in Delphi
    in the temple of Apollo
    beneath the altar floor
    where the tripod of the Oracle once stood
    there is a little slanted cave
    whose tumbled floor
    and topsy-turvy walls
    the archetype of their ancestry belie
    crouched here
    the mists no longer rise
    from fissures magic and alive
    to quell mechanics
    and ignite the veil of time
    I have dipped my pen
    in Castalian waters
    to summon a contemporary muse
    who hunkers here beside me
    in the dark among the blocks
    looking up
    dazzled by the bright Aegean sky

The Temple

Catherine Castle

Chapter 15: The Poetry of the Exalted and Transcendent

Sometimes I dream
Of the quiet
That ringing bells
Breathe and sift
Into the muted form
Of a honeyed mist
Above a faraway temple —
The Saffron Temple of Katmandu.

From exhausted villages
In the sun-blistered country,
Ginger feet plod
Through the yellow dust
Of burning days
With but one thought:
The treasured doors,
The burnished doors
Of the Saffron Temple of Katmandu.

Softly, doors open
And close.
In bronze light,
Jasmine garlands, incense,
Kumquats and sandalwood
Are full upon the shrine.

Shadows from butter lamps
Pale and flicker.
Sages of the ancient walls
Breathe and intone
Rare ethers
Into the air.

Outside, the midday is fierce.

Brown eyes seek alcoves
And archways.
Bells ring brightly
Their brilliant halos
Of sun-hammered foil.

The copper doors are hot
As the day beats
Its staccato patterns
Upon the sun-shattered doors,
The radiant doors
Of the Saffron Temple of Katmandu.

Seeking to Hide

Angela Mailander

Chapter 15: The Poetry of the Exalted and Transcendent

And hiding to seek
I went into a country
Where no man lived

The skeletons of pack mules
Mark the path behind me

Over the next crest I think
A valley and a shining
Sea—there

I breathe the bird-loud air
And am

The lap of tides
Where waves subside

Lament for Lost Silence

Allen Cobb

Published in *Cave Paintings,* by Allen Cobb.

Chapter 15: The Poetry of the Exalted and Transcendent

And why, in the end,
do we think at all?
Stories of forgotten times
recanted in memories
of decanted vintage,
the conversation of a friend
replayed in variations of intensity.
All these are forces summoned
to disrupt the placid surface
of experience when experiencing is extinguished.

We listen to the footfalls
of approaching and departing,
and steel ourselves for conflicts
which are starting in the mist-enfolded battlefields at dawn.
Which even in the knowing
we will know have gone
long before the sun.

These nights enfold more perilously than mist
concocting raptures at once unbearable
and frivolous.
Conundrums pile upon us
like calthrops on a strategic avenue.
We marvel at their interstices.
We play at pick-up-sticks with fragments of understanding
inching each sliver toward precarious equilibrium.
We dictate dialogs to insatiable audiences
who reduce them in repetition to mere memes.

When nothing old arouses from its sleep
to keep us sleeping
we dash headlong into the world
and clutch the first perceptions cast before our senses
savoring them like ship-wrecked sailors
touching lips at last to a mirage of golden grog.
We make old faces at ourselves in secret mirrors
laughing, grimacing, stretching, leering.

How can all these strangers
recapitulate familiar physiognomy?

Behind the reflecting glass
there are no thoughts.
In the silence of not thinking
there is no face.
There is no footstep in the hall.
There is no scrabbling ancient enemy
or tapping new arrival expecting conversation.
Nothing impedes our way
but there is no going.
Nothing shoves us forward or pulls us along behind
for there is no coming
and the going is already gone.

Actions commit themselves
no thanks to acting.
Speech emerges from the lips
no thanks to speaking.
Visions move into and out of sight
no thanks to restless eyes.
Even the pavement, free of calthrops
slides impeccably beneath the feet
no thanks to walking.

Only in old age
does the mental apparatus
impede itself sufficiently for silence.
Only when the wonder of the new
is old.
When all the wonders we behold
are one:
that of the beholding.

That one could know at all
where is thought in that?
Where is the thinking in the knowing?

What are thoughts but babbling accompaniment
to the purity of knowing?
to the searing glare of knowing?
to the long clear tone of knowing?
And when knowing

Chapter 15: The Poetry of the Exalted and Transcendent

in itself accumulates to chords
of harmonies beyond conception
of what purpose is the babble?
What purpose an accompaniment of sand
in these billowings of stellar intervals?

If every thought in every lifetime
could be captured and redacted
polished by the master poet
until each syllable resounds
with natural perfection and evocative grace
charged with meaning
filled with unexpected insight—
no matter.
All this fantastic tapestry of mind
is only thoughts.
Not knowing.

The Egrets

Henry Robert Hau

Published in *For the Bird Sings*, by Henry Robert Hau.

Chapter 15: The Poetry of the Exalted and Transcendent

In a Floridian sky
Lord!

I heard their silence

And leaped from my pond chair
To see them

There, above the stellar pines

All white, sacred and seven

A Hymn to the Moon-Mother

Brother Ludovico

> *FAIR LAMP of night, its ornament and friend,*
> *Who giv'st to Nature's works their destined end,*
> *Queen of the stars, all-wise Selene, hail!*
> *Decked with a graceful robe and ample veil!*
> *Come, blessed Goddess, prudent, starry, bright,*
> *Come celestial Lamp, with chaste and splendid light,*
> *Shine on these sacred rites with prosp'rous rays,*
> *And pleas'ed, accept Thy suppliants' mystic praise!*
>
>> Orpheus: *Hymn To The Moon*
>> — Onomacritus
>> 6th Century B.C. Greek

> *For sucklings of all the savage beasts that lurk in the lonely places, Thou hast sympathy!*
>> — Aeschylus
>> Chorus from *"Agamemnon"*

> *Time.....is a moving image of Eternity.*
>> — Plato: *The Timaeus*

> *Understand that you are another little world, and have within you the sun, the moon, and also the stars.*
>> — Origen
>> Third Century AD

Chapter 15: The Poetry of the Exalted and Transcendent

LAMP
    of Heaven! *Mansion* of the Angels!
O *Thou* who weep'st silver tears of light
Into the gaping maws of primal *Night*,
Till like a virgin snow, night's dark throat spangles!
Thee I invoke, *Thou Governess* of tides,
    And seedtimes, of omens and taboos,
    Of prophets' dreams, and lunatic desires,
Thou Arbitress of coronations, feasts, and ides,
    Brimming the pitcher and cistern with honeydews,
    Enkindling brute bloods with celestial *fire*,
    Until the wolf, the lynx, the owl,
    Adore *Thy Throne* with savage screech and howl!
Thee I invoke, O mystical *Mistress Moon!*
    Mover of tides! *Drencher* of dews! *Sweller* of buds!
Mother of moods, fertilities, and rheums,
    Who stir'st the milks and semens of *Life's* bloods,
Rousing the dormant phallus, to plough and plant the fallow womb!

GODDESS!
    mothering a *Foundling* of dew and dust,
    Laid on a planet's steps by *secret Hands*,
    An *Angel* sleeping, to th' stars flesh-waked as *Man!*
Thou, who distilled into stilled blood a wanderlust
To sail blue seas, fill vales with herd and husbandry,
    Initiating the rites of *wedlock, birth,* and *burial,*
    Foretelling famines and tantrums of the seasons!
Thou, an *hourglass* tallying *Eternity*,
    Whose sands of sparkling silver, first made *visible*,
    Time's swiftest sifting *stuff* to the *Child of Reason*,
    That *Man* might mete and measure,
    His fleeting moments of pain and pleasure!
Hail, *Goddess Mother! Instructress* of cycles and of phases!
Telling the tiller when to yoke the strong ox-team!
The huntsman, when to flush the boar from the greenwood's mazes!
The fisher, when to harvest the salmon-fruited streams!
The maiden, when to lower her veil, and surrender her virgin graces!

This Enduring Gift

WHEN
      kindled new the dawn-fires of *beginning*,
  First trembling the sleeping *Garden of the Earth*,
  Night's Womb first quivering, conceiving *light's birth*,
  Its simple naked *Glory*, pristinely shimmering
On waxen foliage, glossy berry, silkiest petal,
    Purging the turbid ethers to rare *Revelation*,
      Night's murky *Well*, stirred limpid to a *Still Knowing*;
When bloods of stones, plants, beasts, quickened with a *Miracle*,
    That deafened darkness blind with *Realization*;
Earth's soils and stones, diamonded to sheer glowing,
    Prismatic with wave, breeze, and thunder,
    That singing woke from antediluvian slumber;
Then! Then first rose o'er mountains, forests, deserts, seas,
  Thy *Flambeau* burnishing bright the ebony-bosomed night!
A *Rose*, nimbused with fire and gold resplendency!
  God's Eye, now opened, with *Love's Transcendental Light*,
Sparkling *Earth's* blades and blossoms, with the *Universe's Divinity!*

WHEN
    first, *Moon-Mother, Ye* sowed with pearly beams
  The delta fecundity of virgin Night,
  Inseminating, with tears of a mother Light,
  A world darkling, waking the children of Earth's Dream,
Then from hill, wood, and crystal spring, Life's worship sprang!
  The Alleluias of brutish snarl, and howl, and roar!
    The babbling brook! Humming bees! Lilting breeze!
The grasses hissed, croaked, buzzed, and teeming flowering sang!
    Mammoths unearthed! Porpoises leapt! The eagle soared!
Bare boughs bloomed gowns of fruit-gemmed greenery!
    The moth, new-hatched from its cocoon,
      Up-flutter'd first-martyred to Thy Candle's noon!
Then first the fishes, enamoured with Thy lucent lure,
  Splashed in the brooks and pools! Then first dared leap
The hare! First bound the stag! Slug and sly serpent stirred!
  First flocks of nightingales, like midnight virgins sweet,
With sweetest tender throats, choired dulcet anthems vestal pure!

Chapter 15: The Poetry of the Exalted and Transcendent

THEN,
>   from dark grottoes, and deepest forest-hearts,
>   Next roused that lordliest *one* of all *Earth's* kindes,
>   *His* blood, a carnal tide, drawn by *Thy Smile Divine*,
>   To know what rapture thrilled night's sullen dark!
> *Conscious*, as no creature other, the *human Child*,
>   From shadows stepped, rapt with *Thy goddess Wonder*,
>   Bathed and new-baptized in *Thy* luminous *dawn*,
> *His* nerves, new-tingl'd with new *fire*, thawed by beams more mild,
>   Dispelling dreaming ghosts from his ancient slumbers!
>   *Man-lions*, tamed to the timidity of fawns!
>   On hills, cliffs, shores, knelt silhouettes
>   Anoint'd with rarer *Will*, stilled statuesque
> In *God's* own *Gaze*; enamoured, divinely mesmerized,
>   Communing with that *Light* that summed the hosts of stars!
> Their bloods fomenting, urging them to ritualize,
>   To invoke *The Invisible Presence* all things visibly *Are*!
> Dancing and drumming, till mere flesh, prone to *Spir't*, is *miraculized*!

IN
>   exile, war, or sojourn, each tribe of *men*
>   Has lift'd their hearts to *Thee*, O radiant *Mother*!
>   Consulting *Thine Oracle* as no earthly other,
>   Yet beholding *Thy Deity* with varied ken!
> Espying *Thee* enthroned, in battle or parade,
>   As *huntress, cloistress, charioteeress*! Mounting mountains
>   Of stars with sail-cloths, ox-carts, chariots,
> Drawn by each sort of beast-team through the *Milky Way*!
>   Some, seeing silver stags! Others, wing-hoofed stallions,
>   With manes and fetlocks flaming! Or snowy bullocks,
>   Yoked with gay ribbons unto rustic wagons!
>   Leashed lions, some! Some, lightning-breathing dragons!
> Peacocks, celestial tortoises, fishes, writhing snakes,
>   Haling *Thee* through the wilds of heavenly dominion!
> O here! Here where flesh withers, and the proud heart breaks,
>   Where kingdoms crumble with the pins of *Man's* opinions,
> *Earth's* each *Man-child* with *hope, doubt, dream*, adores *Thy* beaming *Face*!

SING,
      Muses, the *Moon-Mother's* constant inconstant glory!
   Her glowing tablets, *Man's* laws; *Her* dreams, *Man's* dreams!
    The waxing and waning of *Her* lustrous *being!*
     Guiding the odyssey of each *man's* quest and story!
   Her ripening sickle silvering, sweetliest suckling
      The fig and olive, the gourd-hung vine, the she-goat's udders!
       Sprouting th' acorn's kernel! Gestating the calf and foal!
 A fortnight to transplant, sow, shear, graft, breed, wean!
       Her maiden *Smile,* a midwife for travailing mothers!
     Herding oysters, through shelly canyons of blue shoals!
      Yeasting the garlic bulbs in garden-dusts,
      Crazing tamed lovers mad with animal lusts!
And as *Her* waxing, sing the waning of *Her* veiling *Face!*
Her wan farewell, death's *deathless* tolling, when widows mourn,—
 When 'tis auspicious to scythe, mulch, prune the rioting grapes,—
   To salt the fish and kill, fell timbers, geld and dehorn!
When *men's* dreams fade, dissolving to a dark and *dreamless place!*

HYMN
    Her full Glory, as ye extol *Her Dark!*
   Her Queening, even as *Her Throne's* abdication!
  Two *Wells of One Light!* Both, *Earth's sanctification!*
 One, fires and dews; the other, a *still pool* in *Her Heart!*
Laud the gold *day-god's* silver *Bride! Her* hymeneal,
  Each candle in the amphitheatre of stars!
   Come, Angels! Stomp with *Man* the purple-blooded grape!
Apple, quince, mushroom, with the ox-eyed daisy cull!
  Sing *Earth's* each heart, dreaming for what their *spirits Are!*
    Each seed in soil and flesh, famished for *Light's* embrace!
     Huntsman and herdsman, the hermit like the lover,
      Wild for *Her manna,* as bees are for clover!
The princess, stepping from the gown let fall to her feet,
 In moonbeams bathing, to swell her bosom for her lord!
Now! The mistletoe's red berries, with jeweled sickles reap!
  Christen the cradle-hood! Anoint the battle-sword!
With *Light's* spread wings, swaddle the belly swelling with *Man's* seed!

CHAPTER 15: THE POETRY OF THE EXALTED AND TRANSCENDENT

WITH
 fruit'd and fatt'd gifts, with timbrel, chant, and pipe,
 Men have *Thy maiden-mother Light* invoked!
 At hilltop temples, under ivy-holy oaks,
 On seashores, deep in glades, high on craggy heights!
 Slaying tusked boars, milk-white bulls, mighty rams!
 Gilt dovecotes offering *Thy* glittering groves!
 With oaten cakes, honeyed apples, wine libations,
 Lilies and loaves and sheaves, with the flower-garlanded lamb,
 Propitiating that *Light* that through *Thee* glows,
 Filling frail bosoms with *Immortal Intimation!*
 Stupendous stones erecting, as earthly dials,
 To measure the seasons of *Thy celestial Smile!*
 Soothsayer, priest, and priestess, agelessly worshipping
 Eclipses, solstices, equinoxes at *Thy* shrines!
 Thy devotees, ringed 'bout their altar-fettered queen,
 Her virgin thighs promiscuously bloomed, like wings sublime,
 To be impregnated with the sparkling *seed* of *Thy pure Beam!*

SING!
 Muses! Sing the *Moon-Mother's* cyclic phases!
 The mystic lovely laws of seed, flower, fruit!
 Life's ages *Parable*, of universal *Truth*,
 That ripens *Whole, Man's Soul*, through its death-dark ages!
 Sing, Angel Muses! With flute, zither, lyre!
 Sing the unveiling of the *Moon-Bride's Smile!*
 Her coyest crescent, lushly blushing *Light's Rebirth!*
 Sound the conch! Gong! Tabor! Kindle the hill's bonfire!
 Exalt *Light's Kiss*, that each creature's heart beguiles,
 Enrapturing with *Hope*, the buds and dreams of *Earth!*
 Hail! *Princess!* From night's sepulcher arisen!
 Hail! *Goddess!* Who with the *Bread of Angels* christens!
 Lead goat and calf a-pasture! Burnish the plough-share bright!
 Cull the wild tansy, poppy, and the cyclamen!
 Hoist sails up oaken masts! Augur the infidel's flight!
 The fruit-tree graft! The fennel, thyme, and dill-seed plant!
 Once more the *Moon-Mother smiles*, sowing the *Promise of Her Light!*

IDOLATRY
    is not idolatry,
  When the *Image* worshipped,— be it god, bull, or maiden,
Is hallowed with a *Light* no chisel's graven,
A violet, sweet-trumpeting an *Eternity*
That blinds the seer's eye, and blasts the hearer's ear,
  Until *Man's Soul*, denuded of its senses,
    Suspends in *Silence* deafened with *Light's Presence!*
A shaft that sunders tombs, and th' stoniest temple sears!
    Surrendered to a *State* defeating all defenses,
  Drunk with a *Wind*, that is *Life's* vial of *Essence!*
    Beyond the veils of idols' marble smiles,
    A *Lover, who* each virgin prayer beguiles,
A *Kingdom*, beyond the crumbling churchyards of the flesh!
A *Tide*, that *Timeless* over this world's threshold bleeds,
Whose *Blood Invisible, Is* a sweet tongue licking blest!
  Man, drowned in *That*, with which *he* may at last breathe!
Light's Angel, glimmering, through a midnight ancient in *Man's* breast!

NIGHT'S
    Gypsy! Mesmerizing with *Thy Medallion*,
  Dangled before *Earth's* pastures, like an amulet,
Man's Heart entrancing, with the myths of *Time* and *Death*,
That we of flesh, bone, and dream, wild as the first stallions,
Might heavenly hearken to *Earth's* holiest *Parable!*
    O lull us with the lullaby of *Thy cosmic dream!*
    Attune us with the cyclic phases of *Thy Heart!*
Yea, from first cusps and crescents, to Thy harvests *full's!*
    That *Man* might *Be* the *Image* of *his Imageless Being!*
  His soul *Awakening* from a deep primeval *dark!*
      Like seeds, tides, seasons, *men's* bloods and minds
      Obeying the rhythms of *Thy laws divine!*
Impart, *Moon*, to the *moon* of *Man's Heart, Thy mysteries!*
  The *Chorus* hymning through the wails of birth and death!
The coexistence of *Time* and *Eternity!*
  The withering of flesh, the blossoming of breath!
The *Light* that flowers through *Man's* ashes with *Divinity!*

Chapter 15: The Poetry of the Exalted and Transcendent

TEACH
    us *Thy* mystic fires burn sacred in *Man's* flesh,
  As atoms are anvils hammered in each star!
  Each seed, pregnant with cycles, of what all things *Are!*
  The *Heartbeat of the Universe*, warbled in *Man's* breast!
Teach *Man* the crystal firmament of *Man's Soul*,
  Mirrors each pebble and orbit of *Life's Scheme!*
  The cosmology of soil, worm, bloom, bird, Sun,
  Birthing the babe of *Man's Heart*, till it screams forth *Whole!*
    God's Fist, breaking Man's ribs with an *Angel's wings*,
  Blooming from ages of ache, a *kingdom Ever come!*
  The spark of a flint, fanned by wings,
    Purging *Earth's* pall with the flame of dream!
Bleed through *Man's Heart, O Moon*, the *Smile* that *Is Man's Breath!*
Both as it wanes with wails and sackcloth unto ashes,
And as it waxes, with its threshing-floors heaped blest!
  Seep *Thy Tide* deep, sweet in the *Sleep* beneath *Man's* lashes,
Flooding *Man's* crypts of *fear*, to drown *his* haunting ghost of *death!*

DIVINE
    sweet *Patroness*, tutor *Man's Soul* to shed
  The winding sheets *Its Angel* has long veiled,
  That *he*, like a melodious nightingale,
  Whose minstrelsies, with *Thy* each coy whim wed,
Pours forth *Love's Mansion* from the thimble of its heart!
  That *Man* might match such *Love!* Die to exhaust
    The *Inexhaustible* welled from his *Heart's springs!*
Smitten with a *Gaze*, abashing worlds of doom and dark!
  That ere *his* dreams, like breaths, are fleeting lost,
  Man might *his moment* in *Eternity* sing!
    Moon-blinded with *Thy Smile* sublime,
    His blood, *moon*-maddened with *Thy Kiss Divine!*
Man's Heart, waked, warbling notes of silver and of gold,
  Drunk with a *Sweetness* that does not wax or wane!
Its *fever*, an *Ecstasy*, to *Thee Moon-Mother* singing told!
  All empires, thrones, and coffers, made void and made vain,
With the *Waking* of the nightingale of *Man's deathless Soul!*

This Enduring Gift

BURN
>>the houses of *Man's* tormented dreams!
>Craze *his* beast to a daisy's sanity!
>Make drunk *his* devils with humility!
>*His temple* ravish with swords of virgin beams!
Combust *Man's* dust to a wild green wheat of fire!
>Trickle through that tomb melting in *Man's* breast,
>>The *Cosmic Consciousness* flooding field and sky!
Free *Man's* chained *Angels* from the hull of *his* desires!
>Evangelize *Man's* demons unto *deathlessness!*
>Drown with *Thy Tide*, the dark mote in *Man's* eye!
>>Bloom, *Moon*, *Man's* creature Full! True! Whole!
>Fulfill the cyclic phases of *Man's* soul!
Imprison *his Instant* bright in *Thy Eternity!*
>*His* toils, *Thy moonbeams*, sowing th' maiden wombs of *Earth!*
Mad with mad rapture, dervishing with *Thy* lunacy,
>Beam through *Man's Heart his* race's *Reason* and *true* worth!
Blanket the cradles of *Man's* graveyards with *Thy Smile's Divinity!*

SING,
>Angels, the *Dark Moon* burning a rarer *Light*,
>That lingers in *Man's Soul* an *Ember* of *Truth's* worth!
>A *Smile*, that *Is* a *Word*, avowing *Light's* rebirth,
>That sparkles skulls, like jewels, on the battlefield of night!
A *Light* to blind the naked eye, to nakedly *Reveal*
>A *bodiless Spir't* embodied in a peasant's *presence!*
>Seeping beneath *death's* shekels, *realms* of *Glory*,
That quickens urns of ashes to honey-hearted wines!
>Splashing no flower, yet drenching each with *Essence!*
>Stunning the prophet dumb with *Silence Revelatory!*
>A barren *Womb*, that through stones bleeds,
>That musters an army in each sleeping seed!
A *Light* first dawning deep in first shepherds' dreams,
>Fermenting *Instinct* through slow eons to *Belief!*
A *Wisdom*, frail as flowers, surrendering to *Heaven's Scheme*,
>The *Alpha* and *Omega* of *Beginningless Endless Being!*
Light's crescent, a chalice, offered *Man's Heart* divinely *Sweet!*

Chapter 15: The Poetry of the Exalted and Transcendent

ILLUMINE
  the ancient darkness in *Man's Heart* and *mind!*
  Cartoon his catacombs with children dreams!
  Bleed through death's shrouds and marble drops of beams!
 Waking *Man's* mummy to its *moment* most *divine!*
From the womb of *Man's cocoon*, bloom an *Angel* long deemed dead!
  With blizzards of *Thy lava* blanket flesh long cold!
   Lover, with murderer, wake warm in arms of Light!
 Eclipse O *Moon* the Sun! Not with locusts of dread,
   But with *that Candle*, quenchless in *Man's Soul*,
   That grants *Man's* blindness a keener kinder *sight!*
    Thaw to the frozen marrow of *Man's Essence!*
    Wake in *his Heart*, a sleeping *Godhead's Presence!*
Drown serpents coiling about the phallus and the womb!
Pumice the crude graffiti from the walls of *Man's heart* scrawled!
 This *Earth's* lost kingdom, with *Man's* new-found *Soul illume!*
  Bring from the caves of *Man*, an *Angel* luminously *full!*
Lead forth that radiant *Child*, who napped for ages in *night's tomb!*

 SING!
  Angel Muses! On ladders of *light* ascend!
  Like budding tendrils trellising, that sunwards climb
   To bloom the treasure of their verdantly-sinewed vine;
  From flesh's roots, lift heavenwards, the *hosannas* of *men!*
  On rungs of alabaster moonbeams scarlet bear
   This moon-flower blossomed from *Man's* bosom's dark,
    That waked with *Glory* from a Winter of death!
  Lay in *Thy* sisters' arms, the thunder of this prayer!
   Accept, *Moon-Mother*, the *moon* of *Man's* bloomed *Heart!*
   That changeling *Thou* did'st nourish in *Man's* breast!
    Suckled with a saturnalia of rites,
    With anthems and bellows of sacrifice!
With virgins' hymens, smoking entrails, fleeces and hides,
 Invoked from every dreaming lover's pillow-fold,
At lambing times, at killing frosts, at harvest-tides,
 An *Image* waxing and waning, till *melted* in *Man's Soul!*
Hail, glorious *Moon-Mother!* Whose *Smile* in *Man's* waked *Heart* abides!

Gates of Dawn

James Tipton

After Kenneth Graham

Chapter 15: The Poetry of the Exalted and Transcendent

At the gates of dawn
They hear the piping and the god
Appears, bearing in his arms
The lost child. They quail
At his feet, themselves lost
In awe and admiration. The
Piping fades as the colors rise.
The river is soundless,
And they remember nothing of
This encounter but a vague memory
Of a song heard at dawn,
Burning at the back of their minds
Like the colors flaring at the horizon,
Like the burning image
Of the compassionate brow
Of the god.

Poem Written Dream-Side

Qin Guan
(Tr. Angela Mailander)

*Translating Chinese Poetry
Without Knowing Chinese*

A poet/translator who works from a language he doesn't know, especially one as different from English as Chinese, draws the poem from depths beyond time, place, and condition, where the original poet also netted it, though, for him, the transformations to land it yielded the surface structure of Chinese, not English.

Like Ezra Pound, the most famous poet/translator to work in this way, such a writer works with a "native informant" who provides a "crib"— that is, a character for character rendition, which often does not result in anything immediately comprehensible in English.

Here, at random, is the crib for a line in a poem:

MOTH SNOW WILLOW GOLD THREAD HAIR NIGHT

No verb in sight, no structure words, nothing to tell what the syntactic relationships among those words could be. The context of the whole poem tells us only that the persona is looking for a girl at a crowded lantern festival in winter. He doesn't find her. But then he says, "I turn: She stands//where light is silent."

Here is how I translate the line: "Moth-**like** snow **in** willows: gold thread **in the** hair **of** night." Accurate? I checked, but there was no need; I was sure. That is the magic that makes such translation possible, the same magic that made Ezra Pound get it right even when his native informant made mistakes.

Published in *Denver Quarterly*, vol. 12, No. 2, Summer 1977, p. 1.

Chapter 15: The Poetry of the Exalted and Transcendent

Spring rain: the path is overrun with flowers;
Flowers stir up the hillside: it swarms with colors.
I walk up-stream and reach the source,
And there's a hundred thousand orioles.

I'm so high clouds fly right by my face,
Bloom into dragons and snakes, and vanish in clear blue;
I'm so high, I lie down under an old wisteria tree,
Where's North? Where's South? Search me...

There are several Chinese cultural symbols in this poem: orioles=subtle, celestial perception; dragon=spring rain, creativity, the emperor, and in this poem especially, the connection between the Absolute and relative spheres of life; snakes=supernatural or siddha powers, especially healing power; wisteria tree=God. The poet, Qin Guan, a Daoist monk, is writing anagoge (i.e. poetic language in which the literal level and the symbolic level coincide in perfect synchronicity and offer expanding commentary on each other). The poem is thus not just about a walk into the mountains after a spring rain, but it also describes the path from ignorance ("the path is overrun with flowers") through transcendence ("I...reach the source") to higher states of consciousness: "Clouds fly...by my face" is an image of witnessing or Cosmic Consciousness; dragons and snakes show what kinds of thoughts (clouds) are being witnessed; "vanish in clear blue" is another image of transcendence, or going beyond even the siddha powers. "I lie down under an old wisteria tree" signifies God-Consciousness; north traditionally signifies heaven, while south signifies earth. "Search me" indicates Unity Consciousness. It may come as a surprise to some that these states of consciousness were known in China. Doubters may consult, for example, *The Practice of Zen* (New York: 1970) by Gharma C.C. C'heng.

Qin Guan, Song-dynasty poet from what is now known as Jiangsu. In 1074, Qin met Su Shi and became his student. After obtaining the jinqu degree at the age of 37, Qin embarked on an official career. However, his association with Su Shi later led to his being given a succession of minor posts. Qin Guan is acclaimed as one of the most outstanding writers of ci song-lyrics of the Northern Song and excelled at poems on the subject of parting and separation.

Unexpected Call

Meredith Briggs Skeath

© Meredith Briggs Skeath, 2003, reprinted with permission from *Soultending*, by Meredith Briggs Skeath (Glanzer Press: Newberry, Florida, 2003).

Chapter 15: The Poetry of the Exalted and Transcendent

As if my love were calling
Come, come to me,
then moving off through olive trees,
I could not see him or hear
his words, only sense the tone
of his longing, how it eddied
the air.

I felt, not words,
but the melted, single yearning one love has
for another. How could God
long for me? I thought all the courting
would be mine to do.

Lovers seek the farthest outcropping
where surf comes, close and cold
with wind-spray mingling their hair
when they bend close, as they must,
to hear each other's words that near
the working sea.
When I close my eyes I think,
this is between God and me, for now
the world can fall away.

Brother Sun Sister Moon

Matthew A. Bovard

Chapter 15: The Poetry of the Exalted and Transcendent

The words flow from my mind with ease,
teasing me along the golden path
as my feet burn to ash.
I am thankful for the heated love
that destroys false flesh
revealing the inner radiance.
Releasing the spirit so it can dance across
the sky with brother sun and sister moon.

At the Speed of God

Michael Hock

> Dedicated to Sri Gary Olsen, current Living Master, and founder of the MasterPath.

Published in *the sky is walking the earth,* by Michael Hock.

Chapter 15: The Poetry of the Exalted and Transcendent

Between night and day
the moment comes.
It comes like a misting rain,
like the ceasing of
some long held pain.
The moment comes
in the scent of lilac on the wind,
a light shining out
from a stranger's eyes,
in the sound of those people talking,
the noise of traffic.
The moment comes in my dreams.
Even when I flail myself
it comes as a distant thunder.
The moment comes,
as I sit listening, intent,
my attention dancing upon Your words,
lifting, enfolding, blessing.
The moment comes
and I swoon in Your love.
It is You, it is me.
At the edge of forever,
the moment comes.

The Poetry of Transition, Surprise, and Ascension

Chapter 16

*Everything must end;
meanwhile we must amuse ourselves.*

— Voltaire, French writer and philosopher (1694-1778)

Contents

644	The Citadel	*Tom Le May*
646	Death Is Coming	*Charlie Hopkins*
648	Shards of Future	*Jason Walls*
650	Lyrebird Song	*Janet Thomas*
652	The Flight	*Libbett Rich*
654	Death's Inheritance	*Brother Ludovico*
658	Days Are Short	*Gale Park*
660	A Man Will Abandon His Face	*Charlie Hopkins*
664	Salaat	*Elizabeth McIsaac*
666	Columbia	*Nancy Berg*
670	Icarus' Lover's Dream	*Andrew Josephs*
672	Consider the Tracks	*Tom Le May*
674	For the Life of Me	*Tom Kepler*
676	View #2	*Thomas Centolella*
678	When a Vessel Breaks	*Patricia Regan Argiro*
680	Near Lindos, Rhodes	*Allen Cobb*
682	Sat Guru	*Michael Hock*
684	When My Body Dies	*Sharalyn Harris*
686	Falling	*Gale Park*
688	When I Lay Down My Treasures	*William Clair Godfrey*
690	Fire Dance - An Invocation of the Light	*Freddy Niagara Fonseca*

*Once the game is over, the king
and the pawn go back into the same box.*

— Italian Proverb

Chapter 16
The Poetry of Transition, Surprise, and Ascension

This passing of reality itself is real...This too is an experience of the soul.
— Kathleen Raine, English poet (1908-2003)

A day will come when we'll leave our problems and worries behind. No one knows what it is like to die, but there's one thing on which we can all agree. If there is a Hereafter, a Heaven, a Nirvana, then there must be a meeting place between Now and Then.

Is that the realm where we come to appreciate everything? Every person, every poem we never comprehended?

Who but the Master Poet will meet us there to receive our ample words of praise — the poems we wrote; the many ideas of a lifetime we infused in our lines, songs, couplets, sonnets, epics; hymns to flowers, trees, grass, rocks, gazelles, birds; odes to clouds, friends, lovers, cities, stars, comets; to mom, dad, you, me, and all who ever were with us?

And as we're finally entering that place we can't describe in words....

This, too, is an experience of the soul....

The Citadel

Tom Le May

Chapter 16: The Poetry of Transition, Surprise, and Ascension

Your approach will be seen from far away —
leagues, really.
Your habits will be studied and correlated.
After breaking camp each morning, your camp fires
will be raked through to see what you've eaten,
what you've discarded or if prayers have been offered.
The broad plains will start to rise slowly
and paths will begin to twist
and become stony.
Which paths you choose will be noted.

And as you rise you'll be challenged
at the first of the checkpoints.
You'll probably pass through to continue on.
And soon the outer wall of the citadel will loom over you.
Not everyone can enter through the outer wall but maybe,
just maybe, you might make it within.
But then there's the moat to cross
and the inner wall which is higher than the first, outer wall.
And within that inner wall is the tower which rises up and up.
And within that tower are stairs descending
to the silent, cold chambers within the mountain itself,
where the hoard is kept in the stronghold.

Now,
if you crane your neck you'll see,
at the very top of the tower above you,
my devoted and wary eye constant upon you.
And if you pass through the guards and are allowed to go down
the stone passageways,
lit only by the occasional flickering sconce,
in one of the silent, cool chambers
you will find my beating child's heart,
kept at a strictly regulated ambient temperature,
ensconced upon an embroidered pillow,
undisturbed by love.

Death Is Coming

Charlie Hopkins

Chapter 16: The Poetry of Transition, Surprise, and Ascension

When it reaches me there will be a marigold of fire
brilliant as an eye opening in my hand.

There will be a light rain of singing
as I am carried down river in a boat of leaves.

When I die there will be one second of fear
as when Carol reaches out at night
to lay her hand on the soft of my throat.
Fear will leave that quickly
as when she rolls against me in our bed.

Even now I hear a voice like three creeks woven into one
with a skin of ice across it.
I see a circle of river rock with a fire burning inside it like an open
eye.

This is one kind of happiness.

Shards of Future

Jason Walls

Chapter 16: The Poetry of Transition, Surprise, and Ascension

Looking up temporarily
From the smell of sweet bean soup

I smile at the times I'll share
Discussing Jasmine tea
With my wrinkled Grandfather, on tatami mats
Behind beige shoji screens

I'll gaze upon staid, imperial processions
With Cherry blossoms scattered on the scene
Falling in a drawn-out way:
Even slowing the steps
Of servants bearing a palanquin

Picturesque

I'll meet a middle aged farmer
With arms knitting into vegetables:
Her words will bloom
Like warm clothes tumbling from a dryer

I'll come across a shy store
Where a plum and an abacus
Talk to each other;
From somewhere, vibrations of a shamisen
Will saturate us like rain

And a boy
With the smile of a pagoda
Looked into the distance
At a slightly worn Go board
Holding pieces of an unfinished game

Lyrebird Song

Janet Thomas

Published in *Leaves by Night, Flowers by Day.*

Chapter 16: The Poetry of Transition, Surprise, and Ascension

I was born near a forest of rags
where gum leaves droop in blistering sun;
and crackling dryness
starves whistling kites, flying foxes,
and frill-necked lizards.

Learning to love like a lyrebird,
I mimicked wattlebirds, lorikeets,
and empty-headed cockatoos.
Tea-time laughter came in white china cups,
familiar antidote to life's sudden venom.

But the day my mother died,
my tongue floated in blood.
Blind words became rumbling rocks,
thrown at darkened windows.

A barrage of bellbirds splintered
the silver spittle of siblings
at her grave.
And when we planted a single boronia
in the orange ground,
a lyrebird sang the rain.

The Flight

Libbett Rich

Chapter 16: The Poetry of Transition, Surprise, and Ascension

The flight begins
I am a seagull
dipping into the sea
for a fish as big as myself
picking up sand in my mouth
stuffing and soaring
but not too long

for an eagle with large wing span
has taken me
and I am protecting my egg in my claws
he is soaring and singing
gliding toward the sun

through mountains of white clouds
following a wind current
we swoop and slide

Suddenly I am dropped
down to the cool water
Safe
I flip on my back
to sun myself

I float in the calm sea
with a belly as big as a walrus

Death's Inheritance

Brother Ludovico

Chapter 16: The Poetry of Transition, Surprise, and Ascension

I

BENEATH THIS SHROUD OF SNOW

An Elegy For My Father
Composed January 8, 2009

BENEATH
    this shroud of snow a heart beats *Still*,
  That fills my breast with lamplight of the Sun;
In these cold bones, and this stopped blood a *Will*,
  Fevering my veins with *Love's Dominion*.
This marble's not my father's monument;
  'Tis the grass, doubling its fists to claw forth Spring,
This grave's no grave, but a throne, whose spleen still vents
  Stern soldier ghosts into my fortune's dreams.
This man was the poem I shall never write.
  In his blunt acts, the meters, rhymes, and verses
That transcribed to *Time's* page poor flesh's rights;
  Within his hammers, tirades, and whiskey curses,
A harp of gold that warbled most when hell it most amused;
Beneath this shroud of snow, sings on my one most noble *muse*.

II

NOW WOULD BE THE LOVELIEST TIME TO CEASE

Composed On A Summer's Afternoon
At The Old MacMillan Place

NOW,
     now would be the loveliest time to cease!
  To hush the echoing hammer of heartbeats,
To deep inhale, from the hookah of this breeze,
  Whose melodies waft, somniferously sweet,
Through the leafy lispings of these cottonwoods;
    To drain this day's wine, drugged with Summery dream,
Poisoned by daisies smiling in henchman hoods,
  Preferring Earth's orgy, to the promise of wings.
To cease, know no more, with death's vial, sip
  Its hemlock seasoned like a honeycomb,
Feeling, as a mother's feathery fingertips,
  On one's eyelids the coins of death's millstones.
At Life's most vulnerable instant: whisper, smile, and nod,
Confessing to flower and cloud: *"I loved thee more than God"*.

III

FIRST FROST

NO
    death mask, nor a mummy's moth-less shroud
  Bandaged o'er bust and hips of *Pharaoic* flesh;
Rather, the crystallizing of a cloud,
  Into a frozen dew dimensionless;
No butcher, mimicking a mad-gone surgeon,
  Who smothers cradles, royal blood-lines freezes,
Rather, *Lust's* heartbeat stilling to a praying virgin,
  Fading till the final cricket's last chirp ceases.
Stillness, frozen in the warm *Womb* of things;
  Not death, but *Life*, melting to its age of rest;
Not Summer's last gasped hour, but *Time's Beginning*;
  No glacial entombment, but a baptism blest;
Ending coquettish roses, and carousing pagan bees;
The winding sheet of death, swaddling all in *Eternity*.

IV

MY BURIAL

I AM
    Being buried in a boundless *Tomb*,
  Deep in a *Silence* that *Awakes* the dead,
Not lowered, but *transcended*, to a doom,
    Where lovers estranged by death, are *deathlessly* wed.
The hinges of this sepulcher groan, shut, lock;
  Its vault, a planetarium *Within*,
The nails of th' stars, driven through boards to rot,
    And drown with *Seas of Light* the dust of sin.
I hear the wailing echoes of the Ages,
  Those widowed of *Love*, those beggared of *Love's* bread,
Ghosts, carnivaling with masks, like rats in mazes,
    Streets of the living, which are streets of the dead.
I am being buried in a *Tomb*, boundlessly, blessedly *Alive*,
Into *That*, which, when Gibraltars crumble, *Its Kingdom* shall survive.

Days Are Short

Gale Park

© Gale Park, 1998.

Chapter 16: The Poetry of Transition, Surprise, and Ascension

A chunk of firewood falls onto the grate
    With a thump
The old man closes the stove door
    Carefully
And adjusts the draft.
It must not burn too fast.

He hoards the wood like his life;
Conserving it,
Burning just one stick at a time.

Enough to keep the chill off.
Not enough to sap the supply.

The winter days are short.
The time of dark drags on.
He sleeps in snatches during the day,
Dresses for bed seriously,
But it's hard for him to sleep long.
His bladder wakes him up.

It is just as well.
The fire might go out.

A Man Will Abandon His Face

Charlie Hopkins

Chapter 16: The Poetry of Transition, Surprise, and Ascension

There was a story my mother told me of a dust storm
in Lubbock, Texas before the war.
Cattle caught in a depression went sand blind
and the green was scoured from 4-door sedans.
But now I am nobody's son.

I am not the boy who fell from the roof of a three-story building
and lived.

From where I lie
I can see the moon like the horns of a bull
and the last star of morning.
But I am not the one who ran with red colts in the field;
who ran with calves kicking up their polished hooves.
I am not the bull with the moon caught in his horns.

There are voices fine as yellow thread that want to call us back saying,
"We know who you are."

Don't listen to them.

Sometimes in early morning I hear my father's voice
drawn from the well he dug by hand through cold volcanic stone.
I hear his words coughed up with smoke and phlegm and red East Texas
clay.

My father's eyes were fields of purple hulled peas
split by a line of thorn tree and sweet gum
with a wave of air running through them.
His anger was one hundred acres of feed corn molded in the husk.

Now I am no body's son.
I am fire burning in a pan of water.

The smokehouse door has fallen from its leather hinges.
The moon has set in the horse pasture where a thousand
blue bottles were thrown.

These memories I put into the ground and smooth them over
with my hand.

This Enduring Gift

We are able to cut the threads that bind us.
We are able to live without idea of who we are.
A man can rise in early morning from the dead
and walk like Christ into the light of day!

A man can abandon his face and have his eyes be everywhere;
become the sky unfurrowed in all directions;
not perceive himself as separate from the blow fly,
or the morning glory vine!
Not care to be less than everything he sees, hears, smells, tastes.
Not care to be more!

I want to go where there is not a whirlwind, not a column of smoke to guide me
where I am ash
and the moon comes down to look me eye to eye.

That is where you find me
one grain of sand tumbling against another.

What I have to show for sixty years of breathing
is the swell of you inside me.
I belong to you.

Chapter 16: The Poetry of Transition, Surprise, and Ascension

Salaat*

Elizabeth McIsaac

*Prayer

Published in *A Sun Palette of Song'ans, Book II*, by Elizabeth McIsaac.

Chapter 16: The Poetry of Transition, Surprise, and Ascension

The sun kissed the mountain
— it smiled gold.

The moon whispered to the mountain
— it laughed pearls.

The rain whistled to the mountain
— it sang silver bells.

I climbed the mountain
— fool's gold.

I climbed the mountain
—faux pearls.

I climbed the mountain
— phantom bells.

I dreamed.

Leaving behind the gold, the pearls, the silver
— I became the sun, the moon, the rain.

I awoke.

Leaving behind the sun, the moon, the rain
— I disappeared.

Columbia

Nancy Berg

Published in *Oracles for Night-Blooming Eccentrics,* by Nancy Berg.

Chapter 16: The Poetry of Transition, Surprise, and Ascension

We should have known by their faces
when they floated on TV—
they had fallen irrevocably in love
with weightlessness.
Blue shirts above,
red shirts below,
they tangled arms and hovered,
a formation reminiscent
of the painted sacred heart.
This was 300-Proof elation,
as rare, almost, as green lips
in genuine grownups.

Four virgins,
three second-timers—
here were seven grateful astronauts
who could hardly believe their luck.
The closest they had come to this rapture
had never been terribly close:
Kalpana from the Punjab
chasing rivers in her small plane,
the Navy flight surgeon spinning, flipping,
that unlikely year before med school
when he briefly dazzled crowds in a circus.
But here, as operatic sunset
filled the overhead flight deck windows,
each could see their own reflection,
and superimposed on one's own mirrored pupil,
the bright and dark sides of the earth, in whole,
with all the endless sky around it.

Red sprites and blue tendrils
awaken the fringes of night;
electrical cousins of lightning
flashing up instead of down.
Roses smell different in space,
yet travel quite easily from bud to bloom.
Silkworms hatch into moths,
puffing out redundant wings.
Without earth's magnetic field,

flames are no longer shaped like teardrops.
The crew sets tiny bouncing fireballs,
dousing them easily with simple fog.
Huge clouds of dust arise and disperse
far, far above the west coast of Africa.
Willie McCool smoothly levitates
to capture a flying spoon with his mouth.
And the crystalline blue marble
finely mottled white with clouds
looks so gentle without borders,
the Aurora Australis
spraying earthshine at the moon.

After 16 days they'd found their space legs,
and who among us could bear to relinquish this?
Who among us could bear to return
where every thought is set in stone?
Strapped tight in orange pressure suits,
the seven as one divested themselves
of their last remaining burden of gravity.

Just four days before the blazing,
Florida Today ran this headline:
"Columbia's Astronauts Find Small Miracles
of Life and Light."
Small miracles, we've heard,
can be especially addictive.
The first one may be free,
but soon you crave bigger and bigger miracles,
signs and wonders all around you.
A vault of light is wide and deep,
and the Helix Nebula, we understand,
is anything but overrated.

Chapter 16: The Poetry of Transition, Surprise, and Ascension

Icarus' Lover's Dream

Andrew Josephs

Chapter 16: The Poetry of Transition, Surprise, and Ascension

Rise to meet me
as I rise
to meet You.
Hold these tired wings;
still these trembling hands
until they come together
finally
to Silence.

(Love is acrophobic bliss.)
We hold each other as we free-fall
through time
in fear of possible pain
in the probable end
and in hope that the power of our gain
in embrace
will cause a suspension
in time and space
for us to love
right there.

Out of habit
we are so upside down
that when we feel love
we feel falling
when it is obvious we are rising
and spinning
to hold and point each other
head and heart first
to meet our shining God.

Consider the Tracks

Tom Le May

Chapter 16: The Poetry of Transition, Surprise, and Ascension

Consider the corroded railroad tracks
that lie behind this building, this old converted factory
where the assembly line hummed long ago,
smacked down in the middle of this Great Plains prairie.
Just a small spur really, a weather-eaten siding that simply
switches off of the principal rails,
the patient, dusty connection.

Now consider the main tracks stretched out, beckoning
like a lover's arms held open and wide, smooth and shining
traveling to the horizon east and west,
then disappearing into the vanishing points:
the vanishing points like mirages: always hopeful.

How I long to ride those rails. Not as a hobo or some other
romantic figure...Old Bill Jones led a hard life after all...
But I wish to board a coach or a freight car — it doesn't matter —
and rattle my white bones out of here,
flying all the way to the wild foaming ocean

to refresh myself in the elements —
the salt spray
the wind
the sun
the sky with its eternal play of clouds,
its myriad of stars and moon.

Every man of an age thinks of death now and again,
perhaps trying it on for size
as if it were a sharp pressed new suit of clothes
he's considering buying.
Looking into the mirror he's pleased,
hopeful.

Sometimes I too long to say my final prayers.
A carnation in my lapel,
I will Hallelujah myself into oblivion,
sing Hosanna Omega Amen.

For the Life of Me

Tom Kepler

Published in *Bare Ruined Choirs,* by Tom Kepler.

Chapter 16: The Poetry of Transition, Surprise, and Ascension

The hardest time for me
was when I told you
your mother was going to die.

Mauve walls and stainless steel chairs,
that sterile, hermetic hospital hum—
your silence as you pruned into tears.

Wondering, for the life of me, why
I couldn't keep your mother from dying—
I, who had done everything for ten years,

who could now do nothing but sit,
watching my restless, empty hands
awkward in their awful leisure,

no metaphors at hand, only this image—
father and son holding one another,
holding on by letting go.

View #2

Thomas Centolella

Published in *Views from Along the Middle Way,* by Thomas Centolella.

Chapter 16: The Poetry of Transition, Surprise, and Ascension

It was just one task to recover the taken-for-granted.
There were others. Such as: simply recover.

And then? And then consider
there's no time off for good behavior,

that the city was a carnival of incandescent streets
but also a dim labyrinth, that the beloved bridge

connecting two wonders of solid ground
provided as well a jumping off point

for those who had lost heart.
That some roads, no matter how far

they take you, will double back.
And then? And then consult the window

for weather. Put on some clothes
and good intentions. Begin again.

When a Vessel Breaks

Patricia Regan Argiro

Published in *Spheres,* by Patricia Regan Argiro.

Chapter 16: The Poetry of Transition, Surprise, and Ascension

When a vessel
breaks,
it is quite possible
to mend it.

But the cracks will show.
And what, oh what
became of the sweet, clear
liquid it contained?

Spilled.
Slipped away.
Irrevocably
soaked back into earth.

Underland,
it travels
to a new
spring.

Near Lindos, Rhodes

Allen Cobb

Published in *Cave Paintings,* by Allen Cobb.

Chapter 16: The Poetry of Transition, Surprise, and Ascension

I walked with an ancient seer
across a wooden bridge
in a shaded forest glade
above a brook

there were others

we stood in silence
then we clapped our hands
ten thousand thousand tiny butterflies
arose from branches
all around us
fluttering in the air
filling the glade in a white cacophony
of aery movement

then they were still
gone to hide again
beneath the leaves

Sat Guru

Michael Hock

> Dedicated to Sri Gary Olsen, current Living Master, and founder of the MasterPath.

Published in *the sky is walking the earth*, by Michael Hock.

Chapter 16: The Poetry of Transition, Surprise, and Ascension

a mighty river
resounds throughout the cosmos.
I am quickened
by the hope of all hopes.
I know He has come.
the sky is walking on the earth

a timeless passage
beckons in my secret chamber.
I am aroused
from my deepest slumber.
I hear Him gently calling.
the sky is walking on the earth.

a ceaseless tide rises
welling deep within my being.
I set my course
with the winds of heaven.
I know He has come for me.
the sky is walking on the earth.

When My Body Dies

Sharalyn Pliler

Chapter 16: The Poetry of Transition, Surprise, and Ascension

When my body dies
The sun will shine undimmed
Over marigolds still bursting into bloom
In unabashed joy,
Flash pearls and rainbows in the sea spray
Over the slick backs of porpoises at play,
And glint like gold from the windows of skyscrapers
Where inside the work does not stop.

On the other side of this spinning globe
The moon will cast soft silver and shadow
Over lovers who do not cease making love
When the last breath passes my lips,
Over the sweet faces of children whose sleep goes undisturbed
And over solemn and stately mountains
Which note no one's passing.

Down the street the junkman
Will keep niggling for rags and tatters
As he has for as long as anyone remembers,
But what small prize would keep me behind?
Were I not eternal,
Would not the very stars expire
When these mortal eyes close?

June 9, 1996

Falling

Gale Park

© Gale Park, 1997.

Chapter 16: The Poetry of Transition, Surprise, and Ascension

Brilliant sun-cured leaves
Adorn the trees
Spicy smells from fall flowers
explode in the cooler air.

A showy thing—the escape of summer,
A defiant act in the face of gray death.

Tomorrow rain will strip the trees of their hosannas
And their bare, twisted knuckles
Will rattle at the heavens.

Their old, creaking bodies will slowly slide into sleep,
And dream awhile
In whiteness,
And dark.

When I Lay down My Treasures at the End of the Trail

William Clair Godfrey

Tune: Polka rhythm

Published in *Lyrical Iowa*.

Chapter 16: The Poetry of Transition, Surprise, and Ascension

When I lay down my treasures at the end of the trail
And I leave them, Good Bye, in the dew.
I know all of life's other treasures will pale
Beside those that I shared with you.

When I unroll the scroll of my life in a line
And I follow it into the blue
I will come to the place where you said you'd be mine,
And I'll walk hand in hand there with you.

Through the flowers in the meadow, the spray on the sea,
The stars in the infinite blue,
Past all of life's pleasures that you shared with me,
The glory that I knew with you.

We will enter the Palace and kneel at the throne
In the light of the Heavenly sun.
With our lips to the chalice, taking you as my own,
We will go on forever as one.

Through the flowers in the meadow, the spray on the sea....

Fire Dance - An Invocation of the Light

Freddy Niagara Fonseca

> *Human beings, vegetables, or cosmic dust, we all dance to a mysterious tune intoned in the distance by an invisible player.*
> — Albert Einstein

Chapter 16: The Poetry of Transition, Surprise, and Ascension

I

Glow, fire, glow!
Whisper, crackle, shimmer!
Grow, fire, grow, grow!
Sparkle, illumine, glimmer!
Soar, fire, soar!
Soar higher, higher! Dance!
Illumine, illuminate, oh, luminous fire,
Illuminate, oh, goddess, illumine us all!
We kindle the fire, and once every year,
In the night of surrender,
We gather in secret here in the clearing
To worship the goddess with magic, fire, and dance
By the radiant light on the face of the moon.

II

Singe, fire, singe!
Glisten, hiss and sizzle!
Leap, fire, leap, leap!
Radiate, scintillate, dazzle!
Dance, fire, dance!
Dance higher, higher! Shine!
We've chosen the virgin. Her eyes are fire.
Enliven, oh, virgin, enliven us all!
We're painted all over with screaming colors—
We glow like embers.
We glitter and gleam in the night
And tremble in front of the goddess of fire and doom
By the terrible light on the face of the moon.

III

Rage, fire, rage!
Soar and glisten! Roar!
Blaze, fire, blaze, blaze!
Fill us with luster! Soar!
Intenser, intenser! Burn!
Shine, fire, shine brighter!
Encircle, oh, fire, encircle us all!
We glare and pant and growl—nothing will stop us,
And out of the blackest of shadows, and from
The bottom of the pit,
The devils arise and revel in row after row
With the ghosts of the dead, and slowly a cloud
Of sulphur and dread enshrouds the face of the moon.

IV

Roar, fire, roar!
Beat, drummers, beat, beat!
The witch doctor screams!
The sound of hundreds of
Pounding bare feet on the
Ground and powerful knuckles and fists on drums
Rebounds and cuts through the jungle around us,
Engulfing, ensnaring, enthralling us all!
We watch an inferno and dance like demons—
The virgin screams!
We prance and growl, completely in trance,
And shake and crawl to the goddess and sprawl
By the light of flaming surrender and fire.

Chapter 16: The Poetry of Transition, Surprise, and Ascension

V

Burn, fire, burn!
Roast and blister! Scorch!
The spirits of fire squirm
And dance on pyre and torch.
As the moon reappears,
We pray for redemption and dash
To the flames and fearlessly dance on the coals.
We cleanse ourselves—each soul is redeemed.
The sacrificed blood of the virgin is burnt,
And the smoke appeases
The nostrils of her, the goddess of fire,
And reaches to all of the stars in the vault of the sky
By the blood red light on the face of the moon.

VI

Glow, fire, glow!
And now we lie down
By the fire and dream.
Glow, fire, glow! Life is a dream,
A brittle illusion—
When is it real? Glow, fire, glow!
Before we know it, life will be over. Glow,
Surround us, oh, fire, envelop us all!
And the light will brighten each feature. The warmth
Will kindle each heart,
And the glow of the stars will show us
The heavenly eyes of the goddess of fire on high
By the radiant light on the face of the moon.

VII

Great goddess of fire,
Soaring higher, higher!
Who has beheld your
Splendor and lived? Oh, goddess!
Radiant, vibrant and bright—
We're awed by your grandeur. Your
Eyes are billions of stars. Your face is the
Sky all ablaze, embracing us all.
Your essence has filled our being—
We love and adore you.
At last we come to ourselves, and sing,
And laugh, and reel. The sky is a witness to joy
By the glorious light on the face of the moon.

VIII

Sing, fire, sing!
The light of the stars
Has touched every soul. The
Children come forward with
Palm leaves, garlands, and fruits.
Sing, fire, sing, dance!
Illumine, illuminate, oh, magical fire!
Illuminate, oh, Spirit, illumine us all!
We chant now with angels, seraphs, and gods.
We're sinless and free.
We rise to the One, the highest of all.
We dwell in ourselves, and we know, and we bow
To the glimmering light in the east—to the dawn . . .

IX

Glow, fire, glow!
And so comes the dawn,
The mystical dawn.
Rise, fire, rise over death!
And here comes the light, the glorious sun.
Oh, *this* is the day of peace and surrender.
We rise from the shadows—we rise from the night.
We look to the east—we reach for the Light.
Oh, Light, oh, all-seeing Light,
Eternal, boundless, loving and bright!
Illumine, illuminate, oh, Light!
Illumine, illuminate, ignite now, oh, Light!
Ignite here the light that has lived and endured in us all!

Who We Are

Epilogue

But I have lived, and have not lived in vain:
My mind may lose its force, my blood its fire,
And my frame perish even in conquering pain,
But there is that within me which shall tire
Torture and Time, and breathe when I expire.

— *Childe Harold's Pilgrimage*
Canto IV, Stanza 137
Byron, British poet (1788-1824)

Sweet vale of Avoca!
how calm could I rest
In thy bosom of shade,
with the friends I love best,
Where the storms that we feel
in this cold world should cease,
And our hearts,
like thy waters,
be mingled in peace.

— From *The Meeting of the Waters* by Thomas Moore,
Irish poet, singer, songwriter (1779-1852)

Epilogue

Who We Are & Poets' Index and Biographies

Now that you've read our poetry, you may want to know who we are and where you'll find us now. Most of us are still writing poetry. Several have moved away from Fairfield, some have returned, and a few have passed on.

Many of us know each other from poetry readings, gatherings, or workshops in Fairfield, and several have met prior to moving to this Midwest town. But there's probably no one who has met all the other poets in person.

Over the years, it has been my privilege to have heard about or become acquainted with almost all of the poets. After I started working on this book in the summer of 2009, I exchanged many phone calls and e-mails with everyone. I was familiar with many of their poems already, and I'm happy I've gotten to know these talented writers even more.

You can read up on some of our personal stories and see some pictures in the following index. You'll also find a listing by page number of all our poems in *This Enduring Gift*.

POETS' INDEX AND BIOGRAPHIES

WHO WE ARE

Patricia Regan Argiro
George K. Attwood
Jasmine Bartolovic
Margo Berdeshevsky
Nancy Berg
Matthew A. Bovard
Phoebe Carter
Catherine Castle
Thomas Centolella
Ken Chawkin
Tracy Chipman
Karla Christensen
Allen Cobb
Carole Lee Connet
Donna Davison
Graham de Freitas
Steven Druker
Ann Du Bois
Linda Egenes
Tony Ellis
Rolf Erickson
Silvine Farnell
Megge Hill Fitz-Randolph
Freddy Niagara Fonseca
Diane Frank
Raven Garland

Leslie Gentry
William Clair Godfrey
Bill Graeser
Henry Robert Hau
Jeffrey Hedquist
Anne Hildenbrand
Michael Hock
Charlie Hopkins
Ruthie Hutchings
Andrew Josephs
Karen Karns
Tom Kepler
Susan Klauber
Rustin Larson
Tom Le May
Judy Liese
Robin Lim
Brother Ludovico
Angela Mailander
Elizabeth McIsaac
James Moore
Susie Niedermeyer
Carol Olicker
Einar Olsen
Gale Park
Nynke Passi

Roger Pelizzari
Sharalyn Pliler
Diana Quinlan
Libbett Rich
River Dog
Megan Robinson
Barry Rosen
Steven P. Schneider
Christopher Seid
Laurie Sewall
Meredith Briggs Skeath
Brian Stains
Para Steinmann
Andrea Dana Stevens
Paul Stokstad
Janet Thomas
Viktor Tichy
James Tipton
Richard K. Wallarab
Leah Marie Waller
Jason Walls
Glenn Watt
Patricia Wood
Jordy Yager

Poets' Index and Biographies

PATRICIA REGAN ARGIRO

170	Rite of Passage
188	Spirals
236	Good Night
542	Advisement
678	When a Vessel Breaks

For 21 years, Patricia Regan Argiro (1934-2001) earned her living as a reporter, photographer, columnist and Associate Editor for Hudson Valley Newspapers, Inc. in New York State. Her weekly column, *Branching*, was a reader's favorite. Her extensive freelance writing included, for several years, monthly features for *SCAN*, a publication devoted to the idea that older citizens are a dynamic, creative population.

Her poetry and prose have appeared in the periodicals *Idiom, Echoes, The Plough, Intaglio,* and in the anthology *Lyrical Iowa* 1997. Her first book of poems, *Spheres*, was published in 1979. She has produced four artist's books combining her poetry with art work. In these books, *Illumination, Pranam, A Rite of Passage,* and *Foundations*, she utilized skills—papermaking, silkscreen, drawing, letterpress, book design, and bookbinding—honed at Women's Studio Workshop in Rosendale, NY.

She has given many poetry readings and lectures at SUNY, New Pfaltz, the Historical Society of Newburgh Bay and the Highlands, Mount St. Mary's College in Newburgh, City College in New York City, and MIU in Fairfield, Iowa. Her exhibit of art works at Unison Learning Center in New Pfaltz opened with a poetry reading sponsored by *Poets and Writers*, New York City.

GEORGE KENNETH ATTWOOD

128	The Moor Park

George Kenneth Attwood (1922-2002) was raised in Oakland, CA and was drawn to the ministry in college. He attended the University of California at Berkeley where he was active in the Lutheran Students' Association. It was

there that he met his future wife, Madge, and became inspired to get a Masters of Divinity at Wittenburg University in Springfield, Ohio after his wedding.

His first church was in Redding, CA where his son Christopher Adrian Attwood was born in 1952. After six months, George was reassigned as assistant pastor at St. Mark's Lutheran Church in San Francisco and three years later became head pastor at Beverly Hills Lutheran Church in Los Angeles. In 1968, George retired from the ministry to follow his passion for teaching and working with young people as a high school biology teacher in Watts during some of the violent riots that occurred in that area in the late sixties and early seventies. During his tenure at Fremont High School, George obtained a Masters in Instructional Design from the University of Southern California and also learned Transcendental Meditation.

Poets' Index and Biographies

After his parents passed away in 1984, he moved to Fairfield, IA to be closer to his son, Chris. There he took a position at Maharishi University of Management (Maharishi Int'l University at that time) selecting instructional software for the various departments. A lifelong learner, George completed his third Masters Degree in Creative Writing at MUM. George was loved by all who knew him. He had a childlike curiosity about everything, a wonderful sense of humor and a deep appreciation of the spiritual aspects of life.

JASMINE BARTOLOVIC
536   If I Could Write

She fancies herself a quiet artist and has been invited to join a quiet art group so maybe she is — and a writer — some say she is. She was a girl in the wild wonderful hills of W. Va. She did a lot of growing up in California. A lot of it with her new group, three children who she calls her "golden watch" — you know: a man works 25 years at a factory, retires and is given a "gold watch". She and her little four footed friend are comfortably at home in Fairfield, IA. She wants to just continue.

MARGO BERDESHEVSKY
358   After the End After the Beginning

Margo Berdeshevsky's *"Beautiful Soon Enough,"* a collection of illustrated short-short stories, just published, September, 2009, by Fiction Collective Two. Her poetry collection, *"But a Passage in Wilderness,"* was published by Sheep Meadow Press in 2007. Her honors include The FC2 Ronald Sukenick/American Book Review Innovative Fiction Award for *"Beautiful Soon Enough,"* The Poetry

Society of America's Robert H. Winner Award, The Chelsea Poetry Awd, Kalliope's Sue Saniel Elkind Awd, and 5 Pushcart Prize nominations (2 Pushcart "Special Mention" citations in 2008 & 2009) for works in leading literary journals including *AGNI, Pleiades, The Southern Review, Kenyon Review, New Letters, Poetry International, Poetry Daily, Fairy Tale Review, Pool, Margie, Nimrod, Runes, Chelsea, Confrontation, Women's Studies Quarterly, Kalliope, Rattapallax, Many Mountains Moving, Poetry Review (UK), The Wolf, (UK.).* Her poetic novel, *"Vagrant"* is forthcoming from Red Hen Press in 2010. Berdeshevsky currently lives in Paris. Here are my web-site addresses: http://www.redroom.com/author/margo-berdeshevsky and http://margoberdeshevsky.blogspot.com/

My book of poetry, *"But a Passage in Wilderness"* (Sheep Meadow Press/ 2007) may be ordered from Sheep Meadow Press: http://tinyurl.com/6p3fhz My newest book of illustrated short stories, *"Beautiful Soon Enough,"* has just been published by Fiction Collective Two (University of Alabama Press, 2009). Order *"Beautiful Soon Enough"* from Amazon.com: http://tinyurl.com/mg9vg4

Poets' Index and Biographies

NANCY BERG
26	Swing Low, Sweet Pontiac
66	Dolphin Report
290	Smallest Dog in the World
390	Chinese Ghost Wedding
474	I Could Have Danced All Night if Hadn't Spontaneously Combusted
666	Columbia

Nancy Berg's book of poems, *Oracles for Night-Blooming Eccentrics*, is winner of the 2009 Blue Light Book Award, and is available through Amazon.com, barnesandnoble.com, and other book selling sites. Her work is widely published, and she has been recipient of a $20,000 Poetry Fellowship from the National Endowment for the Arts, a Stanford University Fellowship, and a number of other awards. Raised by two cartoonists, Nancy literally grew up as a *MAD Magazine* cartoon. She now sells original cartoon art by her late father, Dave Berg, and historical collectibles that belonged to her late husband, a veteran TV and film writer. Nancy now lives in Woodland Hills, California, and is a freelance writer, editor, and instructor. You can reach her at nancyberg@earthlink.net; her accessible-while-still-under-construction website is at http://www.nancyberg.com.

MATTHEW A. BOVARD
210	Atman's Jesus' Buddha's Krishna's God's Flying Spaghetti Monster's Jahweh's Great Spirit's Love
362	Sole of the Shoe
450	Drug Books
544	Poet as Art
638	Brother Sun Sister Moon

Born and raised in Fairfield, Iowa, then went to college at University of Iowa. Really just stumbling through life on the journey of existence painting the world with my poetry that flows from the great beyond. Founded an art magazine by the title of *Knew rEvolution* as a place for the soul to do its painting and spread the word of peace and love.

PHOEBE CARTER
94	A Vague Feeling
244	Cereal Cold Wars
286	Ant Warrior (Snapshot)

CATHERINE CASTLE
612	The Temple

Catherine Castle, R.S. Hom. (N.A.) practices classical homeopathy at Jefferson County Hospital and at her Fairfield Homeopathic Clinic. She is a

Poets' Index and Biographies

lecturer at the U of I Medical School and a faculty member of the American Medical College of Homeopathy. She has traveled widely and enjoys classical music, opera, ballet, art and English literature. She especially enjoys camping in the redwoods, hiking, tennis, and attending polo matches. Her poetry reflects her love of life, nature and the enfolding spirit of the heart.

THOMAS CENTOLELLA
38	View #45
192	The Orders
234	In the Evening We Shall Be Examined on Love
404	The Raptors
442	Lines of Force
676	View #2

Thomas Centolella is the author of *Terra Firma, Lights & Mysteries,* and *Views from along the Middle Way.* He has been the recipient of a Lannan Literary Award, the American Book Award, and the California Book Award from the Commonwealth Club. He has been a Wallace Stegner Fellow in Poetry at Stanford University, and currently teaches creative writing throughout the San Francisco Bay Area. His poems have been featured on National Public Radio and in many magazines and anthologies, including *Don't Tell Mama: The Penguin Book of Italian American Writing.*

KEN CHAWKIN
138	Five Haiku
160	Cold Wet Night
530	Poetry: The Art of the Voice

Ken Chawkin draws his inspiration from the underlying liveliness of nature and feels that the creative process is a subtle collaboration between the two.

He submitted his first poem, *ODE TO THE ARTIST Sketching Lotus Pads at Round Prairie Park*, to Sparrowgrass Poetry Forum and won their 1989 Distinguished Poet Award. That poem and its acknowledgement gave him the encouragement and confidence to keep on writing.

Ken also realizes that the real reward comes from participating in the creative process itself when he experiences the thrill that accompanies the mystery of creation as it unfolds and completes itself in a poem. Of course having your poems published also brings a special kind of satisfaction. This short contribution was taken from a collection of poems written over the last 20 years.

Ken earned a BA in English from Loyola College in Montreal, Canada in 1971, and two MA degrees, one in Education in 1986 from MIU, Maharishi International University, and Maharishi Vedic Science in 2006 from Maharishi University of Management, M.U.M.

Poets' Index and Biographies

Ken has taught the Transcendental Meditation (TM) Program, was a Sales Rep, a Maharishi Ayurveda Health Technician, a Park Caretaker, and a Reading and Writing Facilitator. Currently a publicist for M.U.M., Ken has written articles on TM and Consciousness-Based Education, and assisted other writers, editors, and film and television producers with their news stories and documentary films. He is also the proud father of two wonderful children, Nathanael and Shara. Throughout it all, Ken remains a poet at heart, and continues to transform his life into poetry.

TRACY CHIPMAN
 252   Protection

Traveling, nature, relationships and magical experiences have fueled Tracy's joy of both spoken and written word since she was wee. Presently she divides her time between Fairfield, Iowa and her home in Wisconsin. Please visit her website (up soon); ListentoaTale.com.

KARLA CHRISTENSEN
 78   In the Wind River Mountains
 142   Lullaby Baby Frog
 152   El Dia de los Muertos

Karla Christensen lives in Fairfield Iowa with her four children. She loves reading, travel, backpacking, writing, mosaic work, tile painting and she has worked at many jobs to all of which she brings her gift for creativity.

ALLEN COBB
 242   Waving Man #1
 422   Maine Song #4
 462   Morning
 482   Buildings
 590   These Highest Dreams
 610   Delphi
 616   Lament for Lost Silence
 680   Near Lindos, Rhodes

Composer, photographer, installation artist, sculptor, inventor, essayist, and poet, Allen Cobb has written of his inner and outer experiences for more than half a century. His poetry addresses the wide variety of styles and idioms of the inner world.

CAROLE LEE CONNET
 24   Restoring the Meadow
 190   Lalla
 246   Magic Carpets

Poets' Index and Biographies

260	Red Paste and Rice
340	The Terminal Temple
564	Black Berries All Dried Up Now
572	Retreat from Kandahar

My passions are eclectic, from dancing to dark energy, love to light bodies, nests to natives, paradox to painting, traveling to truth, singing to synergy. All are gifts for my creative expressions. It has always been so, though I am aware that my outpourings of the spirit have not always been fully understood or appreciated by others. As a child of two, I cut my hair to fashion a bird's nest, a work of art which I tenderly placed in a bush. This was right before Easter. My mother had a hard fit when she saw my chopped locks. I tried to explain, but she thought I meant that I had made a bird's nest *in* my hair — in her eyes, a mess. Fortunately, I was fond of hats. On Easter Sunday I wore, not a baby bonnet, but a wide-brimmed lady's hat with a veil, which did not hide my searching eyes.

I wrote my first poem in sixth grade. I can still recite it: Snowflakes, snowflakes everywhere/On the ground and in the air/Dancing softly on the breeze/Gently swirling through the trees/White, white/ Falling softly in the night. Thanks to the teacher whose name I do not recall who pinned it to the bulletin board, my first publication. As an adult, Diane Frank really got me started writing and publishing poetry and still keeps me going. Rustin Larson encouraged me with expert critiques and publication in his *Contemporary Review*, and Robin Lim nurtured me through the publication of my first collection of poems, *Searching for Entrance*, published in Indonesia by Half Angel Press in 2001.

I have years of formal education and pieces of paper to attest that I have a B.A. in psychology and philosophy, a M.A. in history and a M.A. in professional writing, as well as a secondary teacher's certificate. At various times I have taught philosophy, psychology, history, and western civilization as a university instructor, and English literature as a high school teacher. I have worked as an education therapist and counselor. I am a long-time practitioner and teacher of Transcendental Meditation. In addition, I have many more years of informal education and teaching in art, writing, music, dance, outdoor sports, cosmology, nature studies, world cultures, alternative medicine, and spiritual counseling. I write poems and prose, paint, dance and sing to express my innermost feelings. If my offerings resonate with you, I am twice blessed.

DONNA DAVISON

4	Chrysalis

Poetry is the vehicle for the delicate, sensitive, emotional expressions that roam about in this body/personality known as Donna. Poetry is a way for me to process the path of realization.

Poets' Index and Biographies

I love the flow and interweaving of all the threads of the cosmic tapestry of life — from the intense pain to the sublime divinity of all. My poems express moments of complete frustration to times of pensive inquisitiveness to the utter joy of awakening.

That glorious dance with love — both personal and divine — has also been able to find its way into expression through the wondrous medium of poetry. If my poems bring just one moment of clarity or delight, then what a gift for me!

GRAHAM DE FREITAS
    594   This Balloon of Joy

STEVEN DRUKER
    34   Rendezvous

I grew up in Des Moines, Iowa and then attended the University of California, Berkeley (receiving a B.A. in philosophy followed by a J.D. from the Boalt Hall School of Law). I was a founding faculty member of Maharishi International University in 1973 and served many years as Professor of Law and Government. I also served as Executive Vice President during the time the university was laying the groundwork for accreditation. I've been doing public interest law since 1996, when I founded the Alliance for Bio-Integrity. "Rendezvous" was written in 1984.

ANN DU BOIS
    298   Night Heat
    490   High Coos and Buddhist Leanings

LINDA EGENES
    266   New Delhi Street
    452   Hammock

Linda Egenes is a freelance writer, book author and poet who writes for adults and children. One of her poems, "Black Stallion" was published in *Cricket,* the leading literary magazine for kids, and many of her poems are included in her forthcoming retelling of the Ramayana, *The Story of Raam.* Another book by Linda Egenes, *Visits with the Amish: Impressions of the Plain Life*, has recently been re-released by the University of Iowa Press. Linda teaches writing workshops and is an adjunct faculty at Maharishi University of Management in Fairfield, Iowa. Visit her blog at www.LindaEgenes.com.

Poets' Index and Biographies

TONY ELLIS
- 132 Sneaking Free
- 220 I Once Met a God
- 272 My Cambodian God
- 344 One Moment
- 428 Sometimes

Tony Ellis is a free lance writer and poet. Originally from England, he has been a Fairfield resident since 1992. His first book of poems *There is Wisdom in Walnuts: 27 Poems by Tony Ellis and a Couple by His Dad* from which the poems in this collection are taken won a Chelson publishing prize from First World Literary Society in 2004. A second collections of poems, *The Morning Tree: Poems and Reflections on Moving Closer to God*, is due for publication in 2010. He also writes and blogs for the *Iowa Source* magazine. You can read more of his work on his website www.tonyellis.com.

ROLF ERICKSON
- 54 Mirror Lake
- 70 Into the Woods
- 98 There Is a Secret
- 334 Caught Looking at the Moon

Rolf Erickson is a writer, editor, dancer and artist living in Fairfield, Iowa. He was the founder of *Enlightenment* magazine, and served as editor for five years. His poems have been published in the anthology *Leaves By Night, Flowers By Day*.

SILVINE FARNELL
- 532 Somebody Has to Play Mozart

Born and raised in Baltimore, Silvine graduated from Bryn Mawr College in 1963, and went on to graduate school in medieval studies at Yale. She dropped

out before the end of her first year and moved to the Lower East Side of New York City. After a couple of years as a hippie, she discovered a calling to share poetry with others, and returned to grad school in English literature at the City University of New York, completing a Ph.D. there in 1975. She taught for a few years at Dickinson College in Pennsylvania; when her department decided not to support her for tenure, she moved to MIU. There she had the luck to have Tim Truby, director and acting coach, as a colleague; he convinced her that it was a sin to ask anyone to write a paper about a poem until they had prepared it for performance. Teaching people to dive deeper into poetry by preparing it for performance has been her passion ever since. In 1994, she and her husband left MIU, pushed away by what seemed to them a growing rigidity and dogmatism, and moved to Boulder, Colorado. For what she is attempting to do in Boulder, see her website, www.deeperintopoetry.com.

MEGGE HILL FITZ-RANDOLPH
302   The Love of Horses

Megge Hill Fitz-Randolph lives in Iowa City after having lived in Fairfield for over twenty years with her daughter and husband. Megge is a writer, poet, and teacher who has come to understand the true gifts of any writer's life are found in the inner landscape she carries around inside herself.

FREDDY NIAGARA FONSECA
12   Awestruck at Niagara Falls
56   The Language of the Trees
106   The Doe
232   On a Medieval Painting of the Fall of Man
306   The New York City Zoo
342   Statue of an Enraged Lion
374   Carnival in Rio!
520   Poetry Dances, Olé!
546   Books
606   Giant Sequoia - A Hymn
690   Fire Dance - An Invocation of the Light

Poet, narrator, baritone and impresario Freddy Niagara Fonseca hails from South-America. He has absorbed the histories and cultures of Greece, France, Spain, England, Germany, the Netherlands, Italy, and the United States through his travels; worked in graphic design and banking in Amsterdam; studied voice and Italian, and worked in films in Rome, Italy.

He has read extensively in five languages including tens of thousands of poems by authors from Germany, the Netherlands, Great Britain, France, Italy, Spanish speaking countries, and the US, feeling a particular resonance with and a link to American poetry.

As a young adult, he actually disliked poetry. While visiting Rome, Italy, he was moved by a pedestal inscription on a statue of Lord Byron in Villa Borghese Park, and wrote his first poem the next day.

Freddy, who is an expressive performer, has publicly recited his poems, reflective of his visits to various exotic locales, in concert with the accompaniment of musicians, numerous times. In 1990, he staged, produced, and participated in a *Dance, Rhyme & Rhythm Extravaganza* in

Fairfield, Iowa, reciting and dancing to his own poetry with a cast of 30 dancers, accompanied on piano. He lives in Fairfield, Iowa.

His poems have appeared in the US, Canada and England in *The Dryland Fish—An Anthology of Contemporary Iowa Poets, Tower Poetry Society, The Eclectic Muse, The Neovictorian/Cochlea, Candelabrum Poetry Magazine, The Fairfield Ledger, The Iowa Source, Pivot, Inquiring Mind, WinningWriters.com,* and *Passive Fists—An Anthology by Poets for Peace.* Two of Freddy's poems are on permanent display in public buildings in Fairfield, IA, i.e. Revelations Cafe & Bookstore, and the Fairfield Courthouse.

In December 2004, Freddy created the *Candlelight Reading Series* in order to bring entertaining poetry readings with inventive programming and aesthetics on a variety of themes.

The main focus has been on presenting world poetry, classical as well as contemporary and of all cultures, styles and eras. The series regularly invites excellent readers, poets, musicians, dancers, actors, mime artists, story tellers, song writers, comedians, etc.

Freddy has made it his mission to revitalize the oral poetry traditions by modifying them for modern audiences while opening up the gateways of feeling and meaning fearlessly. His fondest desire is to bring poetry back to its rightful home, in the heart of all people; to popularize poetry, using as many imaginative ways as possible.

DIANE FRANK
      16   **Waltz**
     370   **Photograph from Okinawa**
     524   **Iowa Omen**

Diane Frank is an award-winning poet and author of five books of poems, including *Entering the Word Temple, The Winter Life of Shooting Stars* and *The All Night Yemenite Café.* Her friends describe her as a harem of seven women in one very small body. She lives in San Francisco — where she dances, plays cello, and creates her life as an art form. Diane teaches at San Francisco State University, leads workshops for young writers as a Poet in the School, and directs the Blue Light Press On-line Poetry Workshop. She lived in Fairfield, Iowa, from 1989 to 2002 and taught poetry and scriptwriting workshops at Maharishi International University. She is also a documentary scriptwriter with expertise in Eastern and sacred art. *Blackberries in the Dream House,* her first novel, was nominated for the Pulitzer Prize. Her second novel will be published in 2010, and her website is www.dianefrank.net.

RAVEN GARLAND
     468   **The Gray Dress**

Raven is still surprised to find herself in Fairfield, Iowa. Yet, since coming here

Poets' Index and Biographies

in 2005, that is what she has found over and over again. She is a frequent performer at the *Candlelight Reading Series* as a reader/reciter of poems and a eurythmist. Eurythmy is a movement art that makes what is inaudible in language visible. Thank you Freddy for all the opportunities you create for Fairfield to be creative!

LESLIE GENTRY
  590 The Divine Abode of My Own Buddha-Nature

  As a native of Fairfield and descendant of several families who settled Jefferson County in the 1800s, my love of the town and the Iowa prairie is as deep as my roots. Born in 1946, I was welcomed into this life by a dozen grandparents, three grandparents, eight great-grandparents, and a great-great grandmother. I've been very blessed by so much love and nurture. Now, myself a grandmother of eight, I continue to cherish family and home above all else.

  Among many and varied interests is a lifelong love of prose & poetry. My own poetry and other creative efforts are inspired by, and reflect, my appreciation of nature and a life of "simple abundance"; and my enthusiasm for all things numinous and metaphysical. My spiritual journey is one without path or distance; poetry is my "bridge to no-where".

WILLIAM CLAIR GODFREY
  64 Forest Road at Night
  134 Fairy Trifle
  224 God Bless the Universe
  316 So Say the Wise
  472 The Trees Striptease
  500 If You Want to Drop Your Body
  688 When I Lay Down My Treasures at the End of the Trail

  Bill Godfrey is a warrior of the Light, his weapon, song. He is a prospector in the inner vastness, a bushwhacker through the thicket in the dark. His campfire is the light in the heart.

BILL GRAESER
  10 Grandma's Pancakes
  102 Where I Walk
  118 Something to Know
  338 The Black Hearse
  346 Mumbling
  434 Father in His Coffin
  480 Junk Pile
  518 Tag Sale

Poets' Index and Biographies

540 Open Readings On Other Planets

Born and raised on Long Island, Bill has worked as a dairy farmer, carpenter, teacher of Transcendental Meditation and is currently the locksmith at Maharishi University of Management, Fairfield, Iowa. Published in *North American Review, Michigan Avenue Review, Lyrical Iowa, Chiron Review, Long Island Quarterly, Dryland Fish, The Iowa Source,* and *Punk Debris*.

HENRY ROBERT HAU
- 46 A Still Point of the Turning World
- 112 The River Stone
- 270 Blue Heron
- 328 The House Sparrow
- 496 Beauty Hard to Believe
- 602 To the River Is a Place I Go
- 620 The Egrets

Henry Robert Hau was born in Manhattan, raised on Long Island, and in the suburbs of Southern California. His father was a commercial artist and landscape painter, who helped cultivate his son's interests in the arts and nature early in life. Hau has written, " As a child my early years were rife with

poetical lore. Fishing trips to Montauk Point; visits to Teddy Roosevelt's summer home on Sagamore Hill; excursions into the city downtown; The New York Planetarium (absolutely wondrous); Central Park; Mayor Fiorello LaGuardia's great "dead zoo"; The Museum of Natural History (magnificent!); the great art museums and Macy's department store where my father designed the big window displays....I even got to help." He continues, "I went alone on bird sketching trips to the woods of Bethpage, from age five to eleven, several miles from home. The world was safer then. John James Audubon's "*Birds of America*" was my guide." His father also introduced his son to the Korda brothers films: *The Four Feathers, Jungle Book,* and *The Thief of Bagdad* etc. "These films are still relevant, moral and magical. Watch them with your children...."

"My heroes as a kid were naturalists like Audubon and Ivan T. Sanderson, who embarked on zoological expeditions. There were also the stories of circus animal trainer Clyde Beatty and the adventure treks of John Muir. I also read a lot of Jack London as a youngster and almost everything John Steinbeck wrote."

"Southern California was hot, vapid, and cliquish. I left for an education in English Literature and Philosophy at the University of Oregon, where I also took up fly fishing on the Blue River."

After university, Hau lived in Lake Tahoe and Anchorage, and is now a long time resident of Toronto, Canada. As a teacher of Transcendental Meditation, he lectured for nearly twenty years, traveling in the US and Canada. A graduate

Poets' Index and Biographies

of the Canadian School of Eastern Medicine, Hau leads workshops on Ayurveda and the Poetry of Sacred Self.

JEFFREY HEDQUIST
  282   Simon
  304   Squirrel Brain

Jeffrey Hedquist is a radio creator/director/producer/voice actor/storyteller/singer-songwriter/improv performer/organic farmer and occasional poet.

You may have heard his voice on national commercials for dozens of national brands or heard some of the thousands of radio commercials he's produced that have won more than 700 awards for clients, agencies, and producers in 44 states.

His company, Hedquist Productions also produces audio books, including 27 versions of *Chicken Soup for the Soul*.

He continues to conduct hundreds of seminars for broadcast and advertising groups throughout the country and his monthly articles appear in many trade publications and newsletters. http://www.hedquist.com Jeffrey@hedquist.com

ANNE HILDENBRAND
  264   To the Clown Who Had His Eye Blown out by
          Flashlight Powder
  288   An Animal of Ancient Ancestry

Anne Hildenbrand was born May 1, 1900, married in 1932, and widowed in 1957. She attended Bryn Mawr College, receiving her B.A. in 1922, her M.A. in

1923, M.S.S. in 1946. Anne also received an M.A. in the Science of Creative Intelligence from Maharishi International University in 1986.

Over the years her travels took her to many parts of the globe, including a trip around the world in 1963. On New Year's Eve, 1960, she was in Havana when Cubans began celebrating the success of Castro's revolution. She reported that her ship weighed anchor a few hours ahead of schedule and pulled out of the harbor to the accompaniment of rifle fire from the rooftops.

Anne was a Minister of the Age of Enlightenment and made numerous trips to Switzerland to study with His Holiness Maharishi Mahesh Yogi.

One year shy of becoming a centenarian, she passed away in 1999 in Fairfield. She published two books: *Sonnets to Soma* and *Sonnets to Iowa*.

MICHAEL HOCK
  50   This Whisper
  182   Stricken
  354   How Many?

Poets' Index and Biographies

416	The Master's Gift
640	At the Speed of God
682	Sat Guru

Michael Hock lives in Albuquerque, New Mexico. Most of his current professional work involves consulting with the State of New Mexico about how to provide high quality services to people experiencing co-occurring substance abuse and mental illness. He has done many things throughout his life, including ranching, carpentry and psychotherapy, and lived in many different places across the USA. Michael has been a long-time adherent of MasterPath, which naturally evolved from his practice of Transcendental Meditation. He writes a poem almost every day, and nearly all of them are praise and devotion to spiritual essence, and of course, his personal favorite, the Sat Guru and current Living Master of MasterPath, Sri Gary Olsen. He hopes that these poems are inspirational and open enough to include all people who strive to embrace spirituality, and recognize the joy and beauty of the journey homeward, even when it is difficult and challenging.

CHARLIE HOPKINS

42	Four Memories of North West Arkansas
100	Love Poem to a Chinese Tallow Tree
204	I Need to Feel You Every Moment in My Heart
276	House Painter Sitting on the Roof of a Queen Anne Victorian Looking over a Pear Orchard in Bloom
410	Seed Time in Fairfield, Iowa
414	Tenth Anniversary Prayer
430	Middle-Aged Man
582	Three Poems out of Southeast Iowa
596	Hymn of Praise to the Divine Mother in Her Role as Queen of Nature
646	Death Is Coming
660	A Man Will Abandon His Face

I was born in Texas in 1950 and spent five years and seven or eight assorted months living in Fairfield, Iowa. Although I am no longer associated with the

Transcendental Meditation organization, I remember the ordinary people of Fairfield with love, and I respect the community they have created together. Since leaving Iowa in 1988, I have supported myself and my family by house painting and paper hanging. For nine years, along with a close friend and family member, we owned and operated a paint and decorating store in Hood River, Oregon. Now we live just across the Columbia River in Underwood, Washington. Inspiration to write came as a young person reading the King James Version of The Old Testament Prophets, The Song of Solomon, and The Book of Revelations. I wanted to write the way Hank Williams, Johnny Cash, Skeeter Davis, and George Jones sang. Walt Whitman, Allen Ginsberg, Bob Dylan, Federico Garcia Lorca, and Pablo Neruda were

Poets' Index and Biographies

guides. In addition, Juan Ramon Jimenez, Dylan Thomas, James Wright, James Dickey, T.S. Eliot, and friends from a writing group in Fairfield in the 1980s, some of whom are featured here, have been a light. Now I am inspired by the writing of my son Eli Hopkins and the music of my step son, Jeff Lehman. For the last twenty-two years I have experienced Grace in the form of my wife Carol. Everything good in my heart is her. I am always happy to hear from old and new friends at <cah@gorge.net>. Thank you for reading these poems.

RUTHIE HUTCHINGS
492   Toad to My Gray Hairs

Ruthie Hutchings has been writing and editing for many years. She's done graduate work in English Literature and has a Masters degree in Professional Writing. She has taught writing in a community college, and spent years writing user's manuals and marketing materials. Today, she primarily focuses on writing and editing websites and online articles, and occasional poetry and prose poems.

ANDREW JOSEPHS
670   Icarus' Lover's Dream

After finding himself in the Bronx in the mid '50s, Andrew took a learning curve path to Iowa via a few prolonged and valuable stays in Massachusetts, where he found himself as a child and later, as things have it, as an adult. Now, celebrating thirty years in Fairfield, he has found himself again discovering beauty and more of life's depths with and because of his wife, Gina. Andrew enjoys supporting the vertical and horizontal growth of the community through the TM organizations and in founding the short-lived but well-received *Heartland Spirit* newspaper.

KAREN KARNS
30   Meditation
114   Caught
348   Dying

Karen Karns was an English major in college, but went on to receive a Masters Degree in Divinity from Earham School of Religion and a Masters Degree in the Science of Creative Intelligence from Maharishi University of Management. Currently she is on the Invincible America Assembly in the mornings, where she practices the TM and TM-Sidhi program, and works as a pastoral counselor in the afternoons. She lives in Fairfield with her fifty-five year old husband and her 23 year old cat.

Poets' Index and Biographies

TOM KEPLER
    674   For the Life of Me

Tom Kepler is a career classroom teacher and also a teacher of the Transcendental Meditation Program. He currently teaches at Maharishi School of the Age of Enlightenment, Fairfield, Iowa. "For the Life of Me" is a poem from Kepler's recently published book *Bare Ruined Choirs*.

SUSAN KLAUBER
    62   Spring Leaves
    580   Window Decoration

Susan Klauber came to Fairfield in 1983 to participate with 8000 others in the two week "Taste of Utopia" TM course to create harmony and a better quality of life. She never left.

Born in Sudbury, Canada, in 1945, and married to an American, Susan has lived and traveled in North and South America, Europe, and India, always drawn by the personal growth and inner richness that foreign cultures inspire. Retired from business and teaching fitness, she pursues her interests in writing poetry, traveling, and spiritual development. An athlete, she is now transitioning from ardent to occasional golfer and used-to-be hockey player.

Her poetry and prose have appeared in the Harcourt Canada textbook *Elements of English 11*, in the journals *The MacGuffin, Poetry Motel, Iowa Source, Contemporary Review,* and in the anthologies *Eclipsed Moon Coins: Twenty-Six Visionary Poets* and *The Dryland Fish*. Blue Light Press of Fairfield published her first book of poetry and prose, *Face-off at Center Ice*.

She is currently working on publishing a book of poetry and prose based on her 7 winters in India, *Sound of the Sacred Beads: A Poet's Journey into India*.

RUSTIN LARSON
    240   Melons
    296   Cleo
    392   The Gerbils
    370   In the Herb Garden
    454   Teacher
    568   Creatures Nobody Recognizes

Rustin Larson's poetry has appeared in *The New Yorker, The Iowa Review, North American Review, Poetry East, The Atlanta Review* and other magazines. *The Wine-Dark House* is his latest collection (Blue Light Press, 2009). *Crazy Star*, his previous collection, was selected for the Loess Hills Book's Poetry Series in 2005. Larson won 1st Editor's Prize from *Rhino* magazine in 2000 and has won prizes for his poetry from The National Poet Hunt and The

Poets' Index and Biographies

Chester H. Jones Foundation among others. A five-time Pushcart nominee, and graduate of the Vermont College MFA in Writing, Larson was an Iowa Poet at The Des Moines National Poetry Festival in 2002 and 2004, a featured writer in the DMACC Celebration of the Literary Arts in 2007, 2008, and has been highlighted on the public radio programs *Live from Prairie Lights* and *Voices from the Prairie*. He is the host of the radio talk show *Irving Toast, Poetry Ghost* http://www.kruufm.com and lives in Fairfield, Iowa.

TOM LE MAY
- 124 While You Were Gone
- 146 Trying on Your New Hat
- 360 My Hands
- 488 Louie the 14th
- 562 Untitled
- 644 The Citadel
- 672 Consider the Tracks

Tom Le May was born on a sultry summer night in 1949 in New Jersey, the third son of Ernest and Joan Le May who went on to have a total of 7 children. Since then Tom's been around the block a few times and currently resides in Fairfield, Iowa where he maintains a low profile.

JUDY LIESE
- 262 The Bottom of Glass
- 274 This Is How You Hang up Clothes
- 356 Tornado

Judy Liese grew up in Wisconsin and began writing poetry as soon as she learned to print in big block letters. In 1986 she took time out from a busy nursing career to go back to school, earning a BA in Literature and an MA in English and Creative Writing at MIU. After graduation, she returned to nursing, but honed her writing skills in Diane Frank's journal writing and poetry groups. Her poetry has been published in Lyrical Iowa, Embroidered Horizons, The Source, and Eclipsed Moon Coins. Six years ago she and her husband of forty-five years moved from Iowa to Northern California to be closer to their son. She continues to study with Diane Frank in on-line poetry workshops.

ROBIN LIM
- 162 Ode to Dry Starlight
- 350 What Will Never Dry
- 574 Where They Hung a Crucifix

Robin Lim is a grandmother, poet, and midwife. Following in the tradition of her own Filipino *lola*, Vicenta Munar Lim, a *hilot*, she sits at the doorway between life and death, gently tearing and biting angel's wings. Her work is blue as first breath and as ephemeral. Lim lives with her musician husband and

eight gifted children in the traditional village of Nyuh Kuning, Ubud, Bali, Indonesia, where she is intimately involved in a natural-birth community clinic. In 2006 Lim was given the Alexander Langer International Peace Award. Since 1976 "Ibu" Robin and her family have kept a home in Fairfield, Iowa. *Photo (c) Margo Berdeshevsky*

"Robin Lim is what we all should strive to be - a great, abundant, generous, warm and tirelessly running faucet of humanity and grace."

— Elizabeth Gilbert, author of *Eat Pray Love*

BROTHER LUDOVICO

6	I Keep a Flowering Bough
154	Under Orion
214	In Defense of Angels
318	On the Angels among Us
378	The Feminine Mystique, and the Chains that Bind
436	To a Cumulus Cloud
526	These Words Are Wounds
576	We Seep into This World
588	This Lamplight Falling on My Child's Face
622	A Hymn to the Moon-Mother
654	Death's Inheritance

Raised in a blue collar family. Dad was a farmer and trucker. Most of my relatives were uneducated. Some could not read or write. Whiskey, beer, brawls, and oodles and oodles of poverty, and the dark skulking children poverty breeds. A jolly tribe. Much nicer than the PhDs, millionaires, and prima donna man-haters, and self-appointed gurus I've met in my life.

First literary loves when I was a kid: Twain and Stevenson. Still love them. Read them all the time. Simple, elegant, authentic. They did for the novel what Hank Williams did for country music. Modern writers can't touch them, because their stuff's a mental fabrication, and not a child of the blood. One of my childhood's greatest regrets: never being exposed to Dickens.

Eight or nine years later Joyce, Yeats, John Synge and Dylan Thomas sank their teeth into me, and I about read them to death. Started hitchhiking around, coast to coast, some of the time following Ferlinghetti and James Wright. Was a Dylan devotee from the beginning. Wanted to write a book on him, so I used to hitch-hike to Hibbing in the Winter, and interview his relatives and high school teachers. Researched a lot. Wrote nothing. Beautiful old mining era bars, and my own *"Girl From The North Country"* got in the way.

When I was nineteen became part of "The Brotherhood". Became kind of a fake, Leonard Cohen monk. Doomed from the beginning. My brothers first taught me what the ignorant serfs of mankind hadn't: the true meaning of hate.

Poets' Index and Biographies

They hated me, my works, and every other mote that was obviously a sequoia in their eye. More comfortable with karma than the golden rule, I hated them right back. Still hate them. Hate 'em bad. My works were reviled, stolen, burned, shunned, and ultimately banned. I regarded them more as looting Huns, or something straight out of *Mordor* or *Beowulf*, than serene, lentil-fed, turn-the-other-cheek kind of Brothers. My very dreams became spooked with daggers slipped up baggy sleeves, vials of hemlock stuffed in cowls, and a whole lot of Comanche war-cries come from the bushes. Left Dodge.

Wrote and produced some plays. Some pretty successful. Lots of poems, most Keatsean odes. About one thousand sonnets, same kind that were anathematized by the shekel-biting moguls and nirvana-hooded warlords that burned their smiles like crosses before me, those that had come from their pow-wows in their cosmic sanctums. Many idols, too many to mention, but Milton, Synge, Thomas Hardy, Dostoevsky, Richard Wright, Dylan, Mark Twain, David Lean, and the Little Rascals are in the pack. Got idols coming out of my ears and running with their pants on fire through my dreams. The darker and more hell-bound the better.

Live in happy seclusion. Going through some manuscripts. Mostly plays. Got a few revised. If anybody wants to see them, ask Freddy, if he's still talking to me after this humdinger of a bio. *"The Elopement of Megan O'Flagherty With The Ghost From Tinker's Hollow"*, about an Irish barmaid who falls passionately in love with a ghost. *"Tessy"*, an adaptation of Hardy's *"Tess of the D'urbervilles"*, widely regarded as one of the greatest English novels ever written, and one of the most poignant love stories ever told, bar none. *"Huckleberry In Love"*, a spin-off of that flooze *"Shakespeare In Love"* thing, about Huckleberry coming of age, replete with a few hundred lines from *"Romeo And Juliet"*, including the balcony scene on top of a chicken coop. *"Poorest Of The Poor"*, about Mother Teresa, using her favorite song as the play's theme song, a song that was written by an American priest. Strophes and antistrophes sung by choruses of lepers. *"The Death of Shakespeare"*, about the death of Shakespeare in a tavern, surrounded by thieves, tag rags, and drunkards that he immortalized, and that the intelligentsias of the world love to oooh and aaah about.

Oh yeah, the Inquisition hated the heck out of these bleating lambs too. Yup. You got it. I hated their pukey, elitist sitcoms right back with all the the gall my spleen could dish forth for me. I remember Tolkien answering the avalanche of criticism that was heaped on him by his critics, diatribes that have seemed to have evaporated in a cloud of money. "They like their kinds of books, I like mine."

Some favorite quotes: Huckleberry saying, "Conscience, if you was a yaller dog I'd pisen ya." And Hamlet saying to Ophelia, "-marry a fool, for wise men know well enough what monsters you make of them." Most despised word in English: "relationship". The most bastardized word, in my humble opinion, "Democracy". This prince of misnomers, with his coy sweet bride, "Feminism", (that smiling Angel with a bloody ax beneath her gown), torched a planet by letting their brainy brats play with matches. Favorite word is "Silence". Makes me think of cradles, sleep, and tombs.

Poets' Index and Biographies

After the holy brotherhood, lived in trucks, warehouses, campy shacks, and all sorts of places you sure don't take mom to. Got drunk for a few years. That's about it. Thank you. Brother Ludovico.

ANGELA MAILANDER
314   Mushikarati: The Mouse's Poem
484   Fishy Doggerel
504   The Love Song of J. Alfred Frog Prince
614   Seeking to Hide
634   Poem Written Dream-Side (Qin Guan, 1046-1100, tr. Angela Mailander)

Angela Mailander was born in 1940 in Berlin, Germany. She came to the U.S. as a refugee at the age of twelve, fluent in German and Russian. When she was barely fourteen and fluent in English, her mother sent her to a boarding school right outside Paris, France where she perfected her French. Then she moved back to the U.S. and, subsequently, embarked for another boarding school—in Germany this time—making each journey across the Atlantic an adventure via freight ship. She swam with wild dolphins in the Gulf of Mexico, heard whales sing in the North Atlantic, and watched a ship (the Pamir) sink in Hurricane Carrie.

Angela's college education has been entirely in the U.S. Her undergraduate work done was at Kent State University, and she lived in Kent during the time four students were shot there by the National Guard (her story of what happened there differs significantly from the official one).

At Cleveland State University, Angela did her M.A. Thesis on William Blake, specifically on the correspondences between his poetry and his "illuminations" of that poetry through the art of printmaking and watercolor. She concentrated on how Blake "makes vision visible" by consciously using the formal syntax that underlies vision as an organization of visual energies within any framed space.

She then went on to the University of Iowa, for a Ph.D. in Comparative Studies. Having finished the course work and the doctoral exams, she refused to submit a dissertation on the grounds of "philosophical differences" with her professors. They wanted her to say that there was no such thing as "a transcendental signified," while she maintained that without some such thing, translation from one language to another would be impossible. Though she did not submit it, she did write a dissertation, which was subsequently accepted for publication by the most prestigious university press in her field at the time.

Having practiced the art of literary translation since age twelve, she designed and saw to the institution of an M.F.A. program in Translation Studies at the University of Iowa (with the help of subversive friends). Angela is unshakeable in her position that the translation of poetry is as deep (if not deeper) and as original (in the original sense of that word) as the art of writing poetry.

Poets' Index and Biographies

Unable to find a job that paid more than a doctoral fellowship, Angela earned a Ph.D. in English in 1982, again at Kent State University.

Since earning her Ph.D. at Kent, Angela has taught language and literature in the U.S., in Germany, in Greece, in India, and, most recently, in China. She has taught poetry writing at the University of Iowa, at the Chautauqua Institution, and at Mercyhurst College in Erie, PA.

When she is not busy writing poetry or translating it (primarily from the Chinese), she is a practicing artist whose work can be seen at the Teeple Hansen Gallery in Fairfield. She has also been represented by galleries in Ohio and Pennsylvania.

On the side—that is, entirely outside the context of academe — Angela has been developing a teaching methodology (theory and practice) for English as a Second Language. Experimental results (both quantitatively and qualitatively) so far outstripped expected norms that the standardized tests to measure them do not as yet exist. Her approach is related to her work on Blake, as she sees a formality underlying Language (the same in all languages) that also underlies vision. She is about to launch major initiatives in Latin America and in China.

ELIZABETH McISAAC
- 126   Zinnia
- 446   One Hundred Years
- 484   Some Really Nonsense Poems
- 534   Paper Music
- 664   Salaat

I came to Fairfield in 1982. Three weeks later I planned to leave. I am still here. What happened? 2009.

JAMES MOORE
- 72   Jesus in Iowa
- 254   Wild Rabbit in the Woods
- 538   Elvin Ray

James Moore is a freelance writer, musician, and published poet. He is currently general manager of KRUU-LP 100.1 FM, a solar-powered, independent, grassroots community radio station, music editor for the *Iowa Source*, a regional arts and entertainment monthly, and part-time faculty member at Maharishi University of Management in the communications department.

Described as 'a firm member of a why not generation of dreamers by *Des Moines Register* features' writer Mike Kilen and a 'cultural entrepreneur' by Sustainable Living Coalition co-founder Lonnie Gamble, Moore has lived and studied in Spain, France, Switzerland, India, the Philippines, Mexico, England, and

Poets' Index and Biographies

Bahrain, earning an undergraduate degree in the Science of Creative Intelligence and a Masters in business administration.

He resides in Fairfield, Iowa, where he is pursuing his passion for citizen journalism and Canadian literature. His work has appeared in *Modern Drummer, Punk Debris, Lyrical Iowa, Iowa City Press-Citizen*, and *Ottumwa Courier*, among others.

SUSIE NIEDERMEYER
- 36   November Repast
- 166   The Coyotes
- 176   Night Vision
- 196   The Master
- 376   Advent of Autumn
- 556   The Deer
- 570   And if It Happens

Susie Niedermeyer is by education a classical pianist, graduating with a degree in music from the University of Iowa. Her poetry has been published in journals and magazines including *The MacGuffin, Lyrical Iowa, Sierra Magazine* and others; her poem "Diana" won 2nd place in a 2002 contest sponsored by the National Federation of State Poetry Societies. Her poetry also appears in *The Dryland Fish: An Anthology of Contemporary Iowa Poets* (2004) and *Leaves By Night, Flowers by Day* (2006). Niedermeyer won the Blue Light Book Award for 2007 and her first book of poems, *Under a Prairie Moon*, is now available online at Amazon and Barnes and Noble and in Fairfield at Revelations and 21st Century Bookstore.

CAROL OLICKER
- 294   When Ninja Sits

Carol Olicker originally from New York City, has master's degrees in English literature (SUNY at Buffalo, NY) and social work (Univ of Iowa). From her teens, she had been active in the movements for peace, civil rights, and later, women's liberation. In grad school at Buffalo, she taught courses in Women's Studies and helped found the Women's College there. She continued teaching Women's Studies when she moved to San Francisco and founded a women's teaching collective there. In 1971, she learned Transcendental Meditation which instantly opened her heart. Two years later she became a TM teacher and then taught TM in San Francisco, while also substitute teaching in the San Francisco Unified School District. Since 1981 she has lived in Fairfield, Iowa and for the last 6 years worked as a hospice social worker in a neighboring town. Carol is in love with every cat she has ever seen. She has 5 full-time cats and one regular night visitor. She has no human children. "When

Poets' Index and Biographies

Ninja Sits" was a result of the poetry writing class Carol took with teacher par excellence, Diane Frank.

EINAR OLSEN
    208   Shopping

Einar Olsen grew up on the shores of Lake Erie in NE Ohio where his father was a judge and mother a homemaker and nurse. After graduating Phi Beta Kappa and Summa Cum Laude in Philosophy and Religion with a junior year in Varanasi, India with the University of Wisconsin, he has spent half his years working with the Global Country of World Peace, and half in private business in the fields of gems and jewelry, fine incense, and natural health equipment. He and his wife Mary Cathryn are Certified Governors on the Invincible America Assembly in Fairfield, Iowa, in which he has responsibilities for increasing and maintaining attendance.

GALE PARK
    502   My Elephant
    604   A Vision
    658   Days Are Short
    686   Falling

Nature and spirituality are Gale Park's focus and inspiration. She grew up in the shadow of the Great Smoky Mountains of East Tennessee and has written poetry and prose since she was a child. She graduated Top Scholar in the College of Communications at the University of Tennessee, Knoxville, and wrote for large newspapers during her career as a journalist. She has also written free lance for a variety of publications.

NYNKE PASSI

    108   Lullaby for the Universe
    402   We Are Drunk

Nynke Passi is assistant professor of Creative Writing at Maharishi University of Management in Fairfield, Iowa. Her poetry and fiction have appeared in numerous literary magazines and publications, among them *The Gulf Coast Review*, *The Anthology of New England Writers*, and the Anthology of Iowa poets *The Dryland Fish*. Her story *The Kiss* was nominated for a Pushcart prize.

ROGER PELIZZARI

Poets' Index and Biographies

184   The Beginning of Real Time

Roger Pelizzari is a bit invisible these days. In fact, for the past 16 years he's a member of Maharishi's Purusha group. After an MA in writing, after teaching creative writing, after some freelancing and song writing, he took a long look down the long corridor of time, and realized that what he really wanted could not be written.

The Purusha trail has led him through cities and forests, across oceans, and prairies, and delivered him full circle, back to Fairfield. He has been seen walking through fields and standing by waters, and often heard singing inscrutably to himself.

Roger has won poetry awards from *Writer's Digest* and the *Iowa Poetry Association*. His poems have been published in *Collecting Moon Coins*, *The Iowa Source*, *Lyrical Iowa*, *Unfolding Origami*, and *Rasa*.

SHARALYN PLILER
         198   When Will I Awaken
         412   To a Young Waiter
         560   You Left Me
         684   When My Body Dies

Sharalyn Pliler graduated from MIU in 1979 with a philosophy major, and in 1987 with a Master's in Professional Writing. For ten years, she earned her living as a professional writer, specializing in public relations. Besides writing

freelance for various trade journals, newsletters, books and pamphlets, she was a staff writer for *In-Joplin!* magazine for two years, editor for *Builder/Architect Magazine*, and author of numerous other freelance projects, including articles for *Horizon Air*, *Teleconnect Magazine*, *Unity*, and *The Phoenix*. Her poetry has been published in the *Christian Science Monitor*, the *Wittenberg Door*, and *Northwest Review* and various other publications. She has often done dramatic readings of prose and poetry and considers one of her most enjoyable experiences to be the receiving of a standing ovation from several hundred people for a poetry reading on a cruise ship. Her most recent work is *The Reluctant Vegetarian*, released in July, 2009. She lives in Fairfield.

DIANA QUINLAN
         222   He

Diana Quinlan, a seeker.

LIBBETT RICH
         40   A White Veil
         366   I Lie Down

Poets' Index and Biographies

652   The Flight

Libbett has been writing poetry for 30 years. Reading for the *Candlelight Reading Series* in February 2009 was her first public reading of her own work in many years. She has been involved with dance, theatre and spoken word all of her life and enjoys reading for children on KRUU Radio's "Sleepy Time with Grandpa D." What she would most like to be remembered for is to have lived a life where there is no gap between what is art and what is life.

RIVER DOG
136   Water Wings

River Dog is my *nom de plume*. I am not a poet so I don't take responsibility for my imaginary friend's poetry or unconventional lifestyle. River Dog is a nice lady poet in her sixties. She is crazy as a loon and says whatever she wants.

Last year, River Dog sold her one bedroom home in Vedic City for a cool two million and retired as a street performer who juggled a rubber chicken and a hatchet for chump change. She lives alone with her female schnauzer, Deli Lama, whom she named after a sandwich she ate while attending a poetry workshop at Revelations Bookstore.

River Dog and Deli live in a tent on a river raft in the middle of the Skunk

River tethered to a tree. She is not available for comment about her poetry, but granted a brief interview with *The Iowa Source* saying, "Depending on the weather my tent entrance faces all directions. Poetry that goes every which way but east is liberating, I tell you. Thanks for swimming out to see me."

On the move from Vedic City, her big lummox of a boyfriend attempted to load River Dog's laptop into the U-Haul while eating a Hy-Vee bratwurst. He tripped over Deli Lama, dropped the laptop and Deli made off with the bratwurst on three legs. River Dog has a flair for melodrama and true to her credo "Let go and let God," she dumped her boyfriend saying, "'Tis better to have loved and lost a man than a laptop."

The "computer crash" was catastrophic. River Dog could not recover any of the poems she had written since she was six years old. Asked to comment about her devastating loss she said, "Poems about sandcastles on beaches are important these days. It keeps people sane to remember there isn't much use hanging on to anything. It all soon slips away like mud down a river."

Sweet dreams where the river bends, Judy Stevens.

MEGAN D. ROBINSON
388   Song
600   Metamorphosis

Poets' Index and Biographies

Megan has been in love with words all her life. She has been known to write poems on napkins and the backs of grocery lists.

BARRY ROSEN
- 178   Marbles at a San Francisco Sunrise
- 398   Wild Woman
- 508   Laughing Leaves Retreat

Barry Rosen began writing poetry at the University of Illinois in Urbana. During his PhD studies at Indiana University, he specialized in studying the mystical tradition of literature and was always fascinated by peak experiences and mystical experiences as they were expressed in poetry. He was a research assistant and instructor at MIU in 1979-80. He has taught literature at Maharishi  International University as a visiting instructor and also taught film studies and literature at Indiana University and the University of Iowa. In 1994, he began studying with Diane Frank, who was a kind of muse that inspired him and has brought out the best in his poetry. He has continued studying with her through her on-line workshops and personal guidance. Barry currently lives in Sedona, AZ with his wife Bonnie Gould and has a career as a commodity trading advisor. He lived in Fairfield in 1978-1997 with the exception of five years away for graduate school. He can be reached at Barry@fortucast.com.

STEVEN P. SCHNEIDER
- 60   Prairie Air Show
- 84   Walking the Loop
- 268   Chanukah Lights Tonight
- 424   Platte River Liftoff

Steven P. Schneider is Professor of English at the University of Texas Pan American, where he also serves as director of new programs and special projects for the College of Arts and Humanities. Steven is a founding member of the South Texas Literacy Coalition in the Rio Grande Valley and is the recipient of two Big Read grants from the National Endowment for the Arts. He  has used the "Borderlines: Drawing Border Lives" traveling exhibit to promote the teaching of literacy through culturally relevant literature and creativity through poetry and art. Steven offers a variety of workshops on these topics to both high school and college students and teachers.

Steven Schneider has published his poetry widely and given readings throughout the United States, including public performances at the Iowa Summer Writing Festival, the Fort Kearny Writers' Conference, the UTPA Summer Creative Writing Institute, and the South Texas Literary Festival. He has also been interviewed and read his work on NETV. Steven Schneider's poems and essays have been published in national and international journals, including *Critical Quarterly, Prairie Schooner, Tikkun, The Literary Review,* and featured in *American Life in Poetry.*

He is the author of several books, including two collections of poetry, *Prairie Air Show* and *Unexpected Guests,* a scholarly book entitled *A.R. Ammons and the Poetics of Widening Scope* and the editor of *Complexities of Motion: New Essays on A.R. Ammons's Long Poems.* He is a winner of an Anna Davidson Rosenberg Award for Poetry and a Nebraska Arts Council Fellowship.

CHRISTOPHER SEID
    456   Someday I Will Have a Mountain Cabin

Christopher Seid is the author of *Prayers to the Other LIfe,* the 1996 Marianne Moore Poetry Prize from Helicon Nine Editions. Born and raised in Central Iowa, Chris attended Maharishi International University and received his MFA in Creative Writing from Vermont College. He lives with his family in Yarmouth, Maine.

LAURIE SEWALL
    552   Radio City Hall

Laurie Sewall has an MFA in Poetry from New England College and an MA in Counseling Psychology from Lesley University. Born in the northeast, she has lived with her husband and daughter in rural Iowa for the past twenty years. Her poetry is informed by her experience as a counselor, bodyworker, and teacher; her love of the natural landscape; and her devotion to meditation practice. She teaches and writes in Fairfield, IA.

MEREDITH BRIGGS SKEATH
    420   Samoset
    464   Always a Good Time to Grow Up
    636   Unexpected Call

Meredith Briggs Skeath's first poetry collection, *Soultending* focuses on spiritual insights gained through experiences of loss, mothering, and the Divine.

Published by Glanzer Press in 2003, *Soultending* is available at www.amazon.com.

Meredith has an M.A. from M.U.M. and is a former teaching assistant at M.U.M., in both Santa Barbara and Fairfield. She has read her work on National Public Radio, at the Library of Congress, and Yale University, among other venues, and is published widely in periodicals. She has more than 40 years teaching experience and has

Poets' Index and Biographies

taught writing in elementary through college courses.

Meredith lives with her husband and youngest of three children in Silver Spring, Maryland, where she tutors children and adolescents with learning disabilities, trains tutors, writes poetry and songs, and lectures to parents and teachers on educational issues. She can be reached at HYPERLINK "mailto:mbskeath@aol.com"

BRIAN STAINS
    458   Three Non-Haiku

PARA STEINMANN
    164   Night Sketches

Para (Barbara Steinmann) lived and studied in Paris, Amsterdam, and Geneva before joining the PhD program in Vedic Studies at Maharishi European Research University in Switzerland. She worked at the International Capital of the Age of Enlightenment in Seelisberg, Switzerland before joining the Mother Divine program. Her work on Mother Divine took her to Kenya, Brazil, the Philippines, India, Holland, and finally the US, where she settled in Boone, NC before joining the Invincible America Assembly in Fairfield, Iowa in 2006. She spends much of her time in India and is a part-time artist.

ANDREA DANA STEVENS
    300   The Whale's Song
    558   Night Birds

Poetry is compressed language that comes from the human heart. As a poet, teacher, storyteller and writer, I find that poetry is my road to truth, prayer, and the Light of the Divine. I cannot lie when a poem breathes through me. Poetry is the word play across the light of the soul. My poems are mirrors of who I am. These poems are about building and revealing truth of the heart. It is about returning for one another to the only hope of humankind: the promise since the dawn of man. It is the promise of sharing food, hearth, hope, and shelter for this planet which is our only home.

Andrea D. Stevens has been a professional dancer, published poet and writer. She is an artist, college, and high school teacher of literature to students at academic risk on Internet along the east coast of the United States.

She has lived in Canada, France, Mexico, and the USA. She resided in Fairfield, IA from 1986 to 2005 raising her daughter who went to MSAE. She has received numerous awards for her poems, including poet of the year in 2008 from the International Poetry Society, Poetry Award from the Connecticut Poetry Society. At present she resides with her husband Mathias Alig in Terre Haute, Indiana.

Poets' Index and Biographies

Her poem "Melting in the Rain" © Andrea D. Stevens (2009) will be appearing in the forthcoming book *Twin Muses: Art and Poetry* by painter and theologian Amy Kindred.

Andrea has taught workshops in interdisciplinary studies and the arts all along the east coast. Some of her poems are on youtube on Internet. You can find them there under her name.

PAUL JOHAN STOKSTAD

20	New Ache
120	Like the Robin's Egg
226	The Picture of You
408	You're the Most
554	I Turn My Back

Paul Johan Stokstad has worked as a tennis pro, lab assistant, railroad worker, college instructor, dance teacher, meditation teacher, web marketer, and is into partner dance, improv theatre, movies, historical and fantasy books, and poetry.

JANET THOMAS

76	The Stage
110	Tumbling Planets
650	Lyrebird Song

Janet Thomas grew up in Australia within a family besotted with words. She is grateful that her father and his friends filled her ears with their poems, because it helps her understand that reading, writing and listening to poetry is natural and pleasurable.

She likes to think this understanding has helped inform her practice as a teacher and a writer. When she moved to Fairfield in 1987 to further her teaching career at MSAE, she delighted in the opportunity to share her love of language with so many talented students within the school, and later, within the community at large. The vibrant silence of the atmosphere also helped her write a few poems of her own.

After twenty years in Fairfield, she is currently spending time on the exquisite Gold Coast in Queensland, Australia. She continues to write, while teaching workshops in schools throughout the region and pursuing post-graduate research in creativity and talent development. She recently completed certification to teach Nia dance, which she finds to be a wonderful support to poetry.

Her poems have previously been published in *Lyrical Iowa*, 2005, 2007 the anthology *Leaves by Day, Flowers by Night*, 1st *World Publishing* 2006 and she was the 2006 recipient of the *Helen Vaughn Memorial Haiku Award*, established by *Women in the Arts*, Decatur,

Poets' Index and Biographies

Illinois. She has also been published in *Talent Ed*, University of New England, Armidale 2009.

VIKTOR TICHY

8	Fall of an Angel
52	Iowa Meditation
130	The Puzzle Tale
144	When I Die
202	Communion
228	Gaea's Wedding Kiss
250	Bug in My Pants
400	The Sixth Day of Creation
460	"A Fossil, Dad!"
498	Bareback English
566	Territorial Waters

Viktor Tichy grew up in Prague, Czechoslovakia, and lives in Fairfield, Iowa. Father of four, architect-developer, and art and poetry teacher, he also owned a child care center and the Renaissance Preschool in Iowa City. He began to write poetry in Diane Frank's workshop 20 years ago, and has won prizes and publications in over 120 national and state contests. Viktor currently participates in the Invincible America course and writes a nonfiction book about raising renaissance children titled *Genius in Diapers*. He is preparing seminars for parents and child care centers by the same name.

JAMES TIPTON

90	Shepherd on Snowdon
116	The Other Side
150	Riding with Ludwig
528	Lady with an Ermine
632	Gates of Dawn

Born and raised in Berkeley, California (May 31, 1952), with younger brother and older sister; father was a lawyer in San Francisco. In high school, went on peace marches against the Vietnam War with my mother and friends,

sang in a rock group (Virgin Forest), played acoustic guitar and composed songs, read and wrote poetry, and spent as much time as possible hiking in redwoods in Marin County or backpacking in the high Sierra. My favorite authors then (and still among my favorite now): Walt Whitman (with whom I share a birthday), Henry Thoreau, John Muir, Dylan Thomas, Gary Snyder, and J.R.R. Tolkien.

I started reading and writing poetry (and some short fiction) seriously at sixteen, inspired by my high school creative writing teacher, Mr. Sigg. After that, I never looked at books in the same way (but tried to learn something from each new writer), and I knew where my passion lay. After about five years in the rock band (I loved the connection with the audience being on stage), in college I studied classical voice, and ended up singing in the San Francisco Opera Chorus in the great years of the late seventies and early eighties, when Luciano Pavarotti and Placido Domingo were regular principals. I remember one time holding my stage rifle to the back of Domingo (we were about to arrest and hang him), and he sang such a heart-rending aria (on his knees), that it was hard to maintain the angry expression on my face.

In college I pursued the advice, "If you really want to learn to write, read and read and read and write and write," so I received my B.A. and M.A. in English: Emphasis Creative Writing from San Francisco State University, then my PhD in literature from University of California, Davis.

I worked with Gary Snyder on my doctoral dissertation on the California nature poet, Kenneth Rexroth. Since then, I have taught English and creative writing at U.C. Davis, the University of Bordeaux, France, and at colleges around the Bay Area.

Family: Wife, son, stepson and family, cat, and great dog. My son, a poet majoring in playwriting at university, helps me edit my work, as does my wife, who always has a valuable opinion.

RICHARD K. WALLARAB
    326   Doin' What Comes Naturally
    578   The Sandbox

I am a retired Presbyterian minister. Regarding education I have a Doctorate from McCormick Theological Seminary in Chicago. I am a native Iowan. I was born in Davenport. Following college I entered the US Army serving in the Counter Intelligence Corp in Europe. I continued my education following my service and became an ordained Presbyterian minister. I later became an Army Chaplain and lastly was pastor of the Fairfield Presbyterian Church.

LEAH MARIE WALLER
    32   A Word for My Mother
    104   The Rain Is Sun When It Falls in Ireland
    168   Feeding Cats
    258   Hero
    368   My Body
    514   Birth of a Poem

Leah aspires to be an amazing writer, unyielding friend and hopeless romantic. True to her poetic soul she enjoys camping, sushi, coffee and wearing a hat on Mondays.

Poets' Index and Biographies

JASON WALLS
- 96   Imagine You're a River
- 444   Michelle Kwan
- 648   Shards of Future

I'm a student at Union Institute and University studying Writing and Cultural Studies. I plan to graduate in April, and hopefully attend U of I's Creative Nonfiction Writing graduate program. I also have an interest in teaching, particularly abroad in Japan.

GLENN WATT
- 74   Troubles
- 82   On Hope
- 212   Like a Seed
- 330   How They Sometimes Show up
- 352   Ice
- 426   The Fool
- 584   The Forgiven

I am a Wyoming native transplanted to southeastern Iowa in the late 70's and early 80's, where I continue to practice the three R's — reading, 'riting, and roaming — and still miss the mountains every day.

PATRICIA WOOD
- 396   Sparks Flying

As a writer and healer from Northern California, Patricia's poetry and storytelling have been written and told to heal the wounded healer in herself as well as in her friends and family. Her articles on vibrational medicine have been published in alternative health care publications and she has been a main speaker at Evolving Times Expos. She has helped hundreds in her healing practice in California as well as in Iowa and continues to co-create miracles of healing with her clients and friends all over the country.

Patricia began the Candlelight Series of poetry readings with devotional song or bhajans, which is chanting the names of God. Her writing of poetry, story is like a devotional song whether it be written or sung it seems to bring back the experience of a spiritual being having a human experience.

Jordy Yager
- 140   Toilet Poetry
- 172   Swimming through Brooklyn

ACKNOWLEDGEMENTS

All the poems in this book are copyrighted by their creators. Acknowledgements appear on the poems' title pages.

Introductory poems by Brother Ludovico.

The experience of reading each poet who submitted works for this book created a continuous high for me.

I've enjoyed many extensive e-mail exchanges as well as hilarious telephone conversations with Brother Ludovico, Ken Chawkin, Sharalyn Pliler, Christine Fonseca, Henry Robert Hau, Charlie Hopkins, Meredith Briggs Skeath, Bill Godfrey, Leslie Gentry, Einar Olsen, Angela Mailander, Allen Cobb, Tony Ellis, Rustin Larson, Roger Pelizzari, Raven Garland, and others. I thank everyone for your advice, suggestions, and encouragement.

Special thanks to those who helped track down some 'lost' poets that had moved away from Fairfield to parts unknown.

I also thank my editor Diane Rosenberg.

I thank Donovan for his most poetic foreword. Donovan, together with David Lynch, is dedicated to bringing meditation to students all over the world. http://www.davidlynchfoundation.org/

The cover photo is courtesy of
Josie Hannes Design LLC Graphic Design & Photography,
and Fairfield Iowa Convention and Visitors Bureau.
The photo of Sappho is in the public domain.

Jacket design and book layout by Freddy Niagara Fonseca.

Published by 1st World Publishing.

About Freddy Niagara Fonseca

Freddy Niagara Fonseca, Renaissance man, poet, dramatic reader, impresario, and creator of *This Enduring Gift* has immersed himself in the arts all his life and has read tens of thousands of poems in five languages. In 2004 he founded the *Candlelight Reading Series*, and in 2007, the *Chamber Music Society Fairfield*.

With the collaboration of expressive readers, musicians, dancers, and actors, he has presented over 50 poetry readings on universal themes culled from poetry of all styles, eras, and cultures. He regularly invites noteworthy musicians — statewide, nationwide, and internationally — to perform chamber music in Fairfield, Iowa.

Freddy Niagara Fonseca believes that poetry and the whole world will drastically change once a new, spiritual paradigm of consciousness and language emerges. Poetry will then be experienced, written, and appreciated in universal terms, and a sublime awareness of the Earth will manifest.

He has lived in Fairfield for over 20 years and calls it home.

Finis

"They spoke, I think, of perils past.
They spoke, I think, of peace at last.
One thing I remember:
Spring came on forever,
Spring came on forever,"
Said the Chinese nightingale.

— From *The Chinese Nightingale*
by Vachel Lindsay, American poet (1879-1931)

www.ingramcontent.com/pod-product-compliance
Lightning Source LLC
Chambersburg PA
CBHW032011230426
43671CB00005B/48